From International Relations to World Civilizations

This volume explores the work of Robert W. Cox across International Relations, International Political Economy, and International Historical Sociology. Robert W. Cox has been a key figure in so-called critical approaches to world politics, contributing to the inter-paradigm debate in IR, pioneering the Gramscian approach to IPE, developing key insights into international institutions, and the changing nature of capitalism and the state. His more recent work on intercivilizational encounters and intersubjectivity has been no less influential. This comprehensive collection provides an entry-point into Cox's work across these themes of history, theory, political economy, and civilizations, offering a way for researchers and students to engage with Robert W. Cox's rich legacy and deploy the many insights of his thought into contemporary scholarship.

This volume will be of interest to undergraduate and postgraduate students, as well as academics working within world politics.

This book was originally published as a special issue of *Globalizations*.

Shannon Brincat is a Research Fellow at Griffith University, Australia. His research focuses on recognition theory and cosmopolitanism, dialectics, tyrannicide, climate change justice, and Critical Theory. He has been the editor of a number of collections, most recently *Dialectics and World Politics*; *Recognition, Conflict and the Problems of Ethical Community*; and the three volume series *Communism in the Twenty-First Century*. He is also the co-founder and co-editor of the journal *Global Discourse*.

Rethinking Globalizations
Edited by Barry K. Gills, *University of Helsinki, Finland* and
Kevin Gray, *University of Sussex, UK.*

This series is designed to break new ground in the literature on globalization and its academic and popular understanding. Rather than perpetuating or simply reacting to the economic understanding of globalization, this series seeks to capture the term and broaden its meaning to encompass a wide range of issues and disciplines and convey a sense of alternative possibilities for the future.

The Redesign of the Global Financial Architecture
The Return of State Authority
Stuart P.M. Mackintosh

Markets and Development
Civil Society, Citizens and the Politics of Neoliberalism
Edited by Toby Carroll and Darryl S.L. Jarvis

Occupying Subjectivity
Being and Becoming Radical in the 21st Century
Edited by Chris Rossdale

Localization in Development Aid
How Global Institutions enter Local Lifeworlds
Edited by Thorsten Bonacker, Judith von Heusinger and Kerstin Zimmer

The New Global Politics
Global Social Movements in the Twenty-First Century
Edited by Harry E. Vanden, Peter N. Funke and Gary Prevos

The Politics of Food Sovereignty
Concept, Practice and Social Movements
Edited by Annie Shattuck, Christina Schiavoni and Zoe VanGelder

Time and Globalization
An interdisciplinary dialogue
Edited by Paul Huebener, Susie O'Brien, Tony Porter, Liam Stockdale and Rachel Yanqiu Zhou

From International Relations to World Civilizations
The Contributions of Robert W. Cox
Edited by Shannon Brincat

Chinese Labour in the Global Economy
Capitalist Exploitation and Strategies of Resistance
Edited by Andreas Bieler and Chun-Yi Lee

From International Relations to World Civilizations

The Contributions of Robert W. Cox

Edited by
Shannon Brincat

LONDON AND NEW YORK

First published 2017
by Routledge
2 Park Square, Milton Park, Abingdon, Oxon, OX14 4RN, UK

and by Routledge
711 Third Avenue, New York, NY 10017, USA

Routledge is an imprint of the Taylor & Francis Group, an informa business

Chapter 8 © Nicola Phillips, article originally published as Open Access
Statement, Preface, Chapters 1–7 & Chapters 9–11 © 2017 Taylor & Francis

All rights reserved. No part of this book may be reprinted or reproduced
or utilised in any form or by any electronic, mechanical, or other means,
now known or hereafter invented, including photocopying and recording,
or in any information storage or retrieval system, without permission in
writing from the publishers.

Trademark notice: Product or corporate names may be trademarks or
registered trademarks, and are used only for identification and
explanation without intent to infringe.

British Library Cataloguing in Publication Data
A catalogue record for this book is available from the British Library

ISBN 13: 978-1-138-28963-5

Typeset in Times New Roman
by RefineCatch Limited, Bungay, Suffolk

Publisher's Note
The publisher accepts responsibility for any inconsistencies that may have
arisen during the conversion of this book from journal articles to book chapters,
namely the possible inclusion of journal terminology.

Disclaimer
Every effort has been made to contact copyright holders for their permission to
reprint material in this book. The publishers would be grateful to hear from any
copyright holder who is not here acknowledged and will undertake to rectify
any errors or omissions in future editions of this book.

Contents

Citation Information	vii
Notes on Contributors	ix
Statement by Robert W. Cox	1
Preface: On the Legacy of Robert W. Cox *Richard Falk*	2
1. Introduction: From International Relations to World Civilizations: The Contributions of Robert W. Cox *Shannon Brincat*	7
2. Robert W. Cox's Method of Historical Structures Redux *Timothy J. Sinclair*	11
3. The Critical Theorist's Labour: Empirical or Philosophical Historiography for International Relations? *Richard Devetak & Ryan Walter*	21
4. Robert W. Cox and the Idea of History: Political Economy as Philosophy *Randall Germain*	33
5. Neo-Gramscian Theory and Third World Violence: A Time for Broadening *Randolph B. Persaud*	48
6. Traditional, Problem-Solving and Critical Theory: An Analysis of Horkheimer and Cox's Setting of the 'Critical' Divide *Shannon Brincat*	64
7. Framing Robert W. Cox, Framing International Relations *Vendulka Kubálková*	79
8. Labour in Global Production: Reflections on Coxian Insights in a World of Global Value Chains *Nicola Phillips*	95
9. Global Governance and Universities: The Power of Ideas and Knowledge *James H. Mittelman*	109

CONTENTS

10. 'Behemoth Pulls the Peasant's Plough': Convergence and Resistance to Business Civilization in China 122
 George Karavas & Shannon Brincat

11. Rethinking about Civilizations: The Politics of Migration in a New Climate 138
 Samid Suliman

 Index 153

Citation Information

The chapters in this book were originally published in *Globalizations*, volume 13, issue 5 (October 2016). When citing this material, please use the original page numbering for each article, as follows:

Statement
Statement by Robert W. Cox
Globalizations, volume 13, issue 5 (October 2016), pp. 499–500

Preface
On the Legacy of Robert W. Cox
Richard Falk
Globalizations, volume 13, issue 5 (October 2016), pp. 501–505

Chapter 1
Introduction: From International Relations to World Civilizations: The Contributions of Robert W. Cox
Shannon Brincat
Globalizations, volume 13, issue 5 (October 2016), pp. 506–509

Chapter 2
Robert W. Cox's Method of Historical Structures Redux
Timothy J. Sinclair
Globalizations, volume 13, issue 5 (October 2016), pp. 510–519

Chapter 3
The Critical Theorist's Labour: Empirical or Philosophical Historiography for International Relations?
Richard Devetak & Ryan Walter
Globalizations, volume 13, issue 5 (October 2016), pp. 520–531

Chapter 4
Robert W. Cox and the Idea of History: Political Economy as Philosophy
Randall Germain
Globalizations, volume 13, issue 5 (October 2016), pp. 532–546

CITATION INFORMATION

Chapter 5
Neo-Gramscian Theory and Third World Violence: A Time for Broadening
Randolph B. Persaud
Globalizations, volume 13, issue 5 (October 2016), pp. 547–562

Chapter 6
Traditional, Problem-Solving and Critical Theory: An Analysis of Horkheimer and Cox's Setting of the 'Critical' Divide
Shannon Brincat
Globalizations, volume 13, issue 5 (October 2016), pp. 563–577

Chapter 7
Framing Robert W. Cox, Framing International Relations
Vendulka Kubálková
Globalizations, volume 13, issue 5 (October 2016), pp. 578–593

Chapter 8
Labour in Global Production: Reflections on Coxian Insights in a World of Global Value Chains
Nicola Phillips
Globalizations, volume 13, issue 5 (October 2016), pp. 594–607

Chapter 9
Global Governance and Universities: The Power of Ideas and Knowledge
James H. Mittelman
Globalizations, volume 13, issue 5 (October 2016), pp. 608–621

Chapter 10
'Behemoth Pulls the Peasant's Plough': Convergence and Resistance to Business Civilization in China
George Karavas & Shannon Brincat
Globalizations, volume 13, issue 5 (October 2016), pp. 622–637

Chapter 11
Rethinking about Civilizations: The Politics of Migration in a New Climate
Samid Suliman
Globalizations, volume 13, issue 5 (October 2016), pp. 638–652

For any permission-related enquiries please visit:
http://www.tandfonline.com/page/help/permissions

Notes on Contributors

Shannon Brincat is a Research Fellow at Griffith University, Australia. Alongside a number of edited collections, his work on international relations theory and Critical Theory has been published in *The European Journal of International Relations*, *Review of International Studies*, and *Constellations*. He is also the co-founder and co-editor of the journal *Global Discourse*.

Richard Devetak is Associate Professor in International Relations and Head of the School of Political Science and International Studies at the University of Queensland, Australia. He has published on international relations theory and the history of international thought in leading journals in the field, including *International Theory*, *History of European Ideas*, *International Affairs*, *Millennium*, and *Review of International Studies*.

Richard Falk is Milbank Professor of International Law Emeritus, Princeton University, and Research Fellow, Orfalea Center of Global Studies, University of California, Santa Barbara. His most recent books are *Power Shift: On the New Global Order* (2016) and *Palestine's Horizon: Towards a Just Peace* (2017).

Randall Germain is Professor of Political Science at Carleton University, Canada. His teaching and research focus on the political economy of global finance; issues and themes associated with economic and financial governance; and theoretical debates within the field of international political economy. He is the author of *The International Organization of Credit* (CUP, 1997) and *Global Politics and Financial Governance* (Palgrave, 2010).

George Karavas is a Lecturer in Peace and Conflict Studies in the School of Political Science and International Studies at the University of Queensland, Australia. His research focuses on Africa-China relations, the politics of development, and global political economy.

Vendulka Kubálková, Professor of International Studies at the University of Miami, Florida, USA, holds doctorates from Czechoslovakia and England. She held academic positions in New Zealand and Australia before moving to the US. She had written about Marxism (in its different forms) and IR, constructivism and IR, and faiths and religions in world affairs.

James H. Mittelman is Distinguished Scholar in Residence and University Professor Emeritus at the School of International Service, American University, Washington, DC. He is also Honorary Fellow at the Helsinki Collegium for Advanced Studies, and was a member at the Institute of Advanced Study in Princeton.

Randolph B. Persaud is Associate Professor of International Relations at the School of International Service, American University, Washington, DC. He has written extensively on race and international relations.

NOTES ON CONTRIBUTORS

Nicola Phillips is Professor of Political Economy and Head of the Department of Politics at the University of Sheffield, UK. She is a past editor of both the *Review of International Political Economy* and *New Political Economy*. Her work focuses on global economic governance, global production, labour and labour standards, and the political economy of inequality.

Timothy J. Sinclair is Associate Professor of International Political Economy at the University of Warwick, UK. A former official in the New Zealand Treasury (where he worked on public expenditure and the privatization of government agencies), he focuses on researching the politics of global finance and approaches to global governance theory.

Samid Suliman is Lecturer in Migration and Security in the School of Humanities, Languages and Social Science at Griffith University, Australia. He is an interdisciplinary researcher interested in migration, postcolonial political theory, international relations and world politics, global development, climate change, and the politics of knowledge. He is also a member of the Griffith Centre for Social and Cultural Research.

Ryan Walter is Senior Lecturer in the School of Political Science and International Studies at the University of Queensland, Australia. His study of the conceptual foundations of international political economy is published as *A Critical History of the Economy* (Routledge, 2011).

I am grateful to the contributors to this special issue for their views about my work. I am pleased that those taking part in this discussion have felt free to be critical in their comments. I continue to believe that a theory is always for someone and for some purpose. By that I mean a theory is not an abstract concept, but is relevant to a particular process of thought, with specific meaning to a certain time and place. That also applies to my theory. People should be free to apply a theory to their different situations, making it relevant to themselves and their purposes.

Robert W. Cox

PREFACE

On the Legacy of Robert W. Cox

RICHARD FALK

Princeton University, Princeton, NJ, USA

That Robert W. Cox has long been one of the intellectual treasures of the Western world is not as widely appreciated as it should be. This sophisticated series of affirming responses to Cox's work and academic contributions situated outside the box of conventional wisdom should help to establish Cox's scholarly stature with a wider audience. It also helps us understand why many revere Cox as a master mentor who over the years taught his students and readers to swim against the current by looking closely at the slime accumulating beneath the main rocks of international power and wealth. Additionally this publication is extremely timely. It has never seemed quite as crucial to reject the mainstream perceptions of how the world is organized and works, and then use this knowledge to search sympathetically for transformative projects addressing the various historical challenges that menacingly confront the peoples of the world. It is along these lines that Cox's way of interpreting the global setting has become so relevant, even though his most influential publications appeared in the last two decades of the twentieth century.

I would anchor these brief reflections on Cox's importance as a radical thinker in relation to his full embrace and distinctive applications of *critical theory*. As Cox explains, '[i]t is critical in the sense that it stands apart from the prevailing order and asks how it came about' (1996, p. 88). In effect, the critical theorist, unlike the typical positivist, draws into question the way the institutions and social forces brought the existing world order into being, and how it is changing, with regard to an envisioned future. Cox as a critical theorist is insistent upon contextualizing the structures and forces that constitute world order as it related to time present and time future. Citing Machiavelli and Ibn Khaldun, Cox contends that '[a] critical theory is more at the service of the weak than of the strong', which is consistent with his commitment to knowledge as empowerment (1996, p. 504). With more focus on the academic role of what Cox regards as the 'responsible scholar' is to

> to place the process of international organization in the framework of global change, to take the structural, diachronic approach. This critical perspective is particularly necessary in a moment of world history when there is a whole series of interacting fundamental changes. (1996, p. 526)

Here, I find extremely illuminating his juxtaposing of neorealism as a state-centric, status quo-oriented, problem-solving view of world order with his adoption of an approach that he identifies as 'classical realism'. The appeal of the latter is twofold: first, its preoccupation with historical context in which the conflicts of a given time are in the forefront of the political domain along with their economic and social underpinnings, and second its depiction of the ideology and agenda of the powerful as dialectically engaged with the counter-hegemonic strivings of the poor and victimized.

I find Cox's kind of realism liberating as it is so persuasively attentive to 'the real' as contrasted with the self-styled 'realists' who occupy the principal sites of power and are above all dedicated to system maintenance even if and when it unduly risks system annihilation. This quality of attentiveness encourages Cox to posit a post-Westphalian world order. While acknowledging how things are at present, Cox is always sensitive to the contradictions that generate unacceptable risks as well as generate spaces for creative resistance and transformative political behavior. Cox fully understands the role played by states, especially the dominant or hegemonic states, without being a statist who ignores the non-state impacts associated with market forces and civil society. What especially distinguishes Cox's worldview is his acute awareness *as a classical realist* of the somewhat autonomous complementary domain of neoliberal globalization, which has produced the deterritorializing and transnationalizing of business, capital investment, labor markets, production linkages, trade relations, and corporate maneuvers. In other words, state-centrism is diluted and fundamentally altered by the restructuring of the world economy in the post-colonial era.

Additionally, Cox accords importance to the sphere of social, economic, and cultural forces often effective in challenging geopolitical and capitalist frameworks, and putting them under increasing pressures. Considering that Cox's late work is written in a global context that coincides with the ending of the Cold War, he is impressively aware of threats to the biosphere, which he regards as the fallout from ongoing encounters between the rapacious tendencies of globalizing capitalism emphasizing growth at any cost and the well-being of people and the sustainability of the quality of life throughout the planet. In this respect, while the neorealist strives for the stability of existing political and economic arrangements, the classical realist of the twenty-first century, according to Cox, should encourage the pursuit of humane governance at all levels of social organization and emphasize ecological sustainability as a necessary precondition for human well-being. We need to remember that Cox developed this understanding while analyzing the world historical problematique in a period before the actualities of the anthropocene had become clear to most commentators. Such a long Braudelian view of the human condition contrasted with the shortsighted economic and cultural practices of societies, especially the rich ones, which were acting in ways that severely compromised the ecological future without even an awareness of awaiting disaster.

Nowhere is this clash between the ways of neoliberal capitalism and the well-being of peoples, especially those who are most vulnerable, more evident than in relation to the perception and the responses from entrenched elites to the challenges associated with global warming. The 2014 Paris Agreement on Climate Change was negotiated with great fanfare by more than

190 governments under UN auspices. In keeping with the Cox approach, the outcome reflected the problem-solving approach of neorealism that pushed governments and the global private sector to their limits due to the manifested urgency of the situation, but what was agreed upon still fell dangerously short of what an overwhelming scientific consensus prescribed as prudent. In this respect, the severity of the climate change problem posed for world order can be minimized and deferred for now, but since it cannot be solved given the parameters of feasibility set by Westphalian geopolitics and neoliberal capitalism, it is almost certain to reemerge more disruptively in the decades ahead.

Cox also contrasts his 'pessimism' with the 'optimism' of the neorealists, who act as if they have no alternative but to offer feasible solutions to the problems of the day, and yet seem unaware of the insufficiency of their responses because of their failure to admit or even consider the destructive tendencies of statist and capitalist behavior as historically presented (1996, p. 526). When feasibility does not correspond to the imperatives of necessity, system collapse or system transformation becomes the alternatives for the future. In this regard, with neorealists retaining control of the levers of hard power and political authority, the system is heading toward collapse unless effectively challenged. It is the unlikelihood that a sufficient challenge will be mounted that makes Cox pessimistic, and constitutes a refusal on his part to blink, or to follow the neorealists down the lemming path of denial and false consciousness.

Cox situates his own theoretical approach far more broadly than in opposition to neorealism. He challenges structuralism for its failure to address the historical dynamics by which the past became the present and for its inattentiveness to the prospects for change. In that sense, in endorsing classical realism Cox is implicitly insisting that *time* is as important as *space* in the study of world order. This runs against the analytic, ahistorical main current of quantitatively oriented social science. For Cox, the responsible scholar is an interpreter with an eye toward progressive change, and in spirit as well as substance, opposed to the scientific pretensions of positivist epistemologies. The pessimism he identifies with is but an acknowledgement of the forces arrayed in the world that block the pathways of desirable change.

An aspect of Cox's pessimism is a skeptical view of what can be hoped for from the United Nations, and more generally from what he calls 'liberal internationalism'. He does not see an emancipatory future emerging from the technocratic neofunctionalism of David Mitrany or from Karl Deutsch's positive view of the integrative developments unfolding in Europe with the possibility of comparable regionalization taking place elsewhere. In this regard, the UN and the Bretton Woods enablers of global capitalism are instrumentalities relied upon by those with vested interests in the status quo, and are not agents of change but function as incrementally oriented problem-solvers and crisis managers wedded to an ahistorical view of political reality. Hence, it is not at all surprising to Cox that Fukuyama's cockamamie projections of 'the end of history' were taken so seriously throughout the West in the 1990s. These triumphalist projections confused the end of the Cold War phase of geopolitical rivalry with the totally ahistorical contention that systemic stability and ideological consensus along Western lines were now assured forever.

Where Cox sees hope is in the presence of a transformative potential that he situates outside the regulatory structures of dominant states and prevailing market patterns. In his words, '[t]he new order will have to be built from the bottom up, when the present order falters in its attempt to hold things in place from the top down' (Cox, 1996, p. 535). Cox situates the possibility for change in those counter-hegemonic social and political forces that are victimizing and marginalizing the global masses, and putting the future of the human species itself increasingly at risk. Cox's diagnosis helps account for his criticism of world-systems theory as imprisoned by its structuralist explanations of how world order functions, and therefore lacks any capacity to envision an alternate future brought about by a mobilization of the peoples of the world in support of transformative projects.

At the same time Cox is not a world order romantic or utopian. He signals his form of constrained hope by self-describing himself as a pessimist, as well as by suggesting that the future cannot be shaped by the undisciplined energies of desire. Cox writes that his type of realist 'limits the range of choice to alternative orders which are feasible transformations of the existing world' (1996, p. 210). He leaves to others the tasks of concretizing the meaning of 'feasible transformations', which becomes a daunting challenge to our dormant political imaginations, especially as the contours of global crisis become more menacing and undermine foundational beliefs. Even aside from the failure to address the energy/warming challenge, there are ominous signs associated with the global trends toward autocratic rule on the level of the state which is a reflection of underlying social and economic disorder, the various expressions of political expediency and human desperation, exhibited by recourse to severe repressive styles of governance, the return of fascist populisms, the large migration flows of desperate people, the rise of extremism as resistance, and the retreat behind walls of paranoid security consciousness and ultra-nationalist conceptions of political community. Cox does leave us somewhat stranded on this beach of feasibility, and whether there are bridges that connect what is feasible with what is necessary for ecological viability, societal equity, and humane governance. If not, the human species is trapped in fundamental ways that threaten its very existence. There is also some confusion between the emphasis by neorealists on 'feasibility' that Cox repudiates and the feasibility that he adopts with respect to his classical realist search for transformative alternatives to the present to avoid falling prey to utopianism.

It is entirely consistent with his eclectic progressive outlook that Cox should link his worldview with a Gramscian orientation toward the role of the intellectual. As Cox explains,

> ... the essence of the scholarly responsibility lies in the sphere of critical theory ... to take the structural, diachronic approach. The critical perspective is particularly necessary in a moment of world history when there is a whole series of interacting fundamental changes. (1996, p. 526)

It is worth observing that this idea of responsibility is not associated with promoting a particular response to the crisis conditions confronting the peoples of the world, but rather at describing and analyzing as accurately as possible the historical circumstances giving rise to problematic situations and trends, but also to the transformational openings, which is what a diachronic approach encompasses (in contrast to the synchronic approach that ignores the past and future, devoting its energies to finding feasible solutions within the limits set by the established order).

For me, Cox's most valuable contribution is in relation to framing inquiries about political reality in ways that deliberately make thought a tool of emancipatory forces. This tool reminds us that the historical situation is generating urgent challenges that cannot be adequately addressed by elites now in control of the structures of wealth and power nor by their cadre of policy-oriented and technocratically driven think-tank operatives. In this respect, Cox's view is not quite aligned with that of Chomsky or Edward Said who, above all, urge intellectuals to speak truth to power. For Cox, the primary critical task is to induce the realization that the powerful are themselves deeply alienated actors bonded with a doomed system. Accordingly, hopes worth nurturing about the future depend on mobilizing the peoples of the world to adopt an attainable emancipatory vision. To do this Cox believes in the potential agency of a popular movement that is dedicated to achieving transformed relations between structures of authority, the lives of people, and the viability of economic arrangements while taking responsible account of ecological constraints.

Overall, I find Cox's approach to world order illuminating and authoritative in setting forth three imperatives for analysis, reflection, and prescription: first, engage in thick contextualization based on taking account of present historical and material circumstances; second, while acknowledging the persisting importance of states as political actors, also give complementary attention to economic actors associated with market forces and to civil society actors linked to social forces; and third a moral ontology that values knowledge to the degree that it serves to empower the weak, the vulnerable, and the marginal and advance struggles for global justice. I view this volume of critical appreciation as a significant contribution by engaged scholars to the kind of framework that Cox's career as a theorist and practitioner exemplifies.

Reference

Cox, R. W. (1996). *Approaches to world order*. Cambridge: Cambridge University Press.

INTRODUCTION

From International Relations to World Civilizations: The Contributions of Robert W. Cox

SHANNON BRINCAT

Griffith University, Brisbane, Australia

Robert W. Cox has been a key figure in so-called critical approaches to world politics and though his work defies conventional labelling, his deeply historical and relational approach has challenged the very core of the discipline of International Relations (IR). He is said to have the honour of penning the most quoted line in IR from his seminal article in *Millennium* 'Social forces, states and world orders' (1981)—that theory is always 'for someone and some purpose'—a sentiment that continues to push the discipline to engage its theoretical and normative assumptions. The book that followed, *Production, power and world order* (1987), offered one of the first inroads of such a critical engagement within the field developing an account of political transformation through social forces: forms of states, political economy, and the future of world order. In another seminal article, 'Gramsci, Hegemony and IR', also published in *Millennium* (1983), was central to the introduction of Gramscian approaches to both IR and International Political Economy (IPE) that remains so influential today. Across all his work, Cox has furthered an interest in processes of historical change that have seen led to significant developments in International Historical Sociology, especially in terms of method and theory. His contribution to IPE has been no less fundamental than in IR, offering insights into the nature of capitalism, the state, and development. Having worked for two decades in the International Labour Organization, Cox was also a leading scholar in the field of international organizations and his first book *The anatomy of influence* (with Harold Jacobson) (1974) examined eight agencies in the United Nations. His more recent work on inter-civilizational encounters, particularly the essays in *The political economy of a plural world* (2002) and *Universal foreigner* (2013), have served to develop yet another under-theorized dimension of world politics, one that seeks to promote dialogue across civilizations and post-hegemonic forms of human community.[1]

This Special Issue provides an entry-point into Cox's work and came about through discussions around the inaugural International Studies Association Theory Section Distinguished Scholar Award that was presented to Prof. Cox in 2014 (Toronto) and the panel in the following year 'On Robert W. Cox's contribution to International Relations, International Political Economy and International Sociology' (New Orleans). It was at these events that it was agreed a volume dedicated to key aspects of Cox's work—his legacy and future—should be undertaken. Each contributor was selected on the basis of their engagement with Cox's work in their own research and to promote a diverse range of perspectives that ensures a vibrant plurality of voices on the subject. This cross-section of transdisciplinary and heterodox scholars establishes linkages between 'old' and 'new' generations of Coxian researchers, in ways that respectfully engage with the legacy of Cox's work and identify future potentials in this fecund area for the study of world politics. The volume is not, however, a festschrift but a *critical* exercise. Indeed, when Prof. Cox was originally approached about the book, he insisted on this being so—something his opening statement places at the forefront of the volume. Cox's insistence that the project be a 'critical exercise' has meant that the papers do not merely celebrate his work but are intended as a critique to build upon and extend the limits of his scholarship. Whilst each article is distinct, shared themes related to history, theory, political economy, and civilizations do emerge, and the papers have been loosely grouped together in this manner.

After Richard Falk's 'Preface' (2016) that discusses the impact and ongoing legacies of Cox's work, the volume begins with a series of articles looking to themes related to history and historical change. Sinclair (2016) takes up Cox's Method of Historical Structures, extending the pragmatism of this method so it can be more effective as a framework for understanding world order in the twenty-first century. Devetak and Walter (2016) examine the historiography that is required in Cox's version of the 'critical theorist' and their capacity to discern social structures and the possibilities for transformation. Attempting to guard against dangers of systematic anachronism in philosophical history, they put forward Giambattista Vico's historical-empirical approach as better serving Coxian ambitions. Germain (2016) extends these themes, by exploring what he calls the 'historical idealism' in Cox's thought aligned to the work of Collingwood, Vico, Braudel, and Carr. For Germain, this variant of historicism provides deep intellectual coherence across Cox's work, linking historical structures, diachronic change, intersubjectivity, and civilizations.

Bridging these historical concerns with IR theory, Persuad (2016) investigates the limits of the neo-Gramscian theory of hegemony. For Persuad, if this approach is to explain the rise and consolidation of the modern world system, it must pay attention to postcolonial analysis of the persistent violence against the Third World and dominance of racism in the production of successive world orders. Building on this engagement with the implications of Cox's thought related to theory, I (Brincat, 2016) examine the relation between Cox and Max Horkheimer as distinct—though allied—ways of approaching 'critical' theorizing. In contrast, Kubalkova (2016) argues that Cox has been 'framed', even co-opted, as a critical theorist—something that has led to a number of analytical and political problems in Cox's legacy for IR theory.

Turning to themes related to IPE, Phillips (2016) uses Cox's insights to explore production, labour, and governance. She links labour exploitation in the global value chains based global economy to shifts towards transnational private governance and the evolving strategies of organized labour. In similar fashion, Mittelman (2016) uses Cox's understanding of global governance—the ideational dimensions of intersubjectivity—to look at global knowledge production and dissemination. Focusing on universities as specific spheres of authority, Mittelman examines how the actors and processes in the university are redesigning global knowledge governance and how Cox's theorization may be expanded to analyse this dynamic.

Expanding on the growing interest in the theme of civilizations in Cox's later work, Karavas and I (2016) examine the linkage between modernization and development in China as an example of what Cox, following Susan Strange, called 'Business Civilization'. We argue that China's development narrative for the commercialization of agriculture converges with Western conceptions of development exemplified in the World Bank and look to points of resistance against this imposition by traditional civilization. To close the volume, Suliman (2016) rethinks civilizations through the politics of migration in the era of climate change. For Suliman, Cox's idea of 'inter-civilizational' politics helps us to both rethink cosmopolitics in the Anthropocene and envisage alternative, post-hegemonic, world orders.

Acknowledgements

This project would not have been possible without the enthusiasm and support of Barry Gills when I first brought it to him some years ago. I would like to thank the anonymous reviewers who have helped strengthen each of these articles and each author for their contribution and for seeing the project through over such a long period. Finally, I would like to express my gratitude and admiration for Robert W. Cox who will continue to inspire 'critical' thinking well into the future.

Disclosure Statement

No potential conflict of interest was reported by the author.

Note

1. For a detailed introduction to Cox's approach to IR, see Cox and Sinclair (1996). For an account that focuses on his legacy and relation to other approaches, see Leysens (2008). For an interview in which Cox reflects on his own work, see Cox (2012).

References

Brincat, S. (2016). Traditional, problem-solving and critical theory: An analysis of Horkheimer and Cox's setting of the 'critical' divide. *Globalizations*, *13*(5). doi:10.1080/14747731.2015.1130204

Cox, R. W. (1981). Social forces, states, and world orders: Beyond international relations theory. *Millennium*, *10(2)*.

Cox, R. W. (1983). Gramsci, hegemony and international relations. *Millennium*, *12*(2): 162–175.

Cox, R. W. (1987). *Production, power, and world order: Social Forces in the making of history*. New York: Columbia University Press.

Cox, R. W. (2012). For someone and for some purpose. In S. Brincat, L. Lima, & J. Nunes, (Eds.), *Critical theory in international relations and security studies: Interviews and reflections* (pp. 15–34). London: Routledge.

Cox, R. W. (2013). *Universal foreigner: The individual and the world*. Hackensack, NJ: World Scientific.

Cox, R. W., & Jacobson, H. K. (1974). The anatomy of influence. New Haven, CT: Yale University Press.

Cox, R. W., & Schechter, M. G. (2002). *The political economy of a plural world: Critical reflections on power, morals and civilization*. London: Routledge.

Cox, R. W., & Sinclair, T. J. (1996). *Approaches to world order*. Cambridge: Cambridge University Press.

Devetak, R. R., & Walter, R. (2016). The critical theorist's labour: Empirical or philosophical historiography for international relations? *Globalizations*, *13*(5). doi:10.1080/14747731.2015.1133527

Falk, R. (2016). Preface. *Globalizations*, *13*(5). doi:10.1080/14747731.2016.1203050

Germain, R. (2016). Robert W. Cox and the idea of history: Political economy as philosophy. *Globalizations*, *13*(5). doi:10.1080/14747731.2015.1128107

Karavas, G., & Brincat, S. (2016). 'Behemoth pulls the peasant's plough': Convergence and resistance to business civilization in China. *Globalizations*, *13*(5). doi:10.1080/14747731.2016.1204079

Kubalkova, V. (2016). Framing Robert W. Cox, framing international relations. *Globalizations*, *13*(5). doi:10.1080/14747731.2016.1204128

Leysens, A. (2008). *The critical theory of Robert W Cox: Fugitive or guru?* London: Palgrave Macmillan.

Mittelman, J. H. (2016). Global governance and universities: The power of ideas and knowledge. *Globalizations*, *13*(5). doi:10.1080/14747731.2015.1129700

Persuad, R. B. (2016). Neo-Gramscian theory and third world violence: A time for broadening. *Globalizations*, *13*(5). doi:10.1080/14747731.2016.1176758

Phillips, N. (2016). Labour in global production: Reflections on Coxian insights in a world of global value chains. *Globalizations*, *13*(5). doi:10.1080/14747731.2016.1138608

Sinclair, T. J. (2016). Robert W. Cox's method of historical structures redux. *Globalizations*, *13*(5). doi:10.1080/14747731.2016.1143662

Suliman, S. (2016). Re-thinking about civilizations: The politics of migration in a new climate. *Globalizations*, *13*(5). doi:10.1080/14747731.2016.1204129

Robert W. Cox's Method of Historical Structures Redux

TIMOTHY J. SINCLAIR

University of Warwick, Coventry, UK

ABSTRACT   *This article argues that Cox's Method of Historical Structures (MHS), although a highly useful tool for understanding the world, should be adapted to make it more effective as a framework for understanding world order in the twenty-first century. The advent of the method helped rejuvenate critical scholarship in international relations and international political economy during the 1980s. It offered a way out of the excessively structural approaches that had dominated critical thinking in the 1960s and 1970s. Cox's method enabled the unpacking of a structure, so that the components that made up any particular configuration could be considered analytically. Providing guidance on how to look at an historical order, and how to consider the component features of that structure, proved to be a revelation for many critical scholars of international relations. Surprisingly, given Cox's highlighting of the distinction between critical and problem-solving theory introduced in the same* Millennium *article, what really distinguishes Cox's approach, and why it has had the impact it has, is the pragmatism of the method. The MHS offers the possibility of a more closely reasoned analysis of world order than was previously available. It was the practical and somewhat systematic quality of the MHS that made it influential because it offered to facilitate empirical research by critical scholars. Thirty-five years on, the Method looks less satisfactory and this article offers some suggestions for its development.*

The publication in 1981 of Robert W. Cox's essay, 'Social forces, states, and world orders: Beyond international relations theory' was a watershed moment in the development of critical thinking about international relations and international political economy. The context for the article was Cox's disenchantment with the structural Marxist approach that emerged in the late 1960s and his reaction to the popularity of a non-historical version of Realist thinking in the USA, stimulated by publication of Kenneth Waltz's (1979) book, *Theory of international politics*.

The publication of 'Social forces' was crucial to emerging critical thinking in the study of international relations and international political economy because it offered a deeper historical lens than was characteristic of scholarly theorizing in the field of international relations since Second World War. The field was largely preoccupied with the immediate problems of managing American hegemony in the context of the cold war with the Soviet Union. Historical works remained firmly historical. Cox bridged the gap between history and the new field of international relations, suggesting that the immediate problems of the world could be put into a deeper context (Cox, 2013, chapter 8, *passim*).

Although the Method of Historical Structures (MHS) (and Cox's subsequent investigation into Gramsci also published in *Millennium*, in 1983; see Cox, 1996b) are key moments in the evolution of critical thinking in international relations, the Method is not without its problems. This article is concerned with contemporary use of the Method in research. I offer an analysis of the Method, including a discussion of its purpose, and an assessment of the strengths and limitations of the Method. I should clarify that, like Cox, I am not an advocate of a universal or singular purpose to theorizing international relations, although like him I am cognizant of a dominant way of thinking about international relations closely tied to hegemonic forces.

After this discussion, I turn to adapting the method, and consider the scope of the ontology implicit in the MHS, its original purpose, and offer some clarification of agency in the MHS. Finally, in a restatement of a now-reconfigured MHS, I reconsider the purpose of the framework and give a sense of what the 'new' MHS looks like.

What I do not do in the text that follows is offer an evaluation of the foundations of the approach or a comparison with other ways of thinking about the same issues. This is intentional. While those are valid and interesting tasks, they are not the purpose of this article. Here the focus is on updating an established framework that might have some utility for those engaged in empirical and historical research.

Method of Historical Structures

The MHS emerges out of Cox's apparent frustration with the conventional ontology of international relations, which draws a sharp distinction between state and civil society, and focuses on states as if they are essentially alike. For Cox, the basic unit of international relations is the relationship between state and society, or what he calls the 'state/society complex' (Cox, 1996a, p. 86). Rather than there being a singular state form around which all of international relations takes place, there is likely to exist a 'plurality of forms of state, expressing different configurations of state/society complexes' suggests Cox (1996a). Reinforcing this sense of ontological complexity, Cox implores the reader to look at world order 'in the whole' but without 'reifying a world system' (1996a, p. 87), not forgetting that change is a key feature. Cox further suggests we do not underrate state power, but do not neglect social forces either (1996a).

The purpose of the MHS is the generation of critical understanding of some aspect of the world, of an 'initial subdivision of reality' (Cox, 1996a, p. 85). This understanding of a feature of the world is a stepping stone to broader understanding or a 'larger picture', and not an end in itself, as it might be for what Cox calls problem-solving approaches (1996a, p. 89). Problem-solving theory, suggests Cox, dominates our thinking in the social sciences, takes the parameters of the world as it finds them, and seeks to identify and address 'particular sources of trouble' (1996a, p. 88). Problem-solving theory is premised on holding constant all other matters outside the area of concern. This gives it incisive but narrow analytical power, which may exaggerate the veracity of problem-solving thinking in the minds of many.

So how do we explore state/society complexes as the 'constituent entities of a world order', but avoid the static, timelessness of Neorealism, in which motivations are assumed to be fixed (Cox, 1996a, p. 96)? Cox suggests the way to do this is by embracing an historical materialism that actually enlarges the realist perspective through its concern with relationships between structure, which he sees as economic relations, and superstructure (or the 'ethico-political sphere'). These relationships explain why state/society complexes differ, producing the variety of historical forms we encounter in the world.

What are the basic premises of this approach? Cox identifies five main features (Cox, 1996a, p. 97). First, action takes place within a 'framework for action' which limits and constitutes the world. Understanding this requires historical study. Second, theory is also shaped by this framework, in the sense that theorists must be aware of theory's historical character and the continual need for its adjustment as the world changes. Third, the 'framework for action' necessarily changes and the main task of critical theory is understanding this change. Fourth, the framework for action is an historical structure or combination that brings together thought, material conditions, and institutions. An historical structure does not determine action but 'constitutes the context' within which action takes place. Cox's structure can be read as a constraint but also more actively (but less clearly) as constituting action too; so the historical structure does more than limit pre-given agents. Last, frameworks for action, or historical structures, should not be considered in terms of their need for equilibrium maintenance, but more dynamically, in terms of identifying the contradictions and conflicts within them which create the possibility for transformation of the framework for action.

There are two elements that make up the MHS. Each is organized by Cox in the form of a graphic 'triangle', as he put it. These triangles may have greatly aided the communication of the method, and the popularity of the approach. It is the first of these 'triangles' that allows the analyst to map out a particular historical structure (Figure 1). The structure does not determine action, 'but imposes pressures and constraints' creating and limiting what can be done in the circumstances (Cox, 1996a, p. 98). Rival structures are possible, and may push back against a specific structure.

Keeping in mind that Cox's thinking developed in response to 1960s structural Marxism and to the emergence of Neorealism in the 1970s, we need to be clear that Cox's triangles are not analogous to circuit diagrams. Cox did not think of the ontology he laid out in the triangles as fixed or immutable. Nor do they provide the basis for the inference of law-like axioms about social life. They are intended to help undertake more rigorous concrete investigations. The concrete investigations are the things that matter, but like any intellectual undertaking, these are better when their guiding assumptions, in this case ontology, are made explicit.

Cox categorizes circumstances as material capabilities, ideas, and institutions. What determines the relationship between them are empirical conditions, and cannot be assumed in

Figure 1. Forces.

advance. Material capabilities are dynamic productive (and destructive) technologies, physical plant, and natural resources. Ideas are intersubjectively shared notions such as diplomatic immunity. These ideas are what Searle calls social or institutional facts (Searle, 2010, p. 10). Unlike Searle, Cox suggests that although these ideas are durable they are historical. Ideas come and go, albeit slowly. Cox also identifies a crucial second category of ideas. These are competing 'images of social order' held by different groups (1996a, p. 99). There may be several, and they tend to be cast in opposition to each other. Institutions, or as Cox puts it, 'institutionalization', is the way a particular order is stabilized and perpetuated. Institutions are a vehicle for creating hegemony, but they may also take on a life of their own and may also become a 'battleground' for opposing tendencies, or rival institutions may compete with each other. Historical structures are limited and do not represent the whole world (1996a, p. 100). Their partiality can be overcome by juxtaposing related structures. Rather than assuming equilibrium and an abstract model of a smoothly functioning social system, the dialectical character of historical structures can be highlighted by identifying them within historical circumstances and by detecting rival structures.

A little confusingly, Cox suggests the MHS can then be 'applied' via a second triangle to 'three levels, or spheres of activity' (Cox, 1996a; Figure 2). These spheres consist of social forces, or what he terms the 'organization of production', forms of state as derived from the study of state/society complexes, and world orders, or the configuration of forces which define the 'problematic of war or peace for the ensemble of states' (1996a). Like the elements of the first structure, the spheres or levels are interrelated. He cites E.H. Carr's discussion of industrial workers as a new social force, and how this comes to stimulate imperial acquisition (1996a, pp. 100–101). The key to understanding the relationship of the two triangles is that the first triangle (the forces) is applied to each of the elements or spheres of the second triangle. In order to understand forms of state, the analyst needs to consider the configuration of material capabilities, ideas, and institutions it contains. The broader categories of the second triangle of spheres can then be considered in relation to each other for a 'fuller representation of historical process' (1996a, p. 101). Like the forces, the broader spheres do not exist in a relationship linear to each other and we discover how they are linked by historical and empirical study.

The breadth of the approach is impressive. Contrast the wide scope of the MHS if you will with what were then, and still are, the dominant models of social science, which seek law-like understandings of small fields of human behaviour. Cox's ambition has been inspirational to more than one generation of students who have found themselves studying international relations but were frustrated by the limits of the orthodox view.

The non-deterministic character of Cox's understanding of how things relate to each other in an historical structure, and the necessity of empirical and historical research in order to see what is important at specific times, is a great strength of the approach because it undermines inadequate models of social life that assume a mechanistic and ahistorical understanding of our world. Cox's approach makes it quite clear that this sort of understanding is not enough.

Figure 2. Spheres.

The two elements of the MHS allow the analyst to integrate forces and spheres, or the static and the dynamic, so producing a much fuller historical account. The 'forces' analysis allows the researcher to examine how an historical structure, a limited thing in itself, works. Moving these structures to the spheres of Figure 2 allows the theorist to see how these little systems work together to produce broader interactions and contradictions, laying the ground for transformation.

There is no denying that as a simple matter of exposition, the juxtaposition of the two triangles is a source of confusion to many readers. Cox asks us to fit Figure 1 into the elements or spheres of Figure 2. This was perhaps not the best way to organize the Method. It works, but the relationship of these two is a less-than optimal approach.

Many people will want to dispute Cox's ontological choices. Production is considered broadly and inclusively. But where is reproduction and gender relations? Are they not part of history? I think the best response to this problem is to suggest that Cox's categories are not exhaustive as he sets them out in 1981, but are open to redefinition and adaptation over time. One approach to this issue would be to say that the researcher simply elaborates upon the framework given the particular context. I think this is what we do almost all the time. But reproduction, as a basic category of social life, is neglected in the classic formulation of the MHS given in 1981. I see nothing in Cox's views which would be hostile to acknowledging this. Indeed he makes it clear that theory changes as history does, and critical theory must be directed at itself as much as at the world. In the most developed statement (1987) of his views, Cox says that reproduction comprises part of 'material capabilities' as set out in the 1981 *Millennium* outline of his Method (see in particular endnote 7; p. 6 of Cox, 1987). While this may have made sense at the time, it does not seem so convincing now. Being explicit about reproduction puts it on a better ontological (and political) footing.

The last problem is that of agency. Agency in the form of 'history' is everywhere in the MHS, as you would expect. The problem is that it falls between the cracks. The structure and the ontology is clear and visible; however, how things move and why, is not. It is this element that I think is probably unsatisfactory to contemporary audiences. Bieler and Morton have suggested that the best interpretation of Cox's approach to agency and structure, when his subsequent work is considered, is that he 'develops explanations of regularities in human activity within particular historical limits' (Bieler & Morton, 2001, p. 21). What those explanations are, their conceptual sources, is flexible and open, and I suggest potentially allow for the use of problem-solving theory where the analyst finds these relevant.

Adapting the MHS

Broadening the ontology of the first triangle of forces could renew the relevance of the MHS, and making things explicit is, other things equal, good scholarship. Although we could argue that gender issues are implicit in the 1981 framework, 'material capabilities' could be transformed to incorporate reproductive dynamics as well as productive ones. This assumes that reproductive technologies (such as the advent of in vitro fertilization) and the allocation of reproductive tasks (such as childcare) change historically, like other forces in Cox's schema.

As noted, Cox discusses ideas in terms of rival collective images and intersubjectively held norms. Intersubjectivity, or social facts, which have become a major area of social science theorizing, do not sit well with class consciousness, and actually are more like institutions than ideas, given that Cox considers institutions more broadly than mere organizations. Thinking of social facts as ideas gives the false impression that they are somehow voluntary or idiosyncratic. In the new schema, ideas will only refer to consciously held ideas, not social facts.

The broader categories of the spheres' triangle may be easier to live with for some. To others it may seem—ironically—rather state-centric. Instead of 'forms of state' why not stick with the broader category of state/society complex? Surely this would work better here. Or perhaps we could use 'forms of state' but add more categories to reflect social complexity? Cox's sphere of 'social forces' is relatively narrowly understood by him as 'engendered by the production process' (Cox, 1996a, p. 100). But surely this is not enough to capture the other social issues of gender, race, sexual orientation, disability, age and so on that seem central to life in advanced societies but are not easily reducible to production. This is an issue that Marxist scholars have grappled with for decades and I am not aware of a perfect solution. Even when Cox first published this article, it is not clear that the phenomenon of apartheid would have fitted adequately into the social forces sphere. I suggest we add a fourth sphere to be called 'social dynamics'. Into this would fit the vast range of human conflict and cooperation not reducible to production. Struggles by social movements about things such as human rights and the biosphere are manifestly consequential, and need to be recognised as such. Note that I have not made a separate category for 'the environment'. While we are material beings as well as social ones, the struggle over how to address the environment is part of the social dynamic, and how we resolve it will not be reducible to material necessity alone. Note that in adding this fourth sphere of interaction, I have changed the second triangle of spheres or levels into a diamond, neatly ending a source of 35 years of confusion if this innovation is adopted. From two triangles, we now have the triangle and the diamond.

When Cox developed the MHS, he was very conscious of his purpose. If only all scholars were equally as self-aware of their intent. He distinguished between problem-solving and critical theory and it was clear that the purpose of MHS is associated with critical theory. It is premised on the ongoing process of historical change and on the conscious pursuit of change in the interests of improving the lives of most people. But this stark divergence between problem-solving and critical theory is troublesome and in my experience unattractive to those looking for a means of changing the world. Critical theory's objective of transforming the world needs to start somewhere. Transformation is too distant to be very practical and being practical should be an objective for critical theory, unless we are willing to accept that this approach to theory is entirely abstract.

Michael Schechter has written, when considering the report of the Commission on Global Governance, of the merits of what he terms 'policy-relevant critical theory' (Schechter, 1999, p. 247). He suggests that critical theory is particularly adept at the structural and contextual analysis that problem-solving approaches avoid, often by invoking *ceteris paribus*. He also notes how critical theory tends to have a broader, more innovative ontology and thus can include actors and phenomena ignored by problem-solving (Schechter, 1999, p. 248). In contexts like this, critical theory may have a more immediate relevance than it once had, and that relevance can build support for maintaining and developing critical theory. A widening of Cox's purpose for the MHS makes sense.

For those not already sympathetic to Marxist thinking, Cox's approach may seem highly structural. This is ironic given that Cox was responding to excessive structuralism in both Marxist and Realist scholarship in vogue at the time he was writing. But in the context of the time, the 1981 *Millennium* article's attempt to rethink structurally was critical thinking as it opposed mainstream thought, which, like Hollywood movies, gives all the attention to the action. Cox makes it clear again and again that how things work out depends on circumstances.

His agency is in the facts on the ground, and structure does not determine outcome so much as limit the range of possibilities. Cox's understanding of historical structures is that they are 'persistent social practices' which are made (and transformed) by 'collective human activity' (Cox, 1987, p. 4). Is this approach to agency adequate, or does it leave us with an analytical system that is fundamentally structure-centric? The answer may lie in reading Cox's 'lines of force' in terms of the explicitly dialectical political analysis of hegemony (and counter-hegemony) provided by Gramsci. This highlights just how political structures are, and how vulnerable to erosion they remain.

Historical Structures Redux

When Cox's 'Social Forces' article was published in 1981, it was an exciting moment in the emergence of critical international relations scholarship. Here was a framework offering researchers a method to do historically informed empirical investigation that offered to go well beyond the broad categories of existing critical thinking. There is no doubt that Cox's work on international organizations in the 1960s and 1970s, and his subsequent work on critically theorising international relations and international political economy has been very influential (see Randall Germain, 2016). He supervised numerous graduate students at York University who have gone on to undertake research on a wide array of phenomena. Despite this breadth of impact, the results, in terms of completed research closely tied to the Method Historical Structures, did not match the initial enthusiasm for the 1981 article. Some of that can be put down to the incredible flowering of critical international relations theory during the 1980s and 1990s. Scholars were spoilt for choice. It may also be the case, as I contend, that there were problems with the Method which undermined use of the framework to create new knowledge. These problems were three-fold. First, the possible perception that the approach was more structural and determinist than was the case. Second, a seemingly narrow ontology. Last, potential confusion between the purpose of the two 'triangles' and how they related to each other.

In thinking about the MHS Redux, I have tried to give attention to these three problems. The seeming lack of agency in the approach can be addressed by invoking Gramsci because the language of hegemony and counter-hegemony brings to life what may otherwise seem rigid 'forces' or 'spheres'. It also helps remind readers of the link between history, lines of force as Cox terms them, and agency. Agency is very much a lived experience in the Coxian schema, rather than a capacity or box to fill with content. To try to do this a priori with agency is, in the Coxian universe, a mistake of hyperstructuralism. In MHS Redux the ontology has been clarified by moving intersubjectivity to the institutions category in Figure 3, and by distinguishing reproduction and production. On the spheres or levels side (Figures 2 and 4), I have added the new social dynamics level to integrate a key feature of social life given insufficient attention in the classic version of the MHS. Familiarity and use is probably the best route to overcoming confusion about the relationship of forces and spheres. The key insight is that multiple sets of forces exist within each sphere or level, competing for hegemony. 'Forces' provide the static or synchronic analysis, while the broader 'spheres' analysis allows us to think in terms of diachronic potential, as the latent contradictions between forces can be made explicit.

Let us consider what the MHS Redux looks like as depicted in Figures 3 and 4. Figure 3 sticks to the broadest outlines of Cox's ontology of forces, but is adapted as discussed above. Instead of 'ideas', we now have 'competing ideas' which should highlight the focus on the conflict between different collectively held ideas. The conflict between ideas is more apparent in this treatment. As noted, I have moved intersubjectively held ideas from 'ideas' to link up with 'institutions'. I

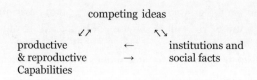

Figure 3. Forces redux.

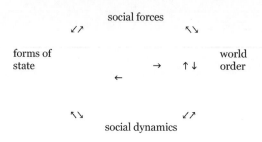

Figure 4. Spheres redux.

did this because intersubjective notions are not ideas in the classic sense but really operate as what Searle calls social facts. These norms and assumptions structure our lives well away from the competition and controversy of competing ideas. I have kept 'institutions' in the title of this force even though social facts are really the same phenomenon in order to capture the everyday understanding of institutions as organizations. Social facts alone might have been abstruse. The last category of forces in the bottom left corner of Figure 3 has been modified from Cox's material capabilities to distinguish productive and reproductive matters. Reproductive issues have been teased out of their implicit location in 'material capabilities'. Although 'production' and 'material' can be and are interpreted by Marxists in all-encompassing ways, I think it is best to acknowledge the distinctiveness of household and gender dynamics, as these are such large dimensions of our lives.

In Cox's schema, Figure 3 provides any number of limited understandings of sets of forces. This structure, let us call it Thatcherism say, can then be understood when applied to Figure 4 as a specific form of state (e.g. confrontational), as a social force (e.g. privatization), as a social dynamic (e.g. conservative values) and as a feature of world order (e.g. reinforcement of cold war competition).

How should we actually go about using the modified MHS in research? We need to be clear about what it will be useful for, and where it will not be useful. It is unlikely to help us produce law-like generalizations about social life. Apart from the obvious observation that Cox is hostile to such knowledge in the absence of a critical theory context, the MHS Redux is best understood as a framework for theorizing consequential phenomena. An example might be contemporary China. We want to understand the rise of China and it is clearly so important we can justify studying it in its own right. But the uniqueness of China as a phenomenon is not going to help us create law-like theories that we can apply to other phenomena. But that does not matter. It is important enough to understand China itself. So Cox's MHS is an aid to theorizing the world, but a world whose historical complexity and uniqueness is the starting (and ending) point. In this sense the MHS is not seeking to produce highly parsimonious knowledge, although highly parsimonious knowledge may prove useful to the understanding of forces in the first triangle. Once the researcher understands and embraces the lack of common ground between the form of understanding Cox seeks and that sought by problem-solving social science she can then undertake her analysis in the two moments. The first, the forces, is the static or synchronic understanding of how things fit together (e.g. Thatcherism) while the spheres of Figure 4 allow for understanding of the broader context and incorporates potential contradictions between elements (Thatcherism vs. Soviet Communism, for example).

Conclusions

In this article I have argued that Cox's MHS, although a useful tool for understanding the world, can and should be adapted to make it more effective as a framework for interpreting world order in the twenty-first century. Cox's method helped rejuvenate critical scholarship in international relations and international political economy during the 1980s. It offered a way out of the rigidly structural approaches that had dominated critical thinking in the 1960s and 1970s. Cox's approach enabled the unpacking of a structure, so that its components could be considered analytically. Providing guidance on how to look at a particular order and how to specify and consider the component features of structures proved a revelation. The MHS offers the possibility of a more closely reasoned analysis of world order than was previously available. Surprisingly, what really distinguishes Cox's approach, and why it has had the impact it has, is its pragmatism. But 35 years on the Method looks less satisfactory than it did. Some of that promise has not been realised. I identified problems with the MHS and suggested some reconfiguring of the framework to acknowledge issues that were never resolved adequately in the classic formula.

The MHS Redux improves on the classic formulation because it acknowledges the core reality of human reproduction and gender relations. This was implicit in the classic model, but it is better made explicit given the scope and depth of this aspect of human life. Sorting out the confusion between competing ideas and intersubjective norms is useful. These two quite different phenomena are not reducible to 'ideas', which gives the false impression of a battle of ideologies, and the rise of constructivism, and especially the work of John Searle has made it clear just how significant is intersubjectivity and social facts. Adding 'social dynamics' to the second 'spheres' triangle gives weight to what are huge human struggles that many Marxists neglected historically.

In offering these adaptations I have also sought to clarify ways in which the MHS can be used in research. One of the glaring weaknesses of critical scholarship in contrast to orthodoxy has been the seeming reluctance to offer guidance on how to do research especially to those new to scholarship. Perhaps this is motivated by a desire to ensure choice is maintained and to avoid the 'training' mentality characteristic of problem-solving social science. In addition to the possibility of better integration of Cox's two triangles—or what in this reformulation becomes the triangle and the diamond—a positive outcome of this development of Cox's method would be greater integration of problem-solving research on specific institutions, mechanisms and relationships within a wider context of diachronic research into context. For me this would truly capitalize on the flexibility and openness of Cox's original formulation and make critical insight stronger and more persuasive. Then, as now, the exciting potential of the MHS lies in the ability of the framework to jump the divide between problem-solving and critical theory, integrating problem-solving synchronic insights into a broader diachronic critical purpose. The depth of understanding this offers versus more sectarian approaches which eschew insights from other methods makes Cox's MHS worth pursuing. The potential to offer more relevant and useful knowledge, as suggested by Schechter, while perhaps a surprising observation, is really in keeping with the pragmatism inherent in the approach from the beginning. In this sense, the MHS Redux seeks to fulfil the potential of Cox's classic 1981 formulation.

Acknowledgements

I thank Shannon Brincat for inviting me to contribute to this special issue, and the two anonymous reviewers for their thoughtful comments on an earlier draft.

Disclosure Statement

No potential conflict of interest was reported by the author.

References

Bieler, A., & Morton, A. D. (2001). The Gordian knot of agency-structure in international relations: A neo-Gramscian perspective. *European Journal of International Relations*, 7(1), 5–35.
Cox, R. W. (1987). *Production, power, and world order: Social forces in the making of history*. New York, NY: Columbia University Press.
Cox, Robert W. (1996a). Social forces, states, and world order: Beyond international relations theory (1981). In R. W. Cox & T. J. Sinclair (Eds.), *Approaches to world order* (pp. 85–123). Cambridge: Cambridge University Press.
Cox, Robert W. (1996b). Gramsci, hegemony, and international relations: An essay in method (1983). In R. W. Cox & T. J. Sinclair (Eds.), *Approaches to world order* (pp. 124–143). Cambridge: Cambridge University Press.
Cox, R. W. (2013). *Universal foreigner: The individual and the world*. Singapore: World Scientific.
Germain, R. (2016). Robert W. Cox and the idea of history: Political economy as philosophy. *Globalizations*. doi:10.1080/14747731.2015.1128107.
Schechter, M. G. (1999). Our global neighborhood: Pushing problem-solving to its limits and the limits of problem-solving theory. In M. Hewson & T. J. Sinclair (Eds.), *Approaches to global governance theory* (pp. 239–258). Albany: State University of New York Press.
Searle, J. R. (2010). *Making the social world: The structure of human civilization*. Oxford: Oxford University Press.
Waltz, K. N. (1979). *Theory of international politics*. Reading, MA: Addison-Wesley.

The Critical Theorist's Labour: Empirical or Philosophical Historiography for International Relations?

RICHARD DEVETAK & RYAN WALTER

University of Queensland, Brisbane, QLD, Australia

ABSTRACT *Robert Cox developed a potent approach to studying world orders that is premised on the capacities of a special intellectual, the critical theorist, to discern social structures and the possibilities for their radical change in the future. While acknowledging the ethical appeal of adopting this intellectual persona, in this paper we are concerned with the style of historiography that it requires. In particular, we argue that the imperative to discover and foster the beginnings of social change leads to a version of philosophical history that will likely produce systematic anachronism. This is not uncommon in the discipline of International Relations, but in the case of Cox it stands in tension with some of his avowed intellectual sources, especially the work of Giambattista Vico, and with the aim of providing critical historical perspective on the present. We argue that Vico stands as an example of an alternative historical-empirical line of research that would better serve Coxian ambitions.*

The Critical Intellectual and Change

One of the most striking features of Robert Cox's reflections on method is the centrality of change in world politics, where change features in two different but related senses. First, change is treated as a fact of human reality, and this means that the concepts of political economy are constantly being outmoded by the world that they are intended to describe. The implication is that theory that is not historically focused is susceptible to mistaking contemporary features of the world for enduring or timeless structures (Cox, 1981, p. 133). This is the occasion for Cox's powerful distinction between problem-solving theory and critical theory.

Problem-solving theory treats the world's leading institutions and power relations as given and tries to optimize their operation or minimize their deficiencies. Waltz's (1979) positivist neo-realism is presented as a case of problem-solving theory that distances itself from history to generate law-like hypotheses regarding international relations, and the history of international relations then serves as a data set to assist with testing and refining hypotheses (Cox, 1981, pp. 131–133; see also Cox, 1996, pp. 52–53). By contrast, critical theory 'stands apart from the prevailing order' to inquire into the origins of this order, and to determine if fundamental change is at hand (Cox, 1981, p. 129). In a recent interview, Cox affirmed this distinction, stating that critical theory 'recognizes that the existing situation is a transitory one', and its task is to 'look for the openings that are likely to bring about structural change in the future' (Cox, 2012, p. 20). A good example of structural change is the emergence of the modern system of states, a development that neo-realism is unable to explain because this system is presupposed as a historical constant, while critical theory is preoccupied with historic shifts of exactly this type (Cox, 1996, pp. 54–58).

The other sense in which change is central to Cox's work relates not to his historical ontology but to the motivating ethos for critical theory. The assumption of structural continuity that characterizes problem-solving theory is treated as an 'ideological bias' by Cox because any existing order will serve some sectional interests (whether national or class) and disadvantage others (Cox, 1981, p. 130). A standing injunction for critical theorists issues from this realization: 'to be critical, to refuse to accept a theory at face value, to look at it and see where it comes from, what it was designed to achieve, the context in which it was developed' (Cox, 2012, p. 19). At this point we can state two characteristics of the Coxian critical theorist. The first is a sensitivity to incipient change in historical structures. The second is a scepticism regarding the purported political neutrality of any given theory.

A third characteristic joins these two together: the role of the critical theorist in making it possible to imagine alternative structures. More explicitly, critical theory transcends the conservative bias inherent in problem-solving theory because it 'allows for a normative choice in favour of a social and political order different from the prevailing order' (Cox, 1981, p. 130). From here a number of sub-tasks unfold. One is to engender a desire for change by exposing 'current doctrines as inadequate in dealing with global problems', while another is to prospect change in world structures by discovering 'other elements that could be thought of, either separately or collectively, as an alternative' (Cox, 2012, p. 20). A further sub-task is to provide the materials for strategic calculations regarding world change: does the current historical moment contain the seeds of change? Which social actors could achieve change on the necessary scale? (Cox, 1996, pp. 54–55). This heady work of motivating, prophesying, and strategizing change raises the issue of who benefits from the critical theorist's labours. Cox has explicitly addressed this issue as follows:

> The role of the critical theorist, then, is to be aware of forces of opposition to the established order, and to bring them to the light so that others are not only aware of them but can evaluate them in terms of their own thinking—assessing whether there are compatibilities and common aims. I'm talking about working from the level of society rather than from a formal institutional structure. We need some sort of feeling at the base of societies, so that people can recognize more concerns with 'others'. (Cox, 2012, p. 21)

In these comments, two familiar figures of western social theory (the 'people' and 'society') emerge as the addressees of critical theory.[1] Ironically, the critical intellectual is likely to benefit from a certain distance from the people and society because they will thereby avoid forming an 'organic relationship to a particular group of people', and this enables thinking that is 'remote, more general, probably more holistic', as Cox described the effects of his own remoteness from 'everyday reality' (quoted in Hoogvelt, Kenny, & Germain, 1999, p. 398).

This sketch of the Coxian critical theorist will be familiar to many readers of this journal even if they have not read Cox's work, for it is a version of the critical intellectual who stands sufficiently apart from the material and ideological determinations of history in order to better apprehend and expose these determinations, thereby transforming formerly anonymous forces into the target of social and political change. The list of eminent thinkers who have acceded to this critical *persona* runs from Hegel to Habermas, and has roots in neo-scholastic and Kantian metaphysical intellectual cultures.[2] In the discipline of International Relations, the leading critical theorists have been Andrew Linklater (1982, 1990), Ken Booth (2007) and the early Richard Ashley (1981). Linklater, for example, cultivated a critical intellectual *persona* committed to a method of philosophical history aimed at providing a normative or emancipatory theory of international relations that traces the progress of universal freedom by identifying obstructions and pathways to change. Like Cox, Linklater (1990, p. 33) explicitly tied the critical theorist's *persona* to the 'commitment to change'. The family resemblance between Cox's critical *persona* and Linklater's should be clear.[3] We now turn to consider the style of historiography that is required to discharge this station.

Cox's Dialectical Production of History

The argument to be developed relates to Cox's admission regarding the empirical character of the historiography necessary for his brand of critical theory. Cox claimed that history is needed to ask 'broader questions about how the whole is changing and what are the points of contradiction within those changes', yet the cost is that such history 'is not going to be as accurate and detailed as a positivistic cutting-up of knowledge and dealing with its attendant bits and pieces' (quoted in Hoogvelt et al., 1999, p. 393). We will suggest that the ethical imperatives that impel the Coxian critical theorist to conceive change in world structures compromise the empirical credentials of their historiography.[4]

The ability to think of the world as a series of structures that might be poised to give way requires that these structures are first erected by dint of theoretical effort.[5] Cox recommended approaching historical structures, or frameworks for action, as composed of material capabilities, ideas, and institutions, and he developed further distinctions between hegemonic and non-hegemonic structures, and distinguished 'spheres of activity', such as production, state, and world order. A structure is a means to simplify and represent one aspect of a complex world. The analysis of change within a structure can then be linked to the analysis of related structures and their development through time, and in this way, critical theory can follow the complex chains of causation that create shifts in world orders (Cox, 1981, pp. 135–138).

Cox mobilized these premises in his description of the rise of the liberal order in his sweeping work, *Production, Power, and World Order*. The liberal order is approached with concepts developed earlier in the book, which included twelve ideal-typical 'modes of social relations of production' and a sketch of their links to three historical processes: simple reproduction, capitalism, and redistributive development. The mode 'central planning', for example, was a consequence of redistributive development in the Soviet Union (Cox, 1987, p. 84). We need to mark that this is a highly theoretical species of intellectual labour, for Cox's modes represent the attempt to 'translate the general category of production into concepts that express concrete historical forms of the ways in which production has been organized'. That is, Cox's modes are theoretical categories deduced from another category—'the general category of production' (1987, p. 1).

Production, in turn, is derived from a Polanyian philosophical anthropology that elevates work as the universal 'transformation of nature for the purpose of satisfying human needs and desires', so that the 'concept of production relations covers the whole universe of work' (Cox, 1987, pp. 13–14). This descending hierarchy—from the general notion of work through production to modes of social relations of production—is joined to a complementary ascending hierarchy from modes of production through states to world orders. States are said to influence modes of social relations of production, and different forms of state will correspond to different world orders (1987, pp. 105–109). Having erected this conceptual edifice through multiple acts of conceptual abstraction, Cox then turned to the history of the liberal order.

The general argument is that a modern system of sovereign states had arrived by the Peace of Westphalia and evolved mercantilism and the balance of power as its operating procedures. This order was replaced when the British bourgeoisie achieved political hegemony internally and the British state achieved military and financial hegemony externally—the 'liberal state and the liberal world order emerged together' (Cox, 1987, p. 123). Prior to the liberal order, the 'world economy was constrained within political boundaries laid down by states', but by the middle of the nineteenth century, the 'world economy achieved autonomy, such that its own laws began to constrain state policies' (1987, p. 107). A key mechanism for change was the calibration of state actions and bourgeois interests as a whole in Britain, especially in relation to the institutional framework and foreign policy. Bourgeois dominance saw the creation of markets for labour at the same time as labour agitation was suppressed, and free trade trumped formal empire as the goal of external negotiations. As an object of desire for the hegemonic class of the world hegemon, the enterprise labour market became the dominant mode of social relations of production in early capitalism, and a liberal world order provided the external conditions for its expansion (1987, pp. 144–150).

One of the crucial conditions that the liberal world order provided was a split between politics and economics, in the sense that the state and state system were to guarantee the operation of the 'open world economy' but refrain from interfering in its actual distributive mechanisms (Cox, 1987, pp. 127, 149–150). Cox treated political economy as the key ideological manifestation of the rise of the bourgeoisie and the coming of the liberal order. In particular, Adam Smith is said to have provided the intellectual rationale for the ideal-typical autonomous liberal state, which facilitated markets by removing mercantile obstructions and producing public goods (Cox, 1987, pp. 129–134). We will return to Cox's account of Smith in our conclusion.

Cox thus links world orders, states, and modes of social relations of production to account for the emergence of the liberal order and its effects. The primary problem with this narrative is that historical investigation is subordinated to the requirements of an abstract and predetermined theoretical framework. To put it more explicitly, before any historical inquiry commences, it is already determined that structures will be found operating at three different levels—modes of production, states, and world orders. This feature of Cox's historiography seems to derive from the imperative of the critical *persona* to discern the potential for epochal change in terms of linked structures. This requirement is realized in the closing pages of *Production, Power, and World Order*, where a 'critical awareness of potentiality for change' flows from Cox's mapping of the existing world order (1987, pp. 393–403). The coherence and power of Cox's historical narrative is less a reflection of the historical record than a product of the philosophically derived unities and the dialectical relations into which they are placed.

From the Critical to the Civil Persona

Another striking feature of Cox's presentation of the critical theorist is that it claims to harness a historical mode of thought that is closely aligned with Renaissance humanism. The realist and historicist thought that he traces from Machiavelli and Meinecke to E. H. Carr and Ludwig Dehio might typically be assumed to be confined to problem-solving as opposed to critical theory, but Cox disagreed (1981, p. 131, 2012, p. 20), arguing that such thought is actually crucial to his version of critical theory (Devetak, 2014). While Cox makes programmatic theory statements of this kind, his historiography does not align with the historicism and realism that he extols.

In what follows we consider a style of historiography that does not derive from the critical theorist's desire to escape the horizon of historical structures and then prophesy their change, but from a far more worldly set of ambitions and purposes pertinent to holders of various political offices. While empirical historiography is not exclusive to Renaissance humanism, this intellectual movement provided a favourable context for its development as a support for the arts of civil government. In this setting, civil *personae* were improvised by humanists and distinguished by disavowing the overtly moralizing and abstract tones of Scholastic philosophy that prefigured the critical *persona*. In their place, humanists developed empirically oriented methods of history and philology. Rather than ignore Cox's remarks about critical theory as a historical mode of knowledge, as many critical theorists are wont to do, they are taken seriously in the following sections in an effort to recover and defend an alternative form of historiography which can only be consigned to 'uncritical' problem-solving on the basis of a sectarian dismissal of its actual history.

One of the defining characteristics of Renaissance humanism was its polemical assault on abstract modes of thought.[6] The scholastic curriculum dominant in schools and universities came under increasing challenge during the fifteenth and sixteenth centuries as the Ciceronian curriculum of *studia humanitatis* forged alternative intellectual tools aimed at cultivating the knowledge and skills essential to a civil persona. In part, humanism grew out of a frustration with the 'proliferating abstractions and superfluous distinctions' of Scholasticism and natural philosophy (Kelley, 1970, p. 29). In their '"selfish" withdrawal into scholarship and contemplation' (Baron, 1966, p. 7), these recondite modes of knowledge were bereft of the practical knowledge, prudence, and wisdom required by those occupying public office. They should thus not intrude into affairs of state.

The Scholastics, in turn, accused humanists of lacking philosophical rigour, being indifferent to truth, and of endorsing ethical relativism (Fubini, 2003, pp. 5–6). Since humanists were not concerned with abstract philosophy, these philosophical criticisms were like water off a duck's back. Uninterested in the moral demands of the philosopher's intellectual persona, humanists were concerned to develop a *persona* grounded in, and serving, the *respublica*. They were more concerned with forming citizens and governing human conduct in everyday life than saving souls. This still allowed humanists to salvage philosophies that accepted their identity as one of several civil sciences (Hankins, 2007, pp. 45–46), but given humanism's commitment to the *vita activa*, or active participation in civil life (*negotium*), and the grooming of a civil *persona*, it was experience and history rather than philosophy which took on greater significance in the world of politics.

This was evident in the fact that several Florentine chancellors—from Coluccio Salutati and Leonardo Bruni to Benedetto Accolti and Bartolomeo Scala—were leading humanist scholars in their day (Black, 1986). In their hostility to the contemplative withdrawal (*otium*) of abstract philosophies, and on the basis of 'the critical-philological spirit', they gave birth to 'a new attitude toward the past' (Baron, 1966, p. 48) and a new articulation of civic republicanism. Their writings, following the exemplary histories of Sallust and Livy, thematized politics by narrating and analysing the ongoing struggles for liberty and good government against empire and tyranny. History became recognized as the preeminent literary genre for understanding the political present.

The revival of historical study, making the past 'the object of knowledge of a specific kind: historical knowledge' (Ianziti, 1991, p. 80), was one of the major achievements of Renaissance humanism. Distinguishing the past from the present, whatever continuities may exist, required the development of new intellectual techniques for uncovering and recovering original sources, and for managing information, both historical and contemporary, considered integral to the maintenance of governments but which were unavailable to (or disavowed by) metaphysical agendas. Documentary sources thus became crucial, which is why chancellors were well-positioned to write histories since they had access to a range of official and private records, as well as laws, ordinances, treaties, diplomatic correspondence, and other archival material. It was philology rather than philosophy that enabled the humanist historian to find and consult primary sources and to avoid relying on ahistorical commentary literature.

In this search for historical knowledge, philosophy's standing declined as it was ill-equipped to search for or examine sources. The task, as humanists understood it, was not to assess past thought against ideas presently believed to be timeless or superior, but to grasp the past more accurately and in its own terms. This meant recovering the actual thought and actions of earlier times, including their idioms and languages, rather than the myths and glosses handed down through generations of interpretation and transported by philosophy to a higher metaphysical plane. In this respect, humanism not only exposed the metaphysics embodied in Scholastic philosophy, it also contributed to the historiographical imperative to contextualize and thus provided more concrete knowledge for political action. As Gilbert (1965, p. 228) observed: 'History moved closer to politics because it was expected that history could teach men about political behaviour, about the functioning of institutions and the conduct of government.' History was a source of political wisdom, supplying virtuous examples to guide political action, but it also incited political action itself (Viroli, 1998, p. 97).

Dismantling the metaphysical agenda of ecclesiastic and Scholastic theologies and replacing them with temporal-political agendas of civil governance was one of the main purposes of humanist historiography (Devetak, 2015; Hunter, 2001, 2014). Given the interest in civil and political life, humanists wrote their histories not 'for the delectation of other scholars and humanists but as a guide for literate statesmen' (Ianziti, 2012, p. 6). Humanist histories had political intent behind them: to preserve and strengthen the *respublica*. Humanists recognized that politics was a historically situated, contingent activity, where actors and institutions interacted in particular contexts and changeable circumstances.

This emphatically historical approach to politics and statecraft is made plain in the writings of one of the most notorious political realists and humanists, Niccolò Machiavelli. His major works are peppered with historical examples offered up as exemplary political lessons (Viroli, 1998, pp. 97–107). Like other humanists, Machiavelli believed that 'classical antiquity constituted a great reservoir of excellence' (Hankins, 2007, p. 32), but not in any simplistic transference from the past to the present. His point was not so much that antiquity should be emulated, but that it offered lessons for those willing to interpret and contextualize political action. The most important thing was to understand the nature of the political moment and the effects of time on the art of government. 'Time sweeps everything along and can bring good as well as evil, evil as well as good', Machiavelli (2003, p. 12) wrote, emphasizing that politics is a temporal activity, always subject to the vagaries of time (history) and place (context). Political actors, therefore, must be able to grasp—in both senses of the word, to comprehend and to seize—the times. Politics and the arts of government therefore call for forms of 'contextual reasoning' (Funkenstein, 1986, p. 206). Without this historical or contextual reasoning, politics risks becoming detached from reality, too abstract, and bereft of practical civil use; or else politics reverts to a normative political theory of the Scholastic type which deals in idealized ethical constructions of 'man' and civil society.

This Renaissance background and the reaction against philosophy is crucial for coming to terms with the one eighteenth-century thinker who Cox credits as a major intellectual influence: the University of Naples' Royal Professor of Eloquence, Giambattista Vico (1668–1744). Cox clearly sees his own critical theory as a continuation of Vico's historical approach, and Vico himself saw his own contribution as an extension of humanism (Vico 1699–1707/1993). Vico's *New Science* was intended to combat the rise of Cartesian philosophy and produce 'a history of the ideas, customs, and deeds of humankind' (Vico 1744/2001, p. 139) by employing the intellectual methods of philology and history. To undertake his history of the 'civil world', Vico developed a historical mode of knowledge that recognized, and was capable of comprehending, the constitutive role played by ideas, myths, and culture in history, the very things that give history its human and civil form.

Intentions, motives, and interests thus become crucial to understanding individual and collective action in the political world, but only if they are understood historically and contextually as the specific responses to actions, events, and institutions in particular places and times. Vico's work thus carried with it a general assault on anachronism, especially scholars who judge past civilizations 'according to the enlightenment, refinement, and magnificence of their [own] age' (Vico, 1744/2001, p. 76). According to Vico's contextualist approach, it is a mistake to assume that we can simply employ our own abstract, refined, intellectualized philosophies to enter into the political imaginations of distant societies (1744/2001, p. 147). Vico's point, as Haddock (1976, p. 515) affirmed, is that 'ideas are contextual'. Our approach to these ideas must therefore be historical; selectively plundering the history of political thought without regard to context, simply to rationalize contemporary theories, tells us more about the present than the past. In attacking anachronism, Vico was denying the 'presentist' or 'transcendentalizing' tendencies to interpret and judge institutions and customs of former times against our own dominant assumptions. For Vico, writing the history of the civil world required a method capable of understanding changing cultural, legal, and political conditions, for these conditions form the contexts within which civil institutions such as nations or states rise and fall. Vico's *New Science* (1744/2001) should thus be seen as an attempt to historicize and contextualize ideas by showing how their modifications over time are part of the history of human civil institutions.

Vico resisted the temptation to evaluate past forms of civil institution according to the criteria of modern philosophical rationality. In fact, the whole thrust of his argument was that philosophy is incapable of meeting the historical challenge of understanding past thinkers and societies free of anachronism. Against the philosophical tendency to erase historical difference, Vico sought to contextualize the ways in which past thinkers and societies have thought about and practised politics. As forms of political and legal arrangement that grow out of the particularities of time and place, civil institutions are best understood as historical phenomena. This is why Vico insisted that civil institutions cannot be grasped independently of the ideas that actors of the time held about them (1744/2001, pp. 119–120). The philological approach advocated by

Vico focuses precisely on the historically different ways in which humans 'have made their world intelligible in terms of certain modes of thought' (Haddock, 1978, p. 165). Vico rejected Cartesian natural philosophy because its abstract scientific method denigrated history and denied the constitutive historical role played by ideas in making human civil institutions. Ultimately, it remained incapable of grasping the interplay of ideas and institutions in the shaping of human interactions, and thus could not contribute to an understanding of 'the world of nations in its historical reality' (Vico, 1744/2001, p. 84). Furthermore, the inner-worldly abstraction of Cartesian natural philosophy did nothing to enrich that 'noble and important branch of studies, the science of the state' (Vico, 1709/1990, p. 33).

As Vico put it in *On the Study Methods of Our Time* (Vico, 1709/1990, p. 35): 'it is an error to apply to the prudent conduct of life the abstract criterion of reasoning that obtains in the domain of science'. Philology, however, offered 'a necessary service to the state' by writing 'commentaries on commonwealths, the customs, laws, institutions, branches of learning, and artifacts of nations and peoples' (Vico, 1720–1722/2009, p. 46). In this regard, Vico not only underscored the importance of a historical method in the study of politics and its institutions, and in understanding the historically different ways that humans have conceived of their civil institutions, he also distanced his approach from contemporary modes of knowledge grounded in Cartesian natural philosophy. The latter do not, because they cannot, determine what counts as practical knowledge or wisdom in the conduct of civil affairs.

Conclusion

After patiently reading all these claims, the reader is entitled to expect a concrete example of the difference between the two styles of historiography in action. One of the starkest contrasts can be seen in relation to the treatment of Smith. As we saw, Cox positioned Smith as programming the ideal-typical capitalist liberal state, which cleared away mercantilist regulations to provide a space for the market to operate free of impediments. Cox then paired this treatment of Smith with a narrative of the concrete political struggles by which the British state approached and receded from this ideal. A drastically different account of Smith is produced, however, if we adopt historicizing and contextualizing forms of historiography, as originally developed by Renaissance humanists.

One of the key tasks of such a historiography is to recover the conceptual languages and idioms that were contextually available to a given author, and then investigate which of these languages the author used and how.[7] In this respect, J. G. A. Pocock and Donald Winch have shown that Smith's *Wealth of Nations* was one of the last great works written in the language of civic humanism, in which understanding the tortured relationship between commerce and civic virtue was a guiding issue (Pocock, 1975; Winch, 1978). The type of liberty that Smith recommended for subjects and the conception of justice with which he connected it were correspondingly non-liberal in character; instead, they related to his theory of moral sentiments in which justice is a virtue emerging from the impartial spectator's sympathetic response to wrongs. In all this, Smith was using a second language simultaneously, a Scottish version of natural law that combined moral sense theory with a reworked version of Pufendorf's voluntarism (Haakonssen, 1981, 2006). Again, there is no point of contact here with liberal accounts of the subject, and economic agency is not a distinct type of agency (Tribe, 1978; Walter, 2008). In fact, engaging in exchange relationships diversified the moral personality by the acquisition of manners and politeness, giving rise not to liberalism but a commercial humanism that could defend commercial society from the allegation of extinguishing virtue (Pocock, 1985, pp. 49–50, 194, 210).

Where Smith does deserve recognition for innovation is his rhetorical construction of a 'mercantile system' that continues today to obfuscate the nature and diversity of early modern writings on trade (Coleman, 1980; Tribe, 1978; Walter, 2015), which are better seen as including the distinct genres of political arithmetic, interest analysis, and counsel on trade (Walter, 2011). By developing his account of mercantilism Smith was being deliberately anachronistic for rhetorical purposes, but when scholars today apply this label their anachronism is likely unconscious. To put the point explicitly, the cost of poor historiography is that we do not know where we came from; in relation to intellectual history in particular, we do not know why we use the categories and think the way that we do.

If the case of Smith can be taken as indicative, then it is necessary to return to Cox's claim that the trade-off inherent to his style of history is that it 'is not going to be as accurate and detailed as a positivistic cutting-up of knowledge in dealing with its attendant bits and pieces' (Cox, 1999, p. 393). For this understates the issue, which is not a loss of accuracy and detail but systematic anachronism: the historical account is not historically reliable, whatever its uses for motivating change in the present. Such a fundamental weakness inhibits Coxian research from realizing one of its motivating aims: 'to be critical, to refuse to accept a theory at face value, to look at it and see where it comes from, what it was designed to achieve, the context in which it was developed' (Cox, 2012, p. 19).

It is worth emphasizing that the burdensome work of producing history that is sensitive to context and can accurately narrate the rise of concepts and categories has never been a politically neutral and merely antiquarian pursuit. The politics of historiography will always be dynamic and disruptive in any society that records its own past in written documents and supports specialized or semi-specialized agents that use the latter to interrogate the former (Pocock, 2005, 2011). We have already described the civil context of early modern Italy that spurred the development of historical inquiry. One need only further consider the fifteenth-century humanist Lorenzo Valla, whose philological attack exposed the *Donation of Constantine* as a forgery and thereby undermined papal claims to imperial political authority, to see that dusty work has political effects.

More recently, the critical function of contextual historiography has been underlined by one of its most well-known exponents, Quentin Skinner. In the final chapter of *Liberty Before Liberalism*, Skinner (1998, p. 112) suggested that we should practise intellectual history because it is 'a repository of values we no longer endorse, of questions we no longer ask'. Gesturing towards an alternative critical *persona*, Skinner continued:

> One corresponding role for the intellectual historian is that of acting as a kind of archaeologist, bringing buried intellectual treasure back to the surface, dusting it down and enabling us to reconsider what we think of it. (Skinner, 1998, p. 112)

The corollary effect is to prompt thinking regarding why some questions and answers have been superseded. The recovered object at the heart of Skinner's book is the neo-roman or republican theory of freedom, which Skinner offered as holding value in the present because of its distance from a liberal theory that has risen 'to a position of hegemony' by presenting itself 'as the only coherent way of thinking about the concept [of freedom]'. The result of this dominance is that in our contemporary thinking we have failed 'to avoid falling under the spell of our own intellectual heritage' (Skinner, 1998, p. 113, 116). Historiography can be critical without the operations of dialectical or philosophical history (Walter, 2011, pp. 117–118).

Viewing the issue from the other side, Coxian critical theory does seem to treat historical knowledge as essential to the enterprise (see, for example, Cox, 2012, p. 20). A subtler tool than narratives based on pre-determined theoretical structures is therefore necessary. We have suggested that the necessary tools have been available as one part of Cox's avowed intellectual inheritance via Vico and humanism, but this reserve has been largely overlooked in favour of philosophical resources. This is no reason to continue to ignore this aspect of Cox's sources when attempting to realize his historical project. For Vico's endeavour to understand the history of civil institutions through changing ideas and contexts of thought is an exemplary case of the historical ethos that has been carried up to the present in the work of figures such as Quentin Skinner, J. G. A. Pocock, and Ian Hunter. All share Vico's antipathy to the 'conceit of scholars', and this is a necessary inoculation against ahistorical theory if International Relations is to become a historical and empirical discipline once more. In this respect, it might be time for Cox's polemical distinction between critical theory and problem-solving theory to be displaced by a distinction between theoretical and historical-empirical inquiry.

Disclosure Statement

No potential conflict of interest was reported by the authors.

Notes

1. For some of the difficulties involved in their invocation, see: Helliwell and Hindess (1999), Hindess (1991), Wickham (2010).
2. For the history of this *persona* and their arts of intellectual grooming, see Hunter (2006, 2008, 2014). We are indebted to Hunter's work generally, and especially Hunter (2001).
3. For a seminal statement on the theoretical framework for a critical theory of international relations that draws heavily on Cox, see Linklater (1990, ch. 1, especially pp. 27–32). For a comparison of Cox and Linklater, see Devetak (2012).
4. Of course, the difficulty here is that Coxian critical theory inoculates itself against this criticism through its distinction between problem-solving and critical theory, where the latter is positioned as ethically superior.
5. The following discussion draws on Walter (2011, pp. 114–117).
6. This section draws upon Devetak (2014).
7. For a concise statement, see Pocock (1985, pp. 1–12).

References

Ashley, R. K. (1981). Political realism and human interests. *International Studies Quarterly, 25*, 204–236. doi:10.2307/2600353

Baron, H. (1966). *The crisis of the early Italian renaissance: Civic humanism and republican liberty in an age of classicism and tyranny* (rev. ed.). Princeton, NJ: Princeton University Press.

Black, R. (1986). The political thought of the Florentine chancellors. *The Historical Journal, 29*, 991–1003. Retrieved from http://www.jstor.org/stable/2639367

Booth, K. (2007). *Theory of world society*. Cambridge: Cambridge University Press.

Coleman, D. C. (1980). Mercantilism revisited. *The Historical Journal, 23*, 773–791. Retrieved from http://www.jstor.org/stable/2638725

Cox, R. W. (1981). Social forces, states and world orders: Beyond international relations theory. *Millennium – Journal of International Studies, 10*, 126–155. doi:10.1177/03058298810100020501

Cox, R. W. (1987). *Production, power, and world order: Social forces in the making of history*. New York, NY: Columbia University Press.

Cox, R. W. (1996). Realism, positivism, and historicism. In R. W. Cox, & T. J. Sinclair (Eds.), *Approaches to world order* (pp. 49–59). Cambridge: Cambridge University Press.

Cox, R. W. (2012). For someone and for some purpose: An interview with Robert W. Cox. In S. Brincat, L. Lima, & J. Nunes (Eds.), *Critical theory in international relations and security studies: Interviews and reflections* (pp. 15–34). London: Routledge.

Devetak, R. (2012). Vico contra Kant: The competing critical theories of Cox and Linklater. In S. Brincat, J. Nunes, & L. Lima (Eds.), *Critical theory in international relations and security studies* (pp. 115–126). London: Routledge.

Devetak, R. (2014). A rival enlightenment? Critical international theory in historical mode. *International Theory*, *6*, 417–453. doi:10.1017/S1752971914000128

Devetak, R. (2015). Historiographical foundations of modern international thought: Histories of the European states-system from Florence to Göttingen. *History of European Ideas*, *41*, 62–77. doi:10.1080/01916599.2014.948291

Fubini, R. (2003). *Humanism and secularization. From Petrarch to Valla*. (M. King, Trans.). London: Duke University Press.

Funkenstein, A. (1986). *Theology and the scientific imagination: From the middle ages to the seventeenth century*. Princeton, NJ: Princeton University Press.

Gilbert, F. (1965). *Machiavelli and Guicciardini: Politics and history in sixteenth-century Florence*. Princeton, NJ: Princeton University Press.

Haakonssen, K. (1981). *The science of a legislator: The natural jurisprudence of David Hume and Adam Smith*. Cambridge: Cambridge University Press.

Haakonssen, K. (2006). *The Cambridge companion to Adam Smith*. Cambridge: Cambridge University Press.

Haddock, B. A. (1976). Vico and the problem of historical reconstruction. *Social Research*, *43*, 512–519. Retrieved from http://search.proquest.com.ezproxy.library.uq.edu.au/docview/1297275587?accountid=14723

Haddock, B. A. (1978). Vico on political wisdom. *European History Quarterly*, *8*, 165–191. doi:10.1177/026569147800800201

Hankins, J. (2007). Humanism, scholasticism, and renaissance philosophy. In J. Hankins (Ed.), *The Cambridge companion to renaissance philosophy* (pp. 30–48). Cambridge: Cambridge University Press.

Helliwell, C., & Hindess, B. (1999). 'Culture', 'society', and the figure of man. *History of the Human Sciences*, *12*(4), 1–20. doi:10.1177/09526959922120441

Hindess, B. (1991). Imaginary presuppositions of democracy. *Economy and Society*, *20*, 173–195. doi:10.1080/03085149100000008

Hoogvelt, A., Kenny, M., & Germain, R. (1999). Conversations with Manuel Castells, Robert Cox and Immanuel Wallerstein. *New Political Economy*, *4*, 379–408. doi:10.1080/13563469908406410

Hunter, I. (2001). *Rival enlightenments: Civil and metaphysical philosophy in early modern Germany*. Cambridge: Cambridge University Press.

Hunter, I. (2006). The history of theory. *Critical Inquiry*, *33*, 78–112. doi:10.1086/509747

Hunter, I. (2008). Talking about my generation. *Critical Inquiry*, *34*, 583–600. doi:10.1086/589481

Hunter, I. (2014). The mythos, ethos, and pathos of the humanities. *History of European Ideas*, *40*, 11–36. doi:10.1080/01916599.2013.784030

Ianziti, G. (1991). Humanism's new science: The history of the future. *I Tatti Studies: Essays in the Renaissance*, *4*, 59–88. doi:10.2307/4603670

Ianziti, G. (2012). *Writing history in renaissance Italy: Leonardo Bruni and the uses of the past*. Cambridge, MA: Harvard University Press.

Kelley, D. R. (1970). *Foundations of modern historical scholarship: Language, law, and history in the French renaissance*. New York, NY: Columbia University Press.

Linklater, A. (1982). *Men and citizens in the theory of international relations*. London: Macmillan.

Linklater, A. (1990). *Beyond realism and Marxism: Critical theory and international relations*. London: Macmillan.

Machiavelli, N. (2003). *The prince*. (G. Bull, Trans.). Harmondsworth: Penguin.

Pocock, J. G. A. (1975). *The Machiavellian moment: Florentine political thought and the Atlantic republican tradition*. Princeton: Princeton University Press.

Pocock, J. G. A. (1985). *Virtue, commerce, and history: Essays on political thought and history, chiefly in the eighteenth century*. Cambridge: Cambridge University Press.

Pocock, J. G. A. (2005). The politics of historiography. *Historical Research*, *78*(199), 1–14. doi:10.1111/j.1468-2281.2005.00233.x

Pocock, J. G. A. (2011). Historiography as a form of political thought. *History of European Ideas*, *37*, 1–6. doi:10.1016/j.histeuroideas.2010.09.002

Skinner, Q. (1998). *Liberty before liberalism*. Cambridge: Cambridge University Press.

Tribe, K. (1978). *Land, labour and economic discourse*. London: Routledge & Kegan Paul.

Vico, G. (1699–1707/1993). *On humanistic education: Six inaugural orations, 1699–1707*. (G. Pinton & A. Shippee, Trans.). Ithaca: Cornell University Press.
Vico, G. (1709/1990). *On the study methods of our time*. (E. Gianturco, Trans.). Ithaca, CA: Cornell University Press.
Vico, G. (1744/2001). *New science: Principles of the new science concerning the common nature of nations*. (D. Marsh Trans.). Harmondsworth: Penguin Books.
Vico, G. (1720–1722/2009). A new science is essayed: From *on the constancy of the jurisprudent*. In T. I. Bayer, & D. P. Verene (Eds.), *Giambattista Vico, keys to the new science: Translations, commentaries, and essays* (pp. 45–59). Ithaca, CA: Cornell University Press.
Viroli, M. (1998). *Machiavelli*. Oxford: Oxford University Press.
Walter, R. (2008). Governmentality accounts of the economy: A liberal bias? *Economy and Society, 37*, 94–114. doi:10.1080/03085140701760890
Walter, R. (2011). *A critical history of the economy: On the birth of the national and international economies*. New York, NY: Routledge.
Walter, R. (2015). Slingsby Bethel's analysis of state interests. *History of European Ideas, 41*, 489–506. doi:10.1080/01916599.2014.926659
Waltz, K. (1979). *Theory of international politics*. New York, NY: McGraw-Hill.
Wickham, G. (2010). Sociology, the public sphere, and modern government: A challenge to the dominance of Habermas. *The British Journal of Sociology, 61*, 155–175. doi:10.1111/j.1468-4446.2009.01306.x
Winch, D. (1978). *Adam Smith's politics: An essay in historiographic revision*. Cambridge: Cambridge University Press.

Robert W. Cox and the Idea of History: Political Economy as Philosophy

RANDALL GERMAIN

Carleton University, Ottawa, ON, Canada K1S 5B6

ABSTRACT *Within the discipline of international political economy (IPE), the work of Robert Cox is usually associated with the tradition of historical materialism, especially its Gramscian-inspired version. In this paper, however, I explore some of the less visible elements of Cox's thought. In particular, I highlight a variant of historicism which, although not without a connection to Gramsci's conception of the philosophy of praxis and absolute historicism, is more fully aligned with the work of Collingwood, Vico, Braudel, and Carr. I identify this as a variant of historical idealism, and I suggest that it is this element of his thought which provides a deep intellectual coherence to his work across the different stages of his career. Furthermore, I argue that this use of the idea of history distinguishes Cox's approach from more radical and constructivist accounts of world order, and allows him to connect his framework of historical structures to his method of diachronic change, which centres ultimately on his conception of intersubjectivity. I close by suggesting that Cox's interest in civilizations is deeply connected to these formative historicist influences, which in turn helps to account for why his later work resonates less well with much contemporary historical materialist IPE analysis.*

Robert W. Cox and IPE

Robert W. Cox is indelibly associated with the emergence of modern international political economy (IPE). He is among the pioneers who helped to establish IPE as a *bona fide* academic field of study, and he is credited—along with Susan Strange—with being a formative influence on the so-called British School of IPE (Cohen, 2008). He has participated in some of the most significant debates within the field, including the debate over the theoretical status of neorealism and the more empirically focused debate on the decline of American hegemony. Successive surveys of international relations (IR) have consistently ranked him among the top 20 influences within the field (e.g. TRIPS, 2012), while his Google Scholar citation record reveals that he has 20 publications with more than 100 citations each, including several with citation counts running well into four figures.[1] He was among the first to use the terms 'neorealism' and 'neo-liberalism', and he coined the well-known distinction between critical and problem-solving theory.

Cox's work is most often associated with the tradition of historical materialism, especially its Gramscian-inspired formulation (e.g. Griffiths, Roach, & Solomon, 2009). This is undoubtedly due to the preference he expresses in a piece devoted to considering how his work intersects with leading IR debates, where he suggests that it is perhaps best simply to refer to him 'as a historical materialist' (Cox, 1986/1996, p. 58). Furthermore, in one of his most widely read (and reprinted) publications, he explores the many contributions which a Gramscian-reading of world order brings to our understanding of contemporary developments (Cox, 1983/1996). And in what is perhaps his most finely balanced and in-depth publication, *Production, power and world order* (Cox, 1987, pp. 408–410), his intellectual debt to Gramscian-inspired concepts is indisputable. Indeed, his Gramscian pedigree is heavily emphasized by a generation of scholars who saw in Cox's work a pathway for their own research.

Nevertheless, the intellectual foundations of Cox's work span a wider set of influences. He has, on several occasions, indicated the importance of a diverse range of scholars in developing key concepts in his work, such as his method of historical structures and the process of diachronic change. Here what becomes critical for understanding the integrity of his thought is not so much the Gramscian influence as that of several scholars who can only be loosely connected to the tradition of historical materialism. I argue below that Cox is profoundly connected to a deeply historicist reading of political economy that relies in turn on a complicated engagement with a very particular form of historical idealism. It is this feature of his work, I contend, that animates and shapes his appropriation of Gramsci.

In what follows, I identify and explore these historicist currents in Cox's thought to rehabilitate their formative intellectual impact on his distinctive approach to political economy and world order. I emphasize, in particular, the work of Collingwood, Vico, Braudel, and Carr, although there are other influences which I could also explore but do not do so for reasons of space.[2] The way that Cox combines their commitments facilitates his interest in Gramsci, and especially his innovative attempt to adapt Gramsci's concepts and categories to conceptualize change at the global level. The aim here, I want to stress, is not to replace one reading of Cox with another; rather it is to recover a less visible dimension of Cox's work so that we might better consider how his concepts and ideas seek to explain contemporary developments. Here, it is interesting to note that much of his later work has become somewhat out of sync with contemporary critical IPE scholarship, which remains overwhelmingly influenced by a set of publications dating from the mid-1980s that are themselves seen almost entirely through a Gramscian prism. By relaxing and even recasting this prism, we can reanimate his work to consider it in the more historically framed light in which it was initially conceived, and which I believe still has much to offer to our understanding of contemporary global order.

Cox and the Idea of History: Assembling an Historical Mode of Thought

Although Cox has authored over 100 publications, he nowhere develops at length his theoretical framework.[3] Nevertheless, in several places, he identifies important components of what he calls an 'historical mode of thought' (Cox, 1981/1996, p. 92), including most importantly his early

1980s articles in *Millennium* (Cox, 1981/1996, 1983/1996); his book *Production, power and world order* (Cox, 1987), the purpose-written essays that are included in his two volumes of collected works (Cox, 1996, 2002), and most recently in his autobiographical reflection *Universal foreigner* (Cox, 2013). As well, during the mid-1970s, as he was abandoning a more explicit behavioural approach to the social sciences in his work, he began to outline a form of historical reasoning that had come to inform his research and thinking (e.g. Cox, 1976/1996, 1977/1996, 1979/1996). Of these publications, perhaps the most elaborate statement of his theoretical framework comes in the postscript penned for the volume on neo-realist theory edited by Keohane in the mid-1980s. In this work, he fully aligns himself with a historicist mode of knowledge directed towards revealing 'the historical structures characteristic of particular eras within which such regularities prevail. Even more important, this research program is to explain transformations from one structure to another' (Cox, 1986/1996, p. 53).

Cox is careful here and elsewhere to distinguish historicism and the historicist approach to social science from both positivism and other structural approaches including variants of Marxism (which Cox associates, e.g., with the work of Althusser and what he sometimes refers to as the 'new scholasticism of the official left'; cf. Cox, 1979/1996, p. 416). What is critical to his understanding of historicism (and indeed, as I will show later, to the way he embraces the idea of historical reasoning) is a refusal to search for either universally applicable laws of behaviour or a conception of causation connected to individual agency. Rather, for Cox, historical research is concerned with uncovering and understanding the intersubjective elements that instantiate structures and their institutions, generate their power, and block (or unleash) transformative social forces (Cox, 1986/1996, pp. 55–56). His conception of the idea of history is most critically connected to the search for meaning and understanding in historically specific political, economic, and social arrangements. In this sense, the idea of history as a research programme—or what he simply calls historicism—is also indistinguishable from his conception of historical materialism as a research programme: both search for 'connections between the mental schema through which people conceive action and the material world which constrains both what people can do and how they can think about doing it' (Cox, 1986/1996, p. 52). In his search for such connections, Cox is inspired by historians like E. P. Thompson, Eric Hobsbawm, and ultimately Antonio Gramsci. But I want to suggest that what Cox found of value in Gramsci was prepared and facilitated by his prior embrace of this version of historical reasoning, or as I will formulate it below, as a particular way of thinking about the idea of history.

We can see how this idea of history developed to inform Cox's work if we consider his scholarship in terms of evolving over three relatively distinct, if also overlapping, phases.[4] His first research phase examines the role and potential of international organization, with the landmark publication of this period being *Anatomy of influence* (Cox & Jacobson, 1972). This work was the culmination of a period of research into how decision-making in international organization occurred, and it was influenced very strongly by the research methods then dominant in American political science (Cox, 1996, p. 26). The publication of *Anatomy of influence* in 1972 coincided with Cox's departure from the International Labor Organization (ILO), where he had worked since 1947. As he notes in an autobiographical reflection published in 1996, he felt a sense of liberation at this moment, which allowed him to begin thinking about the problems of international organization from a much wider angle of vision (Cox, 1996, p. 24). This wider angle was world order and its political economy, which became the principal focus of his second research phase.

During this second period, the problem of international organization ultimately resolved itself into the problem of world order and whether and how it was changing, or decaying, as he described it in a 1980 publication focused precisely on this subject (Cox, 1980, p. 381; cf. Kratochwil & Ruggie, 1986, p. 766). To successfully understand the dynamics of change which he thought confronted the world at the time, Cox returned to a series of thinkers he had initially encountered during his studies in history at McGill University a quarter century earlier, and above all to the work of Collingwood and Vico. What he sought in these thinkers was not just a method of apprehending world order—normally the provenance of IR scholars—but more importantly a way of investigating international political change. Collingwood and Vico helped in particular with the latter; for the former question as we shall see below he turned elsewhere. We can see the influence of Collingwood and his method in what is one of the most prescient publications of his second period, an essay published in the journal *International Organization* called 'Labor and hegemony' (Cox, 1977/1996).

In this essay, which is an exploration of the broader social forces and power relationships shaping the ILO and its operations in the global political economy, Cox for the first time lays out what for him is a new and preliminary method for considering change at the global level. Although he identifies this as the 'historical method', it is not sketched out in any great detail (Cox, 1977/1996, p. 420).[5] However, taking our cue from the article's first footnote, a short detour into the work of Collingwood, an Oxford philosopher and historian, can clarify some of the key determinants of Cox's new method. Of primary importance is Collingwood's insistence on the idea of history as a very particular form of knowledge, which he calls 'human self-knowledge' (Collingwood, 1946, p. 10).

This form of knowledge does not simply enumerate the historical record as a series of accomplishments that might be formulated as data, but seeks instead to understand the interior of events, what might be described as the thoughts and/or thought processes which bring these accomplishments into being. Collingwood's striking formulation—picked up directly by Cox in this article (Cox, 1977/1996, pp. 420–421)—is to distinguish between the 'outside' of an event and its 'inside': the 'outside' of an event is its phenomenology, the concrete movements, articulations, and effects that together describe its occurrence. It is this occurrence which can become, under certain conditions, a fact or datum of history. The 'inside' of an event, on the other hand, is the thought process which brings the event into being: it comprises the thoughts of the actor or actors through which they understand their circumstance and by which they attempt to alter it. It is the 'inside' of events which provides meaning to the historical record; thus the historical method that Collingwood advances and Cox adopts is to look not just for an explanation of events (i.e. of what happened), but rather for their meaning.[6] 'Labor and hegemony' in this sense is an exploration of the meaning for world politics of the American withdrawal from the ILO in 1977.

Although Collingwood provides Cox with a critical element of his method, it is his engagement with the work of Vico that provides social depth to his approach. For despite the considerable attraction which Collingwood exercises in terms of his method, his work tends to focus on individuals as the central actors of history. By this point, however, Cox had become sceptical of the utility of agent-centred social science, precisely because in his mind it failed to adequately comprehend the changing social basis of power relations as manifestations of collective shifts in cognitive mental frameworks. While Collingwood's emphasis on the unity of thought and action was critically important, these mental frameworks could not be considered only in relation to individual actors. It is Vico who provides Cox with the conceptual capacity to think about collective mental frameworks, or *mentalitiés*, thereby cementing the ontological shift in the search for meaning from individual actors to social collectivities.[7]

There are two aspects of Vico's work which Cox picks up on. First, he accepts that Vico's *verum-factum* principle ('the true itself is made') is a reaffirmation of Collingwood's conception of history as human self-knowledge. The *verum-factum* principle states that human beings are uniquely placed to comprehend and understand those *artefacts* which they themselves make:

> For the first indubitable principle posited above is that this world of nations has certainly been made by men, *and its guise must therefore be found within the modifications of our own human mind*. And history cannot be more certain than when he who creates the things also narrates them. (Vico, 1744/1948: para 349 italics added; cf. Cox, 1981/1996, pp. 93–94)

The social and political world, in this sense, is uniquely open to a form of knowledge arrived at through an engagement with the thought processes which generate collective and institutionalized forms of activity. Although Cox came to Vico later in his career (the English language translation of Vico's main treatise was not available until after Cox had completed his graduate studies), the Vichian sensibility towards treating history as a form of philosophy, that is, as an attempt to understand thought processes and their modifications, resonated strongly with Cox's growing conviction that historical rather than behavioural approaches to knowledge provide the best avenue to understand contemporary changes in world politics.

The second aspect of Vico's work which Cox found enormously helpful is the emphasis upon collective mental frameworks as the key to understanding how human institutions evolve. Vico himself was a philologist, engaged in the search for common origins among diverse human histories through the evolution of language and folklore. He discerned three common institutions that all peoples had developed: religion, marriage, and burial customs. Through an imaginative engagement with the folklore and customs of diverse nations, Vico suggested that we could establish a common mental vocabulary—a new science—about these institutions, thus assembling certain knowledge about human affairs that could be used to understand the cycles of history (Vico, 1744/1948, para 338–360). According to Collingwood, Vico offered one of the earliest modern visions of history as a form of self-knowledge, complete with its own method and concepts (Collingwood, 1946, pp. 63–71). For Cox, the seminal advance of Vico is to suggest that we can apprehend historical developments by considering the modifications of the human mind: 'mind is ... the thread connecting the present with the past, a means of access to a knowledge of these changing modes of social reality' (Cox, 1981/1996, p. 93).

Thus, by way of Vico and Collingwood, Cox came to one of his most crucial insights, that the human mind and its collective modifications are the central object of study for the social sciences. This is the essence of what I have elsewhere identified as his 'historical idealism', namely the recognition that the organization of subjectivity lies at the analytical heart of political economy, but that this subjectivity is at the same time the author as well as the object of systematic social practices which form themselves into collective historical structures (Germain, 2007, p. 128). On this reading, it is through our understanding of how we apprehend social reality that we are able to gain insight into our capacity to confront and alter the material conditions of existence. This is, for Cox, the philosophical core of political economy: it is the moment of understanding that is paramount, because it is the set of ideas inherent to any particular form of (collective, intersubjective) understanding which works through evolving social relations to modify existing material conditions. Of course, for Cox as for many who work within the tradition of historical materialism, there is a deep reciprocity between how we understand our relationship to the material conditions of existence, and the organization of those conditions on their own terms. This is not a radical form of idealism, as he emphasizes in his 'Social forces' article (Cox, 1981/1996, p. 93). It is instead a deeply ontological claim which insists that intersubjective mental schema must be considered alongside social relations and material conditions as key determinants of collective agency and outcomes. In this sense, Vico and Collingwood provide Cox with the conceptual tools to account for the shift from international organization to world order: the latter is the substantive grounds upon which the former acts. Without enquiring into the intersubjective construction of world order, our knowledge of how and why international organizations act, and the significance of their global role, is at best incomplete, and at worst entirely misleading.

Interestingly, Cox's ontological commitment to the critical importance of intersubjectivity has led some to characterize his work as constructivist in character (e.g. Adler, 2002, p. 98). However, I think this fails to appreciate the deep connection Cox maintains between intersubjectivity and the material conditions of existence, which is informed by a particular reading of historical structures that comes through an engagement with the work of Carr and Braudel. From Carr, Cox found a way to preserve the critical features of an historical method while also moving beyond Collingwood's narrower concern with *individual* thought processes to connect with larger-scale structural change (Cox, 1996, p. 27). He did this by following Carr's analysis of changing forms of state through the tumultuous decades between 1890 and 1950. Part of Carr's analysis of this period is contained in his best-known publication, *The twenty years crisis* (Carr, 1946), but Cox was more influenced by Carr's wartime tracts (Carr, 1942, 1945), his reflections on history (Carr, 1961), and several of his earlier biographies of nineteenth-century romantic writers and intellectuals, including Bakunin, Dostoyevsky, and Marx. What struck Cox here was the sophisticated way in which Carr situated these writers and/or issues (such as the changing nature of the state, which is the subject of *Nationalism and After*) in a broader conception of their social fabric, through an engagement with how 'thought' was influenced by and became instantiated in collective activity.

Carr himself held fast to the idea of history as 'imaginative understanding', precisely because it could generate insights which, although derived from the mental frameworks of people in one period, might be used as a form of knowledge to illuminate the points of change in another period (1961, p. 24). The idea of history, in this conception, is more than just an investigation of the past; it is centrally concerned with how the future is evolving out of contemporary social, political, and economic arrangements (1951/1957, pp. 17–18). In other words, the past is an avenue of enquiry into the future via the present. For the period in which Carr writes most prolifically on international politics (roughly from the mid-1930s until the early 1950s), what occupies him most centrally are the conjoined processes of state transformation and international political change. There are of course many aspects to these transformations, but Carr is adamant both that they must be considered 'historical' in their origins (i.e. they have a direct relationship with the past) and that we can only properly understand their import when we bring an historical bent of mind to our analysis.[8] For Carr—as for Cox—the idea of history and its imaginative form of understanding resonates methodologically well beyond the discipline of history; it is also a suitable—indeed, a necessary—method of enquiry for the social sciences.

The landmark publication of Cox's second phase of research was *Production, power and world order*. This publication utilized the framework of historical structures to counter-pose elements of continuity in different historical eras to elements of change, with the aim of sketching future possible trajectories of change looking forward from the late 1980s (cf. Germain, 2013). Oddly, however, the method of outlining and then using the framework of historical structures is highly truncated.[9] Rather, Cox refers the reader to his 'Social forces' article for an explication of how he intends to use this framework, where it is presented as an integrated social totality constituted by sets of collective images organically related to specific configurations of material conditions and working at different levels (Cox, 1981/1996, pp. 97–101). Carr is cited in this work as an example of a scholar whose method moves easily between different levels of activity (individual, class, state, and world system) to consider change in its broadest, most structurally complete manifestation. One of the most important advances of *Production, power and world order*, on this reading, lies in how it specifies the continuities and discontinuities of distinct structural totalities. It offers an understanding of the movement from the liberal era to the era of rival imperialisms to the post-war neo-liberal period that hinges on the changing anatomy of these historical structures' political economy.

Here, Cox's definition of historical structures becomes critical. In *Production, power and world order,* he defines them as 'persistent social practices, made by collective human activity and transformed through collective human activity' (Cox, 1987, p. 4). The note appended to this definition, as indicated above, explains that this usage is derived from Vico's conception of collective, social institutions (Cox, 1987, p. 406). But it is clear from how Cox uses the idea of a structure that Braudel's formulation carries much more analytical weight for his definition. Braudel's idea of structure evolved initially out of a pioneering study of the limits imposed on human action by the material world represented by the Mediterranean Sea during the reign of Charles II (Braudel, 1972). But it reached its most advanced formulation in his consideration of the entwined histories of capitalism and civilization during the transitions of the early modern period (Braudel, 1977, 1980, 1982, 1984). What distinguishes Braudel's conception of structure here is the fluid manner in which he knits together collective images that capture the limits of possible human activity with extant material conditions as they are woven into the wide array of institutions that effectively channel such actions. A key aspect of this interweaving of collective subjectivity with material constraints is the way in which Braudel insists on taking account of how differing speeds or tempos of life condition how we think about the enabling conditions of social action. These constraints work in different ways to channel and 'collect' human activity, and Braudel is clear that we need to account for these differences both spatially and temporally. It is the inclusion of temporal considerations that Cox recognizes to be the critical element of what he ultimately calls his framework of historical structures.

For Braudel, humanity experiences time in three distinct but overlapping ways. He identifies these as *l'histoire événementielle*, or the short-term sense of time associated with personal memory; the *conjuncture*, or a medium-term span of time often encompassing decades and associated with identifiably rhythmic patterns of aggregated behaviour such as price levels or business cycles; and the *longue dureé*, a span of time that can stretch for centuries and which many of Braudel's *Annales* colleagues connected to mental frameworks of thought, or *mentaliés* (Braudel, 1977, 1980, 1984; cf. Helleiner, 1997). The conceptual breakthrough which this understanding of time represents is to find a way of moving beyond either a continuous, linear evolution of time—as simple chronology—or a repetitive conception of time—as cycles—to embrace a conception of time that refers directly to lived human experience.[10] Time itself thus becomes 'historical' through the differentiated ways in which it is experienced, with these competing tempos becoming themselves key drivers of change through their differential effects on our intersubjective imaginations. Cox, like Braudel, was most interested in the *longue dureé*, for it was the evolution of mental frameworks of thought that enabled him to consider the diachronic dimension of change, where new material conditions confronted established categories of thought about 'the order of things' (Cox, 2002, p. 32).[11] It is the disruptions and perturbations that new material conditions have on established modes of thought which constitute breaking points in the *longue dureé*. In this sense, Cox's framework of historical structures rests on a Braudelian sensibility about the multiple experiences of time and the rethinking of categories of thought which this stimulates.

Tying these four elements of the historical mode of thought together—Collingwood's sense of the 'inside' and 'outside' of events, Vico's *verum-factum* principle, Carr's conception of history as 'imaginative understanding' and Braudel's specification of the multiple experiences of time—provide the essential framework within which we can situate Cox's embrace of historical materialism. It is an embrace which recognizes the idealist origins of history in terms of the modifications of the human mind, most significantly in its collective form, as it grapples with the ongoing evolution of material conditions, but only where these conditions are understood to have been 'made' by human beings. It is the 'making' which is critical here, and Cox is very happy to follow the more historically oriented Marx in his affirmation that history is made by people but not under conditions of their own choosing (Marx, 1851/1977, p. 300).

However, it is important to recognize that these 'idealist' roots of Cox's mode of historical thought are not themselves entirely and arbitrarily subjective in scope. They are fastened directly to the practices and institutions which humanity 'makes' during the course of the confrontation between material conditions and the (collective) modifications of the human mind. These conditions do not nurture just any old set of ideas; rather, ideas need to emerge, take shape and evolve in a manner that is reinforced by these conditions. This is the basic reciprocity incumbent upon Cox's designation of ideas as 'intersubjective': they exist in a determinate relationship with material conditions that can be specified in their supportive *and/or* subversive attributes. This is why the history of ideas is for Cox a critical dimension of all historical research, as it was for Collingwood, Vico, Carr, and Braudel.[12] We cannot understand historical structures without also and even primarily understanding the intersubjective foundations which hold them together. Crucially, it is the intersubjective core of an historical structure which provides the meaning of each individual action or event that inheres to it. Thus, we can say that a particular conception of historical idealism stands at the heart of Cox's embrace of the tradition of historical materialism. He practices a form of political economy that is effectively historical and philosophical in application.

Such a formulation of the intellectual influences on Cox's thought also help to explain the third phase of his research trajectory, which for many has been the most puzzling aspect of his career. Shortly after the publication of *Production, power and world order*, Cox again began to widen his departure point for thinking about world historical change, from 'world order'—already for many a wide enough angle of vision—to 'civilizations'. During this period, he again returned to scholarship encountered earlier in his career, such as the writings of Oswald Spengler and Arnold Toynbee, to ask questions about the meaning and influence of civilizational forms on world politics and political economy.[13] Many of these explorations are published in his collected volume *The political economy of a plural world*. Why (again) change the angle of vision? For Cox, the answer is straightforward and ethically compelling: the most pressing problem of the contemporary global order he identifies at this point in time is the need to negotiate difference in a world increasingly portrayed in terms of starkly contrasting visions of life, or intersubjectivities (Cox, 2001/2002, p. 157). One aspect of this problem as it emerged in the early 1990s was how to manage irreconcilable differences rooted in competing mental frameworks of thought. Fukuyama (1992), for example, took the end of the Cold War to signal the triumph of a liberal and democratic framework of thought, a kind of 'end of history' in which Western political and economic values were now without competitors. Huntington (1996) replied with a more pessimistic thesis, a 'clash of civilizations', implying a future of deep-seated political conflict. Both views were sustained by the inevitability of globalization as the economic counterpart to the spread of liberal democracy, even if this spread would trail conflict in its wake. Cox saw in both of these views a recipe for epochal conflict that ignored the philosophical and historical grounds for a genuine intersubjective recognition (and accommodation) of difference on a societal basis (Cox, 2001/2002, p. 174).

Cox joined this debate by exploring how thinkers (both contemporary and historical) had considered the question of intersubjectivity understood as a collective spirit animating civilizational coherence. Among the thinkers he considered in this period were Ibn Khaldun, Susan Strange, and Harold Innis, alongside Spengler, Toynbee, and Vico, all of which feature in *The political economy of a plural world*.[14] The key aspect I would highlight about this third phase of Cox's research is that his entry point for considering the 'modifications of the human mind' had reached its logical extension: it had travelled through international organization and the structure of world order to finally rest upon civilizations. Grappling with the changing material conditions of 'difference' together with their associated collective forms of thought formation had taken him from multilateral organizations in the post-1945 era to global structures in the post-Bretton Woods period and finally to civilizational attributes. The method used throughout was 'historical' but the departure point altered over time. In this sense, there is a deep intellectual coherence to Cox's work throughout the last two phases of his career, and in some ways also his first phase. This coherence is predicated upon Cox's particular understanding of historical materialism, which as I have suggested rests upon a form of historical idealism in terms of method and philosophy.

The above remarks serve to situate Cox's very specific appropriation of Gramsci, which crystalized in the middle years of his second phase. Here, he is particularly interested in that part of Gramsci's writing oriented to considering power and intersubjectivity in terms of the interrelationship between culture, ideology, and relations of force. We can see this at work in the concepts which Cox (1983/1996) finds to be most useful to his own enterprise, namely hegemony, passive revolution, and historical bloc. These concepts are distinguished by their cultural and/or intersubjective constitution: they are concepts whose meaning can only be comprehended in terms of a shared and reciprocal conception, by dominant and subordinate forces, of how to act in a world where these forces are the authors of their own histories (i.e. they conduct themselves in certain ways within extant material conditions). But critically, he does not simply lift these concepts out of Gramsci and apply them; rather, he stylizes and grafts them into his own particular conception of the historical method as I have outlined it here. And most critically, he deepens them by emphasizing the element of intersubjectivity which he had come to recognize as the crucial determinant of their evolution. In this sense, Cox came to Gramsci in terms of his engagement with Collingwood, Carr, Braudel, and Vico, finding in Gramsci's own thinking allied concepts which he could adapt and apply precisely because they provided a way to usefully delineate with some precision the social relations he saw as paramount to the construction (or deconstruction) of world order. I would also note that here he was using stylized and/or adapted Gramscian concepts—originally designed for the most part to comprehend national or European developments—on a much larger empirical/historical canvas. In this, he was following the Braudelian injunction to treat concepts as 'ships', testing them to see where and how they 'float' (or make sense) on empirical terrains for which they may not have been originally designed (Braudel, 1980; Cox, 2002, p. 27).[15]

But in Cox's third research phase, it is interesting that the influence of Gramsci becomes muted, although of course it does not disappear. Why? The principle reason I would put forward is that as helpful as the Gramscian concepts identified above were for the exploration of world order, they appeared to him to be less directly beneficial to his new vantage point.

To follow the metaphor just outlined, the Gramscian ship did not sail so effectively on the new empirical terrain Cox was most interested in exploring. Perhaps, Cox believed that the military connotations of hegemony, passive revolution, and wars of movement and position were poorly designed to consider the civilizational features of difference that came to occupy his attention. Or perhaps, they laid too much stress on the direct social relations which characterized the operations of political institutions and the interstate system, whereas Cox had become much more interested in collective thought formation and the ways in which this interacted with changing material conditions (i.e. globalization). For whatever reason, it is noteworthy that while Cox reduced the use of specific Gramscian concepts in his later work, he retained a keen appreciation for Gramsci's conception of 'absolute historicism' as a clear reaffirmation of the utility (and indeed, necessity) of placing the historical mode of thought and its attendant method at the centre of social scientific enquiry.[16] This, I contend, is entirely in keeping with the very specific way in which Cox incorporated Gramsci's work into his own intellectual framework from the start.

Conclusion: Political Economy as Philosophy

What are the implications of making more visible the historical idealist elements of Robert Cox's thought? One implication is to recover a more complete and nuanced appreciation of the intellectual influences on his work. Although he himself has tried to clarify the intellectual *milieu* within which his thinking has evolved, the non-Gramscian influences on his work have remained just off the radar screen, or seen to be ancillary to the main attraction which his works holds for contemporary IPE scholars, which is its innovative adaptation and application of Gramscian concepts. But as I have suggested here, this in a way puts the cart before the horse, for Cox came to Gramsci through an enduring engagement with various forms of historicism and historical idealism that had a profound effect on how he came to appreciate and appropriate Gramsci's concepts for his own use.

A second implication is that Cox's work suggests—although not directly—the utility of an approach to IPE that embraces thinking about political economy as philosophy. What does this mean? First and foremost, it means accepting the importance of thought processes and mental frameworks of thought to the process and meaning of history, where understanding such *mentalitiés* in their collective manifestation provides the entry point to thinking about change and transformation. It elevates intersubjectivity into a principal category of analysis, and specifies a particular formulation of the historical method—imaginative understanding—as a primary means of investigation. The context of investigation, the organization and operation of historical structures, is also critical here as the key material condition or constraint with which collective thought processes engage. The precise form of this engagement might be rendered as 'historical materialism + historical idealism = political economy as philosophy'. There are some parallels between this formulation and what some have suggested that Gramsci articulated (e.g. Thomas, 2009/2013), although I would argue that Cox maintains an 'openness' not always visible in Gramsci's prison writings. Nevertheless, I do not want to argue here that Cox and Gramsci have completely different conceptions of the philosophical basis of political economy, because both are intrinsically concerned to chart the intersubjective dimensions of collective human actions here, even if they come to this effort from rather different starting points.

Thinking about political economy in terms of philosophy furthermore allows questions about how we live and organize our lives to be considered in terms of the possibilities given by the existing terrain of material conditions. In Cox's terms, it is about the modifications of the human mind as informed by and in response to actually existing circumstances. Neither pure philosophical idealism nor blunt empirical materialism suffices to capture the reciprocal dynamic embodied in Cox's conception of the intersubjective basis of human action and potential. At the same time, this potential is always constrained by pathways and opportunities that are given to and confront agents; this is another reason why he often ends his analyses by setting out two or three alternative scenarios, each anchored by a clear-sighted assessment of the material conditions and ideational templates specific to differently situated social actors. This sense of realism Cox also certainly shared with Gramsci, who famously distinguished, in a letter written from prison in 1929, between the pessimism of the intellect and the optimism of the will.[17]

This is perhaps a fitting place to close, by noting that the foregoing does not counsel us to separate the historical idealism of Cox from the historical materialism of Gramsci. Cox is very much influenced by the historicist currents in Gramsci's thought, just as he has been clearly influenced by the more historical and philosophical writings of Marx. We all pick, choose, and adapt with care from among those thinkers and writers in whose work we see something of value. Rather, the point I make here is that Cox came to Gramsci with a strongly entrenched sense of historical enquiry, a form of historical idealism as I have described it, that inclined him to focus on those parts of Gramsci's work which paid greater attention to the formation of thought in collective terms, or what Cox came to identify as intersubjectivity. This was the Gramsci he appropriated and used so brilliantly during the second phase of his research into the changing structures of world order. That he subsequently moved on to explore questions connected to civilizational orders, where he might have seen less utility in these same Gramscian concepts, is not to downgrade Gramsci's overall influence on Cox. It is rather to place it alongside other influences which are equally foundational to his thinking.

And this last point, I think goes some way to accounting for why Cox's later work is less central to contemporary debates in critical political economy as compared with his work in the 1980s and early 1990s. His third phase resonates less clearly with current scholarship, for two reasons. One reason is that the idea of civilization has not captured the scholarly imagination of critical IPE, much of which remains focused on neoliberalism, American hegemony and class in its transnational formulation. This is not an area where political economy as philosophy garners an immediately obvious reception. But equally importantly, Cox's historical mode of thought, and especially his peculiar sense of historical idealism, is almost wholly out of tune with contemporary mainstream IPE scholarship, focused as it is on rational choice and constructivism as theoretical departure points. The historical method that is the intellectual heir to the kind of imaginative understanding recognized by Collingwood, Vico, and Carr, and one that is attuned to very long time spans postulated by Braudel, is today quite simply out of fashion across a broad spectrum of IPE. Instead, other traditions are picking up these themes, such as historical sociology, postcolonial accounts of international politics, and feminist analyses.

Nevertheless, the Coxian sensibility towards history as imaginative understanding retains its ability to tell us much of value about the contemporary organization of the global political economy and world order. First of all, it draws our attention to the changing intersubjective dimensions of global order, which today are dominated by the erosion and decay of liberalism as a chief animating force of social action. As the commitment to liberalism mutates, capitalism is becoming redefined and the political forces connected to it are evolving. Cox's mode of historical thought is well positioned to capture this longer term trend and extrapolate from it. Second, although the move to think about the impact of civilizational elements on political institutions and world order is replete with conceptual and measurement issues of all kinds, such a large and powerful intersubjective potential should command our attention, especially if we agree with Cox that it is the modifications of the human mind which both drive forward and provide meaning to history. At the very least, taking intersubjectivity seriously demands that we investigate the potential ways in which civilizational influences shape and constrain the possibilities of transformation in world order structures. It is here where a Coxian approach continues to provide significant value added to our analysis.

Acknowledgements

I would like to thank Shannon Brincat for the invitation to contribute to this special issue, and to two anonymous reviewers for their helpful and constructive comments on an earlier draft. As well, I benefited from comments received from participants at a seminar at Ryerson University and from students in the PECO 6000 Ph.D. Core Course Seminar at Carleton University, where earlier versions of this essay were presented. I am of course responsible for any remaining errors and omissions.

Disclosure Statement

No potential conflict of interest was reported by the author.

Notes

1. My count of his Google Scholar citations hit 12,838 by the 14th page of the list that included his name. The highest count was his 'Social forces' article (3066), while the lowest count was 'Labor and hegemony': A reply (16). Google Scholar accessed May 26, 2015.
2. Such influences would include, for example, the work of Georges Sorel and Max Weber. Here, I am picking up on the rich contextualization of Cox's work begun in the edited volume dedicated to Cox (and his wife, Jessie Rankin Cox) and published as *Innovation and transformation in international studies* (Gill & Mittelman, 1997; also see Mittelman, 1998), but yet which was never followed up on, with the partial (and useful) exception of Ayers (2008).
3. The bibliography of Cox's work at the end of *Approaches to world order* numbers 79 publications, but ends in 1996 and does not include either *Approaches to world order* itself or the chapter he wrote for it. I estimate that he has published at least 20 new pieces over the subsequent 2 decades, including work on multilateralism, civil society, and civilizations.
4. As I detail below, these phases—especially the second and third ones—are not discrete chronological time periods. Rather, they overlap in certain ways. However, conceiving them as organized around different problematics and animated by evolving conceptual formulations helps to comprehend the overall trajectory of his thinking.
5. While Cox does not reference his article 'On thinking about future world order' (Cox, 1976/1996) published the previous year, he might well have done so, as this was a review of different ways of conceptualizing world order that traversed some of the same intellectual terrain. What distinguishes 'Labor and hegemony', however, is that this constitutes the first active application of what would become Cox's trademark framework of historical structures. Interestingly, both Collingwood and Gramsci are cited in this piece, albeit only once each and without elaboration.
6. As Collingwood puts it: the historian's work

    may begin by discovering the outside of an event, but it can never end there; he must always remember that the event was an action, and that his main task is to think himself into this action, to discern the thought of its agent. (1946, p. 213)

7. A footnote in 'On thinking about future world order' published a year earlier makes precisely this point with reference to Vico and Collingwood (Cox, 1976/1996, p. 79).
8. As Carr (1951/1957, p. 118) phrased it: 'the world of politics—and what is not political today?—is the world of history'.

9. The derivation of Cox's use of the idea of historical structures is not at all straightforward. In *Production, power and world order*, Vico is the inspiration (Cox, 1987, p. 406). In his 'Social forces' article, Gramsci and Carr are highlighted (Cox, 1981/1996, p. 119; but see the reference to Machiavelli in note 15 of this article). And yet, when he reflects on the evolution of his thought, Braudel is often credited with the idea of historical structures (e.g. Cox, 1992/1996, p. 149, Cox, 1996, p. 29, Cox, 2002, p. 29). For a useful discussion of how this framework operates, see Sinclair (1996, pp. 8–12).
10. I would argue that it is this conceptual advance—by moving beyond Carr's chronological conception of time and Vico's cyclical version—that enables Cox to breathe social life into his framework of historical structures.
11. Interestingly, although Cox is most intrigued by transformational breaking points in world order, this does not necessarily sit comfortably within Braudel's notion of the *longue dureé*, as the transition from the *Pax Britannica* to the *Pax Americana* is more accurately a conjunctural change rather than a *longue dureé* break. As Cox notes in *Production, power and world order*, the move from a British to an American-led world order did not involve a fundamental break in the social structure of accumulation (Cox, 1987, p. 212).
12. Indeed, as I shall detail below, in his third research phase, he became keenly interested in the intellectual history of key ideas such as civil society and the 'international' (e.g. Cox, 1999/2002, 2007).
13. He was also influenced here by Braudel, who in one of his final works attempted a history of civilizations and civilizational encounters (Braudel, 1994).
14. The essay on Khaldun, although published in *Approaches to world order* (along with an essay on Susan Strange, both written in the early 1990s), is particularly important in this respect, as it marks one of Cox's first attempts to bring his mature historical mode of thought to bear on how intersubjective images animate inter-civilizational encounters. In this essay, he flatly declares that 'how this objective world is made and remade through changes in intersubjectivity is the principal question to be answered in any attempt to understand the process of historical change' (Cox, 1992/1996, p. 150).
15. In his 'Social forces' article, Cox elaborates on the idea of concepts and the need for them to be flexible, citing E. P. Thompson's claim that concepts, in order to be historically useful, also need to be quite 'elastic' in their application (Cox, 1981/1996, p. 117).
16. It needs to be noted clearly that Cox did not abandon Gramscian concepts entirely in his later work; he merely reduced their import for his historical mode of thought. For example, when he considers the changing idea of civil society, or the part played by world order in civilizational encounters, Gramsci and Gramscian concepts remain prominent (e.g. Cox with Schechter, 2002, Chaps 6 & 9). It is also worthwhile remarking that there are many passages in *The prison notebooks* and other of Gramsci's writings devoted to matters directly relevant to understanding how cultural and indeed civilizational considerations affect social and political relations. The point here is not that Gramsci himself did not explore these ideas, but that Cox did not avail himself of them as much in his third research phase as he had previously done.
17. This phrase, written in a letter to his wife, is usually attributed to Roman Rolland. Gramsci's phrasing is: 'my mind is pessimistic, but my will is optimistic' (Gramsci, 1973, p. 159).

References

Adler, E. (2002). Constructivism and international relations. In W. Carlsnaes, T. Risse, & B. Simmons (Eds.), *Handbook of international relations* (pp. 95–118). London: Sage.

Ayers, A. (Ed.). (2008). *Gramsci, political economy, and international relations theory*. Basingstoke: Palgrave.

Braudel, F. (1972). *The Mediterranean and the Mediterranean world in the age of Philip II*. (S. Reynolds, Trans.). New York, NY: Harper & Row.

Braudel, F. (1977). *Afterthoughts on material civilization and capitalism*. (P. Ranuum, Trans.). Baltimore: Johns Hopkins University Press.

Braudel, F. (1980). *On history*. (S. Matthews, Trans.). Chicago, IL: University of Chicago Press.

Braudel, F. (1982). *Civilization and capitalism: 15th to 18th centuries, Vol. 2: The wheels of commerce*. (S. Reynolds, Trans.). London: Collins/Fontana.

Braudel, F. (1984). *Civilization and capitalism: 15th to 18th centuries, Vol. 3: The perspective of the world*. (S. Reynolds, Trans.). London: Collins/Fontana.

Braudel, F. (1994). *A history of civilizations*. (R. Mayne, Trans.). New York: A. Lane.

Carr, E. H. (1942). *Conditions of peace*. London: Macmillan Press.

Carr, E. H. (1945). *Nationalism and after*. London: Macmillan Press.

Carr, E. H. (1946). *The twenty years crisis* (2nd ed.). London: Macmillan Press.

Carr, E. H. (1951/1957). *The new society*. Boston, MA: The Beacon Press.

Carr, E. H. (1961). *What is history?* London: Penguin Books.
Cohen, B. (2008). *International political economy: An intellectual history.* Princeton, NJ: Princeton University Press.
Collingwood, R. G. (1946). *The idea of history.* Oxford: Clarendon Press.
Cox, R. W. (1976/1996). On thinking about future world order. *World Politics, 28*(2), 175–196; re-published in Cox with Sinclair (1996).
Cox, R. W. (1977/1996). Labor and hegemony. *International Organization, 31*(3), 385–424; re-published in Cox with Sinclair (1996).
Cox, R. W. (1979/1996). Ideologies and the new international economic order: Reflections on some recent literature. *International Organization, 33*(2), 257–302; re-published in Cox with Sinclair (1996).
Cox, R. W. (1980). The crisis of world order and the problem of international organization in the 1980s. *International Journal, 35*(2), 370–395.
Cox, R. W. (1981/1996). Social forces, states and world orders: Beyond international relations theory. *Millennium, 10*(2), 126–155; re-published in Cox with Sinclair (1996).
Cox, R. W. (1983/1996). Gramsci, hegemony and international relations: An essay in method. *Millennium, 12*(2), 162–175; re-published in Cox with Sinclair (1996).
Cox, R. W. (1986/1996). Realism, positivism and historicism. In R. Keohane (Ed.), *Neorealism and its critics.* (pp. 239–249) New York, NY: Columbia University Press; re-published in Cox with Sinclair (1996).
Cox, R. W. (1987). *Production, power and world order: Social forces in the Making of History.* New York, NY: Columbia University Press.
Cox, R. W. (1992/1996). Towards a posthegemonic conceptualization of world order: Reflections on the relevancy of Ibn Khaldun. In J. Rosenau & E.-O. Czempiel (Eds.), *Governance without government: Order and change in world politics* (pp. 132–159). Cambridge: Cambridge University Press; re-published in Cox with Sinclair (1996).
Cox, R. W. (1996). Influences and commitments. In R. W. Cox with T. Sinclair (Eds.), *Approaches to world order* (pp. 19–38). Cambridge: Cambridge University Press.
Cox, R. W. (1999/2002). Civil society at the turn of the millennium: Prospects for an alternative world order. *Review of International Studies, 25*(1), 3–28; reprinted in Cox with Schechter (2002).
Cox, R. W. (2001/2002). Civilizations and the twenty-first century: Some theoretical considerations. *International Relations of the Asia-Pacific, 1*(1), 105–130; re-published in Cox with Schechter (2002).
Cox, R. W. (2002). Reflections and transitions. In R. W. Cox with M. Schechter (Eds.), *The political economy of a plural world* (pp. 26–43). London: Routledge.
Cox, R. W. (2007). The 'international' in evolution. *Millennium, 35*(3), 513–527.
Cox, R. W. (2013). *Universal foreigner: The individual and the world.* Singapore: World Scientific.
Cox, R. W., & Jacobson, H. K. (1972). *The anatomy of influence: Decision making in international organization.* New Haven: Yale University Press.
Cox, R. W. with Schechter, M. (2002). *The political economy of a plural world.* London: Routledge.
Cox, R. W. with Sinclair, T. (1996). *Approaches to world order.* Cambridge: Cambridge University Press.
Fukuyama, F. (1992). *The end of history and the last man.* New York, NY: The Free Press.
Germain, R. (2007). 'Critical' political economy, historical materialism and Adam Morton. *Politics, 27*(2), 127–131.
Germain, R. (2013). The making of IR/IPE: Robert W. Cox's production, power and world order. In H. Bliddal, C. Sylvest, & P. Wilson (Eds.), *Classics of international relations* (pp. 187–196). London: Routledge.
Gill, S., & Mittelman, J. (Eds.). (1997). *Innovation and transformation in international studies.* Cambridge: Cambridge University Press.
Gramsci, A. (1973). *Antonio Gramsci: Letters from prison.* (L. Lawner, Trans. and introduced). New York, NY: Harper & Row.
Griffiths, M., Roach, S., & Solomon, S. (2009). *Fifty key thinkers in international relations.* London: Routledge.
Helleiner, E. (1997). Braudelian reflections on economic globalisation: The historian as pioneer. In S. Gill, & J. H. Mittelman (Eds.), *Innovation and transformation in international studies* (pp. 90–104). Cambridge: Cambridge University Press.
Huntington, S. (1996). *The clash of civilizations and the remaking of world order.* New York, NY: Simon & Schuster.
Kratochwil, F., & Ruggie, J. G. (1986). International organization: A state of the art on an art of the state. *International Organization, 40*(4), 753–775.
Marx, K. (1851/1977). The eighteenth Brumaire of Louis Bonaparte. In D. McLellan (Ed.), *Karl Marx: Selected writings.* (pp. 300–325) Oxford: Oxford University Press.
Mittelman, J. (1998). Coxian historicism as an alternative perspective in international studies. *Alternatives, 23*(1), 63–92.
Sinclair, T. (1996). Beyond international relations theory: Robert W. Cox and approaches to world order. In R. W. Cox with T. Sinclair (Eds.), *Approaches to world order* (pp. 3–18). Cambridge: Cambridge University Press.

Thomas, P. (2009/2013). *The Gramscian moment: Philosophy, hegemony and Marxism*. Delhi: Aakar Books.

TRIPS. (2012). *Trip around the world: Teaching, research and policy views among international relations faculty in 20 countries*. Daniel Malniak, Susan Peterson, and Tierney, M. J. Williamsburg. Virginia: The Institute for Theory and Practice of International Relations. Retrieved November 20, 2014 from http://www.wm.edu/offices/itpir/_documents/trip/trip_around_the_world_2011.pdf

Vico, G. (1744/1948). *The new science of Giambattista Vico*. (Thomas Goddard Bergin and Max Harold Fisch, Trans.). Ithaca: Cornell University Press.

Neo-Gramscian Theory and Third World Violence: A Time for Broadening

RANDOLPH B. PERSAUD

American University, Washington, DC, USA

ABSTRACT *This article argues that the neo-Gramscian theory of hegemony is not as useful in explaining the rise and consolidation of the modern world system. In particular, while the force-consensus approach may indeed be relevant in examining relations among the Western countries, it is fundamentally wanting when applied to the third world. The two main reasons concern the persistent violence against the third world, and the dominance of race and racism as social forces in the production and maintenance of successive world orders. Neo-Gramscian theory needs to be broadened perhaps by paying attention to the relevant thinking in postcolonialism.*

The West won the world not by the superiority of its ideas or values or religion [. . .] but rather by its superiority in applying organized violence. Westerners often forget this fact; non-Westerners never do. (Huntington, 1996)

. . . despite major accomplishments and promises, the neo-Gramscian turn appears to have lost its nerve. (Pasha, 2008, p. 199)

Introduction

My contention is with one of the most important aspects of neo-Gramscian *international* theory, namely, hegemonic consensus and coercion on a global scale. I argue that the application of neo-Gramscian hegemonic consensus theory in international relations is actually more relevant to intra-Euro-American relations than to the global system as a whole, and only minimally to the relationship *between* Western countries and the Third World. In contradistinction to consensus, the West—that is, Euro-America, has engaged in persistent, sometimes savage, but always debilitating violence, including full-scale wars, against the Third World (Beckert, 2014; Burleigh, 2013). The history of this carnage goes back to conquest and colonization, followed by various forms of coercive domination delivered through militaristic imperialism and other forms of foreign interference. I endeavor to show that it is violence, *not* consensus that has been the definitive, consequential, and most enduring aspect of Euro-American relationship with the Third World. I also argue that outside the writings of postcolonial scholars, race has been a missing factor in the neo-Gramscian analysis, and this despite the massive constitutivity of race and racism in the making of the international system and world orders (Persaud, 1997; Mills, 1999; Mittelman, 2009; Anievas, Manchanda, & Shilliam, 2015; Krishna, 2001). Some major exceptions are noted and discussed below.

The Coxian Method of Historical Structure

Robert W. Cox's contribution to international theory is immense by any measure. Pasha is correct when he notes that Cox's work is important in '...a critical project of resistance, counter-hegemony, and emancipation' (Pasha, 2008, p. 199). From his seminal 1981and 1983 articles in *Millennium*, through his *magnum opus—Production power and world order*—and then onto his work on civilizations, Cox has provided a durable platform for critical theory. The robustness of his contribution led to a veritable intellectual movement in international theory aimed at constructively ruining the intellectual prestige of the hitherto and perhaps still hegemonic literature in traditional international relations. The fact that he formulated neorealism as a 'problem-solving theory' (Keohane, 1986, pp. 18–19) is symptomatic of his innovative critique of the regnant Cartesian and non-agential structuralism, which at least up to 1989 formed a kind of essentialist last instance in international theory. If his work did not reach the status of epistemological revolution, it certainly produced massive discursive disturbance of what then looked like the settled options in realism, liberalism, and Marxism.

Cox's most significant contributions are to be found in his development of the method of historical structure, itself built around two principal configurations, namely ideas, institutions, and material capabilities, and social forces, forms of state, and world order (Cox, 1987; Germain & Kenny, 1998; Gill, 1993; Gill & Mittelam, 1997; Mittelman & Pasha, 1997; Persaud, 1996; Sinclair, 2016). Some key concepts culled from Gramsci—hegemony, historic bloc, *transformismo*, organic intellectual, passive revolution, war of position, and war of movement, among others, provided the building blocks for a more general materialist but non-reductionist political theory of global (as distinct from international) power (Rupert, 1995). Historical structure is operationalized both synchronically and diachronically (with emphasis on the latter), and at a more abstract level, it is located in Gramsci's 'genetic' historicism (Jameson, 1988, p. 154; Persaud, 2001a, p. 199).

Apart from its trenchant critique of neorealism, Coxian international theory liberated Marxism from economic reductionism, anti-historical scientific structuralism (*a la* Althusser), and compellingly also from 'activistic' voluntarism such as embedded in Luckas' *History and class consciousness*. Now, despite the complexity of Cox's work, most neo-Gramscians have tended to focus on the theory of hegemony, much of it counter-posed to the centrality of dominance (Bieler & Morton, 2004).

Cox's own neo-Gramscian scholarship became even more influential because of a number of scholars who either commenced using a Coxian interpretation of Gramsci or started to use Gramscian analysis though without direct Coxian influence. Stephen R. Gill, James H. Mittelman, Enrico Aguelli and Craig Murphy, William I. Robinson, and Mark Rupert, among others, made major contributions in the early stages of neo-Gramscian international relations theory (Rupert 1995; Robinson 1996). Gill and Law's 'Global hegemony and the structural power of capital', published in *International Studies Quarterly* (1989), did much to bring the new neo-Gramscian approach to the mainstream international relations community, and to younger critical theorists working in the political economy tradition.[1] A textbook by the same authors, *The global political economy*, published the year before was widely used by senior undergraduates as well as graduate students. Gill's edited volume *Gramsci, historical materialism and international relations* (1993) also made an impact; his article 'Globalisation, market civilisation and disciplinary neoliberalism' (Gill, 1995) was widely read and the citation count now stands well over one thousand. Mittelman also published heavily within the neo-Gramscian framework. *The globalization syndrome* (2000) made quite an impact with over a thousand citations, and *Out from underdevelopment revisited* co-authored with Pasha (1996) was one of the earlier works that applied Gramscian theory and the work of Cox to the political economy of the Third World. Robinson's 1996 *Promoting polyarchy: Globalization, US intervention and hegemony* was hugely successful and a major contribution to the emergence of broader neo-Gramscian international relations. Notably, Robinson's work, much like Augelli and Murphy, demonstrated convincingly that theorizing (American) hegemony really can and ought to be done with considerable emphasis on coercion against the Third World. Robinson showed the ways in which polyarchy, global society, and Third World domination are part of a globally structured and interconnected totality.

The work of Enrico Augelli and Craig Murphy deserve special attention. Murphy came to the Gramscian analysis of international relations *via* postcolonial theorists, and especially through the writings of Partha Chatterjee and Gayatri Chavrovorty Spivak (Murphy, correspondence with the author, 2015). Augelli was a senior diplomat in the Italian Foreign Service with several assignments in Africa, including North Africa. Aguelli's time as the Italian Ambassador to Somalia is noteworthy for its grounded approach (Kennedy, 1993). Perhaps most importantly, Augelli and Murphy used the concept *supremacy* instead of hegemony precisely because the former is more applicable to the Third World. In many ways, supremacy is a combination of violence plus cultural domination, instead of coercion plus consensus. As Murphy puts it,

> ... we were much more careful about describing the supremacy of the inter-imperial system and neocolonial systems as something that involved hegemony that was confined to the core; and there, not to the 'periphery within the core.' Force and fraud has always ruled elsewhere and even minor attention to the memoirs of Western and Japanese military commanders, let alone the rank and file, would make that perfectly apparent. (Murphy, 16 February 2015, correspondence with the author)

Usually, neo-Gramscian scholars (despite notable exceptions) have mostly employed the consensual aspects of the consensus–coercive dialectic of hegemony as originally theorized by Antonio Gramsci. In my view, the main reason for the emphasis on consensus in the neo-Gramscian literature is that the principal concern is restricted to the crisis of capitalism and, even so, within the narrow spacio-cultural cartography of the North Atlantic.[2] Neo-Gramscian international theory needs to go beyond what I shall call a *northernist* ontology, and beyond ideas and culture restricted to processes of legitimation. For Radice

> ... the question is to what extent Gramsci's concepts are adequate to the task set for them by Cox and other neo-Gramscian scholars, or more specifically, do they carry forward a mode of enquiry that is both critical and historical in the ways specified by Cox and closely echoed in subsequent neo-Gramscian studies? (2008, p. 55)

If indeed culture and ideas are so important then perhaps one of the first reconstructed iterations out of neo-Gramscian self-reflection and broadening could very well be that problems of race and racism have been critical social forces to conquest, empire, cultural hegemony, and to the reproduction of both capitalist economies and societies, not to mention the rather central role of race in the configuration of forms of state and world orders (Ayers, 2008; Drainville, 2012; Gabriel & Pellerin, 2008; Morton, 2013; Persaud, 2001b; Persuad & Walker, 2001). What we may call here the *racial dynamic* in history-*making* is a particularly notable gap in neo-Gramscian scholarship because Cox's framework of historical structure explicitly and methodically employs 'social forces' as a key element of his problematic as many postcolonial and gender theorists have shown (Blaney & Inayatullah, 2010; Chin, 1998; Muppidi, 2012; Shilliam, 2008; Whitworth, 2005). Race is one of the most enduring social forces for the past 500 years in both relations of physical/territorial security and the configuration of social formations and macro-systems of accumulation (Beckert, 2014; Mittelman & Pasha, 1996). Neo-Gramscian theory needs to systematically engage the postcolonial literature from this angle, a move that would call for notable adjustments in the ontologies and historiography of the extant neo-Gramscian theoretical practices.

Another important adjustment that has to be made if global coloniality were to be addressed is the systematic incorporation of violence against the Third World when making claims and propositions about world order *as a whole* (Beier, 2005; Doty, 1996; Laffey, 2016). Violence against the Third World is not simply a means to an end, but more often than not an integral aspect of the relationships between the West and various Others. The incorporation of the 'coloniality of power' would facilitate the theorization of what I have called *primitive hegemony* (see below) where violence is the preponderant practice in the consensus–coercion nexus (Chatterjee, 2012; Dabashi, 2015; Henderson, 2015; Quijano, 2007; Tirman, 2011; Turse, 2013). In fact the consensus aspect is so weak between the Third World and Euro-America that it might be better to posit a dialectic of coercion/domination, rather than coercion/consensus in understanding the making of the modern global political economy and inter-state system.

In the meantime, critical scholars outside the neo-Gramscian tradition have made significant contributions to security studies that have systematically included race and are about violence by Euro-America against the Third World. Tarak Barkawi and Mark Laffey, Roxanne Doty, Marshall Beier, and others have offered sustained critiques of the Eurocentric character of security studies as it has developed since World War II (Acharya, 2014; Barkawi & Laffey, 2006; Barkawi & Stanski, 2013; Beier, 2005; Doty, 1996). A recent edited volume by Brincat, Lima, and Nunes is also a step in the right direction, although it must be noted that while the work is on critical international relations, including security studies, not all of the contributors are neo-Gramscians (Brincat, Lima, & Nunes, 2011). Columba Peoples has used the work of Gramsci and Cox, combined with that of Sean Wyn Jones, in interrogating the legitimation processes of ballistic missile defense. Peoples concluded that a ballistic missile defense as a viable defense program is partly explained by the ways in which technology has been deeply socialized as a form of common sense, meaning that complex social and political problems can be solved through the use of military technology (Peoples, 2010). Outside of IR Judith Butler, with great epistemological sophistication, has shown how the lives lost in the Third World do not count, and are rendered '*ungrievable*'. The Israeli invasion of Gaza in December 2008/January 2009 led Butler to conclude that 'Righteous coldness is not only what it takes to kill, but also what is required to look at the destruction of life with moral satisfaction, even moral triumph' (p. xxiv).

Approaches to Hegemony

Hegemony is not a new concept in international relations. It had been central to the power-politics school but became even more forceful through the aggressive 'offensive neorealism' of thinkers such as John Mearsheimer.[3] Liberals and neoliberal institutionalists also use hegemony in both explanatory and prescriptive ways. Joseph Nye's notion of *soft power* is an iteration of a liberal hegemonic project aimed at *leading* through socialization of the values of the 'hegemon', in his reckoning, those being the values of the United States.

In contradistinction to the zero-sum perspective of neorealism, where the 'winner takes all', neoliberal institutionalists claim that absolute gains (across the system) is an incentive for cooperation. The institutional form of neoliberal institutionalism is regimes in different 'issues areas'. Cooperation is housed in hierarchical institutions where the hierarchical character reflects the state-centricity of this form of liberalism. Regimes are supposed to provide better information, coordination, and reduce externalities such as cheating. Regimes, however, cannot and do not just naturally spring up from the groundwork of the international system. Rather, they are the products of *leadership* by a hegemonic power. It takes a state with both resources and credibility to build an international order that would be both efficient (defined as reduction in transactional costs) and legitimate, meaning that followership would not be based on coercion (Keohane, 1984; Krasner, 1983).

Soft power and regimes as central articulating concepts bring to mind Slater's astute observation that

> ... a regular series of statements, emphases, themes, priorities and recommendations needed to be created as a way of providing a vision, an explanation and also a frame for the practical construction of a strategy that will be deployed through the appropriate international and national organizations and apparatuses of rule. (2004, p. 98)

Neoliberal institutionalism is pre-occupied with forms of cooperation in the global economy, with added focus on how leadership is organized. Security is a by-product of economics.

Now, the neo-Gramscians also emphasize the making of consensus but go to great lengths to demonstrate how this consensus is a form of benign domination, while the liberals, as noted above, usually prefer to emphasize hegemonic practice as a form of leadership, a public good. Either way, the concern is with legitimacy, although for the neo-Gramscians the preoccupation is with the *processes* of legitimation, and particularly the fit among production (and more latterly finance), state power, and ideology.

While the *northernist* neo-Gramscian employment of hegemony is absolutely useful in the analysis of domestic politics and Euro-American relations, I argue that it is only partially so at the international/global level, and even then, only since the end of World War II. Moreover, in theorizing hegemony, neo-Gramscianism has almost exclusively focused on the analysis of culture as related to social formations in the West. As Pasha notes, 'the shortcomings of neo-Gramscian theory, with references to culture, reproduce erasures and enclosures that bind the IR enterprise to the Western story of modernity, global political economy, and hegemony' (2005, p. 200). Yes, there was definitely consensus among the West European countries and Canada, New Zealand, and Australia. The Third World, however, has never been in this company. In fact, the exact opposite can be documented. While Western countries accommodated each other's interest in alliances and various forms of multilateral cooperation, they willingly (though by no means always unanimously) participated in coercive and outright violent forms of intervention in the Third World.

These interventions began in colonial times and have survived through various phases of the global expansion of capitalism and military domination. This is why Grovougi and Leonard express concern '... that Cox's representations of hegemony and dominance validate historic forms of violence associated with primitive accumulation' (2008, p. 222). Grovougi and Leonard, in this instance, questioned the periodization and more broadly the historiography of Coxian hegemonic theory. In my own view what is called hegemony in the *northernist* neo-Gramscian sense can alternatively be understood as intra-colonial and intra-imperialist *cooperation* among the West, combined with *collaboration* with undemocratic and authoritarian regimes in the Third World, many of them the direct product of Western policies (Chalcraft and Noorani, 2007). Pasrsons points to abundant empirical evidence of the fine distinction between cooperation and collaboration (2010, p. 441).

I previously identified three distinct kinds of hegemonic practice, namely the primitive, the enlightened, and the benevolent (Persaud, 2004). The key here is to understand each as an ideal type. Primitive hegemony exists where the use of force or outright violence is employed to achieve desired outcomes, including coercive forms of capital accumulation, or what Beckert has called *war capitalism* (2014). Enlightened hegemony is based on a balance of coercion and cooperation in shaping and maintaining a social order domestically, and world order at the regional/global levels. Benevolent hegemony is a form of cultural power exercised where the practicing agent (states, NGOs, and individuals) assumes that its own culture is superior, and where lesser recipients can benefit from various kinds of 'support' or engagement. The support may be material, or 'spiritual', and according to Augelli and Murphy, may be traced back to the Calvinist notion of the Elect which articulates a discourse of a 'chosen people' (1988, p. 29). The three kinds of hegemony are not mutually exclusive, but one form may be dominant in a historical structure. Primitive and benevolent forms of hegemony have characterized the Euro-American relationship with the Third World. Enlightened hegemony has characterized North Atlantic and OECD relations, this perhaps best theorized by Gill in *American hegemony and the trilateral commission* (1992). In what follows, I apply the concept of primitive hegemony to describe and demonstrate that violence, not consensus, has been the definitive relationship between Euro-America and the Third World for the *greater part* of their contact since the age of colonialism.

Primitive Hegemony in the Third World

The collaboration of Western states in the *violent control* of the Third World can be empirically established in the two grand historical structures represented as global hegemony (in all realist, liberal, and neo-Gramscian theories), namely *Pax Britannica* and *Pax Americana* (Grovougi & Leonard, 2008, p. 223; Hobson, 2012; Persaud, 2002, 2004; Vitalis, 2015). Empirical evidence in the form of data alone cannot refute theory, but a quick scanning of the relevant data on violence in the *same periods* of supposed hegemonic consensus (i.e. British and American global leadership) is a good place as any to begin. The period covered here is from the late nineteenth century through the early twenty-first century, again, a span of time that is purposely selected to fit with the neo-Gramscian hegemony as consensus historiography and theory of international relations. In what follows, I review this violence by the West against the Third World after which it should be evident that the neo-Gramscian theory of international relations based on hegemonic consent needs serious revision when applied to the global political economy *as a whole*.

Table 1. Western and Third World casualties 1886–2006

Period	Western deaths	Third World deaths	Source TW
1886–1908 Belgium vs. Congo Free State	16	10,000,000	Hoch
1898–1902 United States vs. Philippines	4165	212,000	
Germany vs. Namibia	676	65,000	UN Rep
1936 Italy vs. Ethiopia	10,000	275,000	Del Boca
1945–1949 The Netherlands vs. Indonesia	5000	70,000	A. Vickers
1946–1954 France vs. Vietnam	175,000	518,714	M. Clodfelter Incls Cambodians
1948–1960 UK vs. Malaya	719	11,000	Olson and Shadle
1950–1954 United States vs. Korea	33,686	511,000, S. Korea 400,000, People's Volunteer Army (PVA) 215,000, Korean People's Army (KPA) 290,000, N. Korea	Does not include N. Korea civilian deaths (M. Hickey; Yan Xu)
1952 UK. vs. Kenya	100 Europeans	13,970	Olson and Schadle
1954– France vs. Algeria	25,000	880,000	Horne Incl. post-war reprisal
1955–1975 United States vs. Vietnam	58,220	950,765	(US Def. Dept)
1961–1975 Portugal vs. Angola and Mozambique	4000 3500	75,000 60,000	Hartman World Atlas of Mil His.
1979–1989 USSR vs. Afghanistan	14,453	850,000	Khalidi + Sliwinski
United States/United Kingdom vs. Iraq	4287 (Glob Sec.Org)	500,000	PLoMedecine

Table 1 shows that violence against the Third World has been both pervasive and continuous. In what follows, however, I have considered only those instances where there were more than 1000 deaths, and for the most part used established minimum estimates. In some cases the differences are enormous and if the upper estimates were used, the magnitude and kill ratio would be significantly more tragic. In the Belgium/Congo war, for instance, I use a lower credible estimate—10,000,000,[4] instead of the highest estimate of 30,000,000. The same is true for the Dutch war against Indonesia, where the lower estimate is 70,000 and the maximum estimate is 200,000. I use the minimum of 500,000 for the Iraqis killed due to the 2003 invasion (and subsequent occupation) despite the quite credible estimate of 654,965 offered by John Hopkins University and Al Mustansiriya University in Baghdad (http://www.jhsph.edu/news/news-releases/

2006/burnham-iraq-2006.html). Even higher estimates have been arrived at by prestigious sources such as *The Lancet*.

Three other points must be taken into consideration. First, I include the Soviet War against Afghanistan (using the minimum estimate 850,000 vs. 1,500,000) despite the fact that the USSR was for the most part considered outside the West. It is indeed, but it is still basically European. Second, I do *not* include the 511,000 South Korean deaths from the Korean War, nor do I include any deaths from the 'war on terror' in Afghanistan. A reliable overall (minimum) estimate for deaths in the Third World caused by Euro-American war or other kinds of violence between 1886 and 2013 is 15,386,449, compared to the very reliable number of Euro-American deaths which stands at 338,822. With these numbers the death ratio of Third World people to Euro-Americans is 45:1. A credible objection might be that the Soviet war against Afghanistan should not be included because it has nothing to do with the way neo-Gramscians have theorized global hegemony, and more particularly the consensus–coercion problem. If we take out those USSR–Afghan death figures on both sides we have 14,536,449 Third World deaths and 324,369 Western deaths, for a ratio of 44.8:1—that is, the general picture is not much different. Finally if we drop the two highest death counts (10,000,000 Congo deaths vs. Belgium and 175,000 French vs. Vietnam) we end up with 5,386,449 Third World deaths; and 149,369 Western deaths, for a ratio of 36:1.

Some further consideration needs elaboration. First is the span of time covered and diversity of situations involved and the number of countries covered. As the Table 1 shows we are dealing with constant wars for more than the past 125 years—including Belgium vs. Congo Free State (1886–1908), United States vs. Philippines (1899–1902), Germany vs. Namibia (1904), Italy vs. Ethiopia (1936), the Netherlands vs. Indonesia (1945–1949), Britain vs. Kenya (1952–1956), Britain vs. Malaysia (1948–1960), France vs. Algeria (1954–1962), Portugal vs. Angola (1961–1975), Portugal vs. Mozambique (1961–1975), France vs. Vietnam (1946–1954), United States vs. Korea (1950–1954), United States vs. Vietnam (1954–1975), USSR vs. Afghanistan (1979–1989), and United States vs. Iraq (2003–2012).

The persistent aggression against the Third World noted above makes it difficult to speak of consensual hegemony in the international system. It does not exist. The neo-Gramscian employment of the concept of 'hegemony as consensus' is at best applicable only to Euro-America, and fundamentally wrong when applied to the international system as a whole. Perhaps this is why Barkawi and Laffey observe that '… Eurocentric security studies regards the weak and the powerless as marginal or derivative elements of world politics, at best the site of liberal good intentions or at worst a potential source of threats' (2006, p. 332).

Pervasive though the violence has been as noted above, not all the carnage is covered here. Missing is a catalog of violence that is so widespread and so persistent that it is almost impossible to detail in an article of this length. What we may do, however, is to construct categories of violence that might be employed in a more comprehensive study. Consider the following: (1) *Small Wars against the Third World*: a large amount of violent interventions that were catastrophic but that did not produce comparatively large numbers of death but destructive all the same are not but should be factored in when doing a more comprehensive analysis. Think randomly of Grenada, Panama, Honduras, and Nicaragua in the Americas alone; (2) *Violent Destabilization:* many governments were toppled leading to long periods of not only repression through police states, but also sustained violence—Iran, Guatemala, Argentina, Chile, Brazil, Mozambique, Angola, and Zaire (now Zimbabwe), this being just a short list (Prashad, 2012); (3) *Participatory Silence*: next, we should consider all those places where the West stood by in active silence in situations of universal moral repugnance or outright catastrophic violence. In many instances, the supposed 'ethnic violence' has a direct lineage to the way in which colonial powers parceled out state power and economic privileges. South Africa and Rhodesia fit the former and the latter has a long list, namely Rwanda, Darfur, Syria, and the Congo; (4) *Internal Violence:* the United States is routinely described as the global hegemonic leader, but this claim would be considerably tempered if one were to examine the fit between domestic social forces and world order, consistent with the Coxian framework. In the case of the United States, therefore, there is only a lopsided hegemony because of the violence against African-Americans during slavery, Jim Crow (lynching), the Civil Rights era, and currently through the prison-industrial-complex situated in the age of global neoliberalism. Those of us using the work of Gramsci and Cox might consider the proposition that hegemony pace Gramsci has been for White America, while violence has been the preferred mode of 'governance' for African-Americans. I myself consider the United States to be a *dual society by design*, rather than a melting pot. Further, even if the focus is only on capitalism as is the case with most neo-Gramscian writers, then the role of racialized institutions and ideas (two key elements of historical structures) should figure heavily in the analyses of structures of accumulation and various developments; (5) *Colonial Bodies as War Resource*: the periods when the West was not visiting violence on the Third World were, ironically, exactly when the 'colonials' were helping the West fight against other Western states (and fellow colonizers). The British Indian Army numbered more than one million. India was the jewel in the crown not only for economic resources, but also for strategic and military purposes. The Indian army was active on behalf of the British Empire from South Asia, all the way deep down into Southeast Asia, reaching Singapore during World War II. Troops from Africa played a key role in the French efforts against Germany in Africa itself, but also on the front lines in Europe. Colonial subjects from as far away as the Caribbean reaching way down in British Guiana on the South American coast were pressed into service against Germany in both World Wars. The French *troupes indigènes* played key roles in World War I and World War II. In August 1914, France had 90,000 of these troupes at hand (Fogarty, 2008, p. 24).

Apart from the sustained violence detailed above we should also take cognizance of other practices, such as the voting behavior of Western states at the United Nations on the issue of apartheid in Rhodesia (now Zimbabwe) and South Africa. Even the states that were pursuing more moderate policies *vis-à-vis* the Third World often abstained on roll call votes intended to condemn or sanction those countries. The leader of the Western alliance had a policy of *constructive engagement* with apartheid in South Africa at a time when the entire Third World was engaged in determined action to put an end to the diabolical practices of racial domination. Further, practically all the Western states have and continue to practice some form of coercive immigration, quite often constructed on the bases of racialized if not racist 'white only' criteria.

On the question of colonialism, the intra-imperialist cooperation was witnessed as late as the 1970s when many Western states stood with Portugal, first against India in 1961 regarding Goa, and then active support of violence in Mozambique and Angola. Much of this was done through the racist regime in South Africa with linkages attributed to the CIA (Mamdani, 2002, 775–776). Western support for RENAMO in Mozambique, and UNITA in Angola took cover behind the Cold War. Mamdani notes that the Western-supported RENAMO was responsible for almost 100,000 deaths in Mozambique and the same support for UNITA led to widespread maiming due to the use of land mines, mostly against peasants (2002, p. 769).

In the more recent period, especially *after* the Cold War, and against the determined struggles of the masses in the Middle East, the West has consistently shown its hands in coercive 'diplomacy' against the Third World[5] (Prashad, 2012). Western support for undemocratic regimes in the Middle East is legendary (Engdahl, 2004) and only recently more proof came when Western states first held on to strongman Hosni Mubarak and, after that cause was lost, helped to depose the democratically elected Morsi government. The West then actively and openly participated in the restoration of a military regime in Egypt, while they also propped up the government of Bahrain even though the same government has been one of the worst violators of human rights associated with the Arab Revolutions. Western countries also actively participated in the overthrow of Mummar Gadaffi. Only a few years before Prime Minister Blair had congratulated the 'Mad Dog' for his accomplishments in the war on terror, renditions, and all. In 2007, the British Prime Minister abandoned the 'Mad Dog' label and sent a 'Dear Muammar' letter to Gadaffi. Blair signed off the letter 'Best Wishes yours ever, Tony'.[6] As this paper is being written, the United States is providing coordinates for air strikes by Saudi Arabia in Yemen with a good deal of these resulting in huge civilian casualties. It is reasonable, therefore, to suggest that the trajectory of Western violence continues today through commission and omission (such as the silence on Syria), most pointedly so in the language and practices of humanitarian intervention and counter-insurgency warfare, the latter especially linked to the current war on terror. Recent declassified documents from the Clinton Administration show in convincing fashion that the United States and others were well aware of both the impending genocide in Rwanda and the actual genocide as it was unfolding.

The discussion above also allows us to offer a classificatory schema of primitive hegemony in the Third World—(1) *Violent Conquest* of 'new areas' resulting in quick annihilation of the domestic population and then subsequent exploitative repression of those who survived—the Americas, Australia, and New Zeeland; (2) *Gradual Entry* over an extended period carried out through violent displacement of the local leadership and then collaboration with locals who were cultivated to administer imperial domination and economic exploitation (e.g. India and Indonesia); (3) *Invasion*, bombing, and/or occupation of independent/sovereign countries that do not collaborate with imperialism—Vietnam and Iraq; (4) *Covert Operations/Support* to topple ideologically 'deviant' or non-cooperative (non-consensual) governments followed by instillation of a collaborator (enforcer is probably more accurate) who employs violence to maintain the social order—for example, Chile, Brazil, Iran, Guatemala, Congo, Egypt, Tunisia, and Yemen, just to name a few current or recent ones. These categories roughly correspond to the different kinds of violence noted above.

Cox himself is clear that as you move to the Third World consensus gets thinner (1981). This crucial aspect of Cox's work needs to be more fully integrated into neo-Gramscian theorization and operationalized in historical/empirical analyses. The emphasis on the consensual dimension of hegemony and the near abandonment of violence (often racialized) itself needs explanation.

Firstly, most of the neo-Gramscian analyses that have been done to date have been through critical political economy, and very little on international and global security.[7] The closest that neo-Gramscians come to security questions are in the three following ways—human security, imperialism, and resistance. Let us examine these below.

Generally, neo-Gramscians have accepted the liberal concept of human security, and even so, mostly on the freedom from want side of the equation. This should be no surprise because some forms of human security are actually neo-Marxist political economy in the language of critiques of globalization. Here neo-Gramscians focus on transformations in the global structure of production (especially internationalization/globalization), the structural power of international capital, the rise of financial capitalism, cultural developments associated with globalization mostly focused on the rise of commodification and the rise of consumerism, expansion and intensification of exploitation, and global inequality. This analysis of the contradictions in global capitalism need not detract from analysis of violence against and in the Third World. Barkawi and Laffey have done exactly this kind of critical security analysis linked to the global structure of capital (Barkawi & Laffey, 1999). It is worth noting that some aspects of neo-Gramscian political economy are actually indistinguishable from liberal approaches to human security. David Held's cosmopolitan multilateralism, for instance, or the 'freedom from want work' of Mary Kaldor or Caroline Thomas could easily be housed in an edited volume on neo-Gramscian approaches to global governance. The obvious difference of course would be around the use of social classes and more broadly the class character of globalization.

Secondly, neo-Gramscians make references to violence against the Third World (including in the form of war) usually as an *extension*, an end point of the logic of imperialism where imperialism itself is theorized as a dynamic of international capital or global capitalism. Here, the neo-Gramscians are keen to explore the *contradictions* of capitalism in Euro-America (includes Canada, Australia, and New Zealand) and *where necessary*, the violent aspect of Western imperialism are then drawn in, though not systematically analyzed. Some writers working within the neo-Gramscian tradition such as Robinson have, in fact, shown that the analysis of global capitalism and the practice of violence sometimes go together (2003).

Too often the Third World is used either as an *illustration* of the excesses and limitations of capitalism. Much of the critiques of the violence in places like Iraq are outside of neo-Gramscian international theory per se. These critiques rather are expressions of genuine outrage. Hobson makes the argument that the anti-imperialism of the neo-Gramscians is within a framework of 'subliminal anti-paternalist Eurocentrism' which is remarkably similar to the 'anti-imperialism and subliminal Eurocentrism' of classical realism, with further resemblance to the 'explicit anti-imperialism but defensive Eurocentrism' of 'cultural realism' (2012, pp. 332–333).

Thirdly, and in my view most tragically, neo-Gramscian international theory, having basically abandoned violence against the Third World from its core *theoretical* infrastructure, is forced to retrieve it in order to facilitate one of the most important epistemological *requirement* of critical theory, that is, resistance (Shilliam, 2008, p. 240). In the old Marxism, the endpoint was always revolution (not reform), but since 1989, the destination has been tweaked. No 'war of position' and much less no revolutionary upheaval is possible in Europe in the foreseeable future, and given the import of transformation and change embedded in the claims and propositions of neo-Gramscianism, it has had no alternative but to factor in 'the declivity where an authentic upheaval can be born' (Fanon, 2008). The resistance aspect of neo-Gramscianism does not so much concern the internal structures of power, that is to say, on its own terms in the Third World, but is mostly resistance to imperialism which in the more recent period is associated with neoliberal globalization. Perhaps the best illustration of this was the widespread 'adoption' of Chiapas by left intellectuals, including in the writings of Prof. Cox. Yashar has usefully drawn our attention to the fact that thousands of activists, NGOs, etc. descended on Chiapas following the January 1994 rebellions (Yasar, 2007, p. 161).

While neo-Gramscians absolutely and unequivocally criticize violence against the Third World, (the older) Marxism has a long history going back to Marx himself who not only bought into, but aggressively advocated European imperialism as a civilizing mission. Bill Warren notes that even though Marx and Engels knew that force was being used to implant European imperialism, it did not affect their perspective. Warren notes that 'violence did not necessarily mean retrogressive disruption or greater suffering than peaceful reaction' (1980, p. 39). In footnote sixty-eight of chapter two of *Imperialism pioneer of capitalism*, Warren causally notes that Barrington Moore supports the same theme. He himself calls the concepts underdevelopment and neocolonialism 'fictions', and chastises Marxists who ' ... cavil at the thought that progress sometimes requires the use of force' (Warren, 1980, p. 127).

Conclusion

Radice's 'pessimistic reading' of the question of resistance and/or counterhegemony is that ' ... while neo-Gramscianism may have become established in the IPE wing of academia, it is unlikely to be of much help in seeking to build a global "movement of movements" that can seriously challenge the present order' (2008, p. 67). This problem may be partly addressed by making greater use of the postcolonial literature in international relations (see Bhambra, 2007; Chowdhry & Nair, 2002; Jones, 2008; Krishna, 2008; Said, 1978; Sajed, 2013).

There is an obvious gap, if not divide, between the *northernist* neo-Gramscians and Gramscian postcolonial theories of the international (Hobson, 2012; Persaud, 2015b; Srivastava & Battacharya, 2013). Several points come to mind. Firstly, the former almost always begins with Euro-America; the latter almost always with the Third World.[8] Secondly, the former is always keen on demonstrating how the contradictions of capitalism do not (but perhaps should) lead to a cataclysmic rupture of the social order at home (meaning Euro-America), hence the stress on *consensuality*. By contrast, the postcolonial Gramscians are always keen on theorizing and demonstrating how race as a social force and Eurocentrism as an epistemological technology are at the center of the constitution and reproduction of not only Euro-centered solidarity, but also neocolonial globalization.[9] Thirdly, while neo-Gramscian ontology is grounded in *exploitation* of the working class in the process of capitalist accumulation, the postcolonials foreground this same exploitation in the historical structures of colonialism and the resurrection of relations of domination in the new coloniality of power (Persaud & Chin 2015; Quijano, 2007; Seth 2013). Fourthly, while neo-Gramscians construct resistance as a sort of theoretical last instance (in the sense used by Althusser in a different context), the postcolonial Gramscians place counterhegemony on an equal spacio-temporal footing, that is, as a simultaneous *act of movement* in the dialectic of hegemonization (Hobson, 2012, p. 240; Persaud, 1996, 2001). Jacques Depelchin's critique of 'major histories' such as that of Fernand Braudel adds to our understanding of the denial of Third World agency. Depelchin argues '... that African history is usually approached with a series of preconceptions which are derived from how these major histories, namely Western European and North American, have been written' (2005). I have myself previously argued that:

> Resistance and counter-hegemony are too often seen as *responses* to interests already formed, rather than theorized as dialectically defining the conditions which make hegemonic practices historically 'necessary' in the first place ... As such, counter-hegemonic practices must be seen as a fluid and unstable *engagement*, rather than a settled response to hegemony. (Persaud, 1996, 2001a, my italics)

It is in this context that John Hobson provides detailed references to a number of major neo-Gramscian writers who, despite the language of double movement, routinely attach Third World resistance/counterhegemony as an addendum, and well after the theorization is completed.

Finally, there is no doubt about the contributions of the Coxian variant of neo-Gramscian international theory by a slew of scholars who have made an especially significant mark in international political economy. Neo-Gramscian theory has played a major role in democratizing international theory. We are at a stage now where the occasion calls for a broadening of neo-Gramscian theory within international relations, a broadening that must pay equal attention to the violent repression and racial domination of the Third World in building and maintaining the international system in its several historical forms.

Acknowledgements

I received important feedback for the paper from Craig Murphy, James Mittelman, John Hobson, Nicola Phillips, Sankaran Krishna, and Christine B.N. Chin. I also gratefully acknowledge the first-rate research assistance of Davina Durgana for this paper. I would also like to thank Shelley A. Barry for outstanding editorial guidance.

Disclosure Statement

No potential conflict of interest was reported by the author.

Notes

1. Among the students at York University (Toronto) who came under the direct influence of the neo-Gramscian theory through Robert W. Cox (or some through Stephen Gill) were André Drainville, Randall Germain, Eric Helliner, Martin Hewson, W. Andy Knight, Laura MacDonald, Robert O'Brien, Hélène Pellerin, Magnus Ryner, Timothy Sinclair, Deborah Stienstra, and Sandra Whitworth. The author was also a student of Professors Cox and Gill. I am grateful to Stephen Gill who suggested that perhaps I should take race more seriously in writing about international relations.
2. Major exceptions are included but not restricted to Augelli and Murphy, William I. Robinson, and Adam Morton. Note that Cox is clear about the political economy orientation of his work. Referring to his well-known article, and one that is definitive in the rise of neo-Gramscian theory, he writes that the 1983 Millennium article '... was an application of some of Gramsci's concepts to a way of thinking about world order in a *political economy perspective*' (Cox, 1983, 2014, p. 215).
3. Defensive neo-realism is ultimately based on balance of power theory in both the realist and neorealist forms. Hans Morgenthau, a realist, and Kenneth Waltz, a neorealist, are both defensive realists. Offensive neorealism, however, theorizes that states (great powers) seek hegemony, not merely survival. Mearsheimer writes:

    > Offensive realism parts company with defensive realism over the question of how much power states want. For defensive realists, the international structure provides states with little incentive to seek additional increments of power; instead it pushes them to maintain the existing balance of power. Preserving power, rather than increasing it, is the main goal of states. Offensive realists, on the other hand, believe that status quo power are rarely found in world politics, because the international system creates powerful incentives for states to look for opportunities to gain power at the expense of rivals, and to take advantage of those situations when the benefits outweigh the costs. A state's ultimate goal is to be the hegemon is the system. (2001, p. 21)

4. There is a lower estimate at 5,000,000.
5. I would like to thank an anonymous reviewer for highlighting the struggle of the masses in the Middle East against foreign domination, almost always in collaboration with local rulers.
6. 'Blair's letter of thanks to Gadaffi' (*Daily Mail*, 24 January 2015).
7. A major exception is Augelli and Murphy (1988).
8. Major exceptions include but are not restricted to important books by William I. Robinson and Adam David Morton.
9. For a critique of postcolonial constructions of war, see Porter (2013).

References

Acharya, A. (2014). Global international relations (IR) and regional worlds. *International Studies Quarterly*, 58(4), 1–13.

Anievas, A., Manchanda, N. & Shilliam, R. (Eds.). (2015). *Race and racism in international relations: Confronting the global color line*. New York, NY: Routledge.
Augelli, E., & Murphy, C. (1988). *America's quest for supremacy in the third world: A Gramscian analysis*. New York, NY: Pinter.
Ayers, A. J. (Ed.). (2008). *Gramsci, political economy, and international relations theory*. New York, NY: Palgrave-Macmillan.
Ayoob, M. (1995). *The third world security predicament*. Boulder, CO: Lynne Rienner
Barkawi, T., & Laffey, M. (1999). The imperial peace: Democracy, force and globalization. *European Journal of International Relations, 5*(4), 403–434.
Barkawi, T., & Laffey, M. (2006). The postcolonial colonial moment in security studies. *Review of International Studies, 32*(2), 329–352.
Barkawi, T., & Stanski, K. (Eds.). (2013). *Orientalism and war*. New York, NY: Columbia University Press.
Beckert, S. (2014). *Empire of cotton: A global history*. New York, NY: Vintage Books.
Beier, J. M. (2005). *International relations in uncommon places: Indigeneity, cosmology, and the limits of international theory*. Basingstoke: Palgrave Macmillan.
Bhambra, G. (2007). *Rethinking modernity: Postcolonialism and the sociological imagination*. New York, NY: Palgrave Macmillan.
Bieler, A., & Morton, A. D. (2004). A critical theory route to hegemony, world order and historical change, neo-Gramscian perspectives in international relations. *Capital and Class, 28*(1), 85–113.
Blaney, D., & Inayatullah, N. (2010). *Savage economics: Wealth, poverty and the temporal walls of capitalism*. New York, NY: Routledge.
Brincat, S., Lima, L., & Nunes, J. (Eds.). (2011). *Critical theory in international relations and security studies: Interviews and reflections*. New York, NY: Routledge.
Burleigh, M. (2013). *Small wars, faraway places: Global insurrection and the making of the modern world, 1945–1965*. New York, NY: Penguin.
Butler, J. (2010). *Frames of war: When is life grievable?* London: Verso.
Chalcraft, J., & Noorani, Y. (2007). *Counterhegemony in the colony and postcolony*. New York, NY: Palgrave Macmillan.
Chatterjee, P. (2012). *The black hole of empire*. Princeton, NJ: Princeton University Press.
Chin, C. B. (1998). *In service and servitude*. New York, NY: Columbia University Press.
Chowdhry, G., & Nair, S. (Eds.). (2002). *Power, postcolonialism and international relations*. New York, NY: Routledge.
Cox, R. W. (1981). Social forces, forms of state and world order. *Millennium, 10*(2), 126–155.
Cox, R. W. (1983). Gramsci, hegemony and international relations: An essay in method. *Millennium, 12*(2), 162–175.
Cox, R. W. (1987). *Production, power, and world order: Social forces in the making of history*. New York, NY: Columbia University Press.
Cox, R. W. (2014). *Universal foreigner: The individual and the world*. Singapore: World Scientific.
Dabashi, H. (2015). *Can non-Europeans think?* London: Zed Books.
Depelchin, J. (2005). *Silences in African history: Between the syndromes of discovery and abolition*. Dar Es Salaam: Mkuki na Nyota.
Doty, R. (1996). *Imperial encounters: The politics of representation in north-south relations*. Minneapolis: University of Minnesota Press.
Drainville, A. (2012). *A history of world order and resistance: The making and unmaking of global subjects*. New York, NY: Routledge.
Engdahl, W. (2004). *A century of war: Anglo-American oil politics and the new world order*. London: Pluto Press.
Fanon, F. (2008). *Black skin, white masks*. New York, NY: Grove Press.
Fogarty, R. S. (2012). *Race & war in France: Colonial subjects in the French Army, 1914–1918*. Baltimore: Johns Hopkins University Press.
Gabriel, C., & Pellerin, H. (Eds.). (2008). *Governing international labour migration*. New York, NY: Routledge.
Germain, R., & Kenny, M. (1998). Engaging Gramsci: International relations theory and the new Gramscians. *Review of International Studies, 24*(1), 3–21.
Gill, S. (Ed.). (1993). *Gramsci, historical materialism and international relations*. Cambridge, MA: Cambridge University Press.
Gill, S. R. (1989). Global hegemony and the structural power of capital. *International Studies Quarterly, 33*(4), 475–499.
Gill, S. R. (1992). *Hegemony and the trilateral commission*. New York, NY: Cambridge University Press.
Gill, S. R. (1995). Globalisation, market civilisation, and disciplinary neorealism. *Millennium, 24*, 399–423.
Gill, S. R., & Law, D. (1989). *The global political economy*. Baltimore, MD: Johns Hopkins University Press.

Gill, S. R., & Mittelam, J. H. (Eds.). (1997). *Innovation and transformation in international relations.* New York, NY: Cambridge University Press.

Grovogui, S. N., & Leonard, L. (2008). Uncivil society: Interrogations at the margins of neo-Gramscian theory. In A. J. Ayers (Ed.), *Gramsci, political economy, and international relations theory.* New York, NY: Palgrave Macmillan.

Henderson, E. A. (2015). *African realism? International relations theory and Africa's wars in the postcolonial era.* Lanham, MD: Roman and Littlefield.

Hobson, J. M. (2012). *The Eurocentric conception of world politics.* Cambridge: Cambridge University Press.

Huntington, S. P. (1996). *The clash of civilizations: Remaking of world order.* New York: Simon & Schuster.

Jameson, F. (1988). *Ideologies of theory: Essays, 1971–1986, Vol. 2— syntax of history.* Minneapolis: University of Minnesota Press.

Jones, B. G. (2008). Race in the ontology of international order. *Political Studies,* 56(4), 907–927.

Kennedy, F. (1993, July 22). In Somalia, Machiavelli vs. Rambo. *The New York Times,* p. A23.

Keohane, R. O. (1984). *After hegemony: Cooperation and discord in the world political economy.* Princeton, NJ: Princeton University Press.

Keohane, R. W. (Ed.). (1986). *Neorealism and its critics.* New York, NY: Columbia University Press.

Krasner, S. (Ed.). (1983). *International regimes.* Ithaca: Cornell University Press.

Krishna, S. (2001). Race, amnesia, and the education of international relations. *Alternatives,* 26(4), 401–424.

Krishna, S. (2008). *Globalization and postcolonialism: Hegemony and resistance in the twentieth-first century.* Lanham, MD: Rowman and Littlefield.

Laffey, M. (2016). Postcolonialism. In A. Collins (Eds.), *Contemporary security studies* (pp. 122–138). New York, NY: Oxford University Press.

Mamdani, M. (2002). Good Muslim, bad Muslim: A political perspective on culture and terrorism. *American Anthropologist,* 104, 766–775.

Mearsheimer, J. (2001). *The tragedy of great power politics.* New York, NY: W.W. Norton.

Mills, C. W. (1999). *The racial contract.* Ithaca, NY: Cornell University Press.

Mittelman, J. (2000). *The globalization syndrome.* Princeton, NJ: Princeton University Press.

Mittelman, J. H. (2009). The salience of race. *International Studies Perspective,* 10(1), 99–107.

Mittelman, J. H., & Pasha, M. K. (1996). *Out from underdevelopment revisited: Changing global structures and the remaking of the third world.* New York, NY: Palgrave-Macmillan.

Morton, A. D. (2013). *Revolution and state in modern Mexico: The political economy of uneven development.* Lanham, MA: Rowman and Littlefield.

Muppidi, H. (2012). *The colonial signs of international relations.* New York, NY: Columbia University Press.

Murphy, C. N. (2015, February 16). *Email correspondence with the author.*

Pasha, M. K. (1996). Security as hegemony. *Alternatives,* 21(3), 283–302.

Pasha, M. K. (2008). Return to the source: Gramsci, culture, and international relations. In A. J. Ayers (Ed.), *Gramsci, political economy, and international relations theory.* New York, NY: Palgrave Macmillan.

Pasrsons, T. H. (2010). *The rule of empires: Those who built them, those who endured them and why they always fail.* New York, NY: Oxford University Press.

Peoples, C. (2010). *Justifying ballistic missile defence: Technology, security and culture.* New York, NY: Cambridge University Press.

Persaud, R. B. (1996). *Hegemony and foreign policy: The case of Jamaica 1960–1980* (Doctoral dissertation). York University, Canada.

Persaud, R. B. (1997). Frantz Fanon, race and world order. In S. Gill & J. H. Mittelman (Eds.), *Innovation and transformation in international studies* (pp. 170–184). New York, NY: Cambridge University Press.

Persaud, R. B. (2001a). *Counter-hegemony and foreign policy.* Albany: State University of New York Press.

Persaud, R. B. (2001b). The racial assumptions of global labour recruitment and supply. *Alternatives,* 26(4), 377–399.

Persaud, R. B. (2002). Situating race in international relations: The dialectics of civilizational security in American immigration. In G. Chowdhry & S. Nair (Eds.), *Power, postcolonialism and international relations* (pp. 56–81). New York, NY: Routledge.

Persaud, R. B. (2004). Shades of American hegemony: The primitive, the enlightened, and the benevolent. *Connecticut Journal of International Law,* 19(2), 263–274.

Persaud, R. B. (2015a). Colonial violence: Race and gender on the plantation of British Guiana. In A. Avievas, N. Manchanda, & R. Shilliam (Eds.), *Race and racism in international relations* (pp. 117–138). New York, NY: Routledge.

Persaud, R. B. (Guest editor). (2015b). Race, de-coloniality and international relations. *Alternatives* (Special Issue), 40(2).

Persaud, R. B., & Chin, C. B. N. (2015). From sexation to sexualization: Dispersed submission in the racialized global sex industry. *Cambridge Review of International Affairs*. Retrieved from http://www.tandfonline.com/doi/full/10.1080/09557571.2015.1077617

Persaud, R. B., & Walker, R. B. J. (Eds.). (2001). Race and international relations. *Alternatives* (Special Issue), *40*(2).

Porter, P. (2013). *Military orientalism: Eastern war through western eyes*. New York, NY: Oxford University Press.

Prashad, V. (2012). *Arab spring, Libyan winter*. Baltimore, MD: AK Press.

Press Association. (2015, January 24). Blair's letter of thanks to Gaddafi. *Daily Mail Online*. Retrieved from http://www.dailymail.co.uk/wires/pa/article-2924273/Blairs-letter-thanks-Gaddafi.html

Quijano, A. (2007). Coloniality and modernity/rationality. *Cultural Studies*, *21*(23), 168–178.

Radice, H. (2008). Gramsci and neo-Gramscianism: To what purpose? In A. J. Ayers (Ed.), *Gramsci, political economy, and international relations theory*. New York, NY: Palgrave Macmillan.

Robinson, W. I. (1996). *Promoting polyarchy: Globalization, US intervention, and hegemony*. Cambridge: Cambridge University Press.

Robinson, W. I. (2003). *Transnational conflicts: Central America, social change, and globalization*. London: Verso.

Rupert, M. (1995). *Producing hegemony*. New York, NY: Cambridge University Press.

Said, E. (1978). *Orientalism*. New York, NY: Vintage.

Sajed, A. (2013). *Postcolonial encounters in international relations: The politics of transgression in the Maghreb*. New York, NY: Routledge.

Seth, S. (2013). *Postcolonial theory and international relations: A critical introduction*. New York, NY: Routledge.

Shilliam, R. (2008). Jacobinism: The ghost in the Gramscian machine of counter-hegemony. In A. J. Ayers (Ed.), *Gramsci, political economy, and international relations theory*. New York, NY: Palgrave Macmillan.

Sinclair, T. J. (2016). Robert W. Cox's method of historical structures redux. *Globalizations* (published online Feb. 16, 2016). Retrieved from http://www-tandfonline-com.proxyau.wrlc.org/doi/full/10.1080/14747731.2016.1143662

Slater, D. (2004). *Geopolitics and the post-colonial: Rethinking north-south relations*. Oxford: Blackwell.

Srivastava, N., & Battacharya, B. (2013). *The postcolonial Gramsci*. New York, NY: Routledge.

Tirman, J. (2011). *The death of others: The fate of civilians in America's wars*. New York, NY: Oxford University Press.

Turse, N. (2013). *Kill anything that move: The real American War in Vietnam*. New York, NY: Picador.

Vitalis, R. (2015). *White world order, black power politics: The birth of American international relations*. Ithaca, NY: Cornell University Press.

Warren, B. (1980). *Imperialism: Pioneer of capitalism*. London: NLB and Verso.

Whitworth, S. (2005). Militarized masculinities and the politics of peacekeeping: The Canadian case. In K. Booth (Ed.), *Critical security studies* (pp. 89–106). Boulder, CO: Lynn Rienner.

Yasar, D. (2007, March). Resistance and identity politics in an age of globalization. *The Annals of the American Academy of Political and Social Science*, *610*, 160–181.

Traditional, Problem-Solving and Critical Theory: An Analysis of Horkheimer and Cox's Setting of the 'Critical' Divide

SHANNON BRINCAT

Griffith University, Brisbane, Australia

ABSTRACT *Robert W. Cox's dictum that '(t)heory is for someone and for some purpose' (emphasis in the original) is said to be the most-quoted line in International Relations (IR) theory. Yet whilst this spurred a revolution in critical thinking in IR, it echoed a far older conception of Critical Theory advanced by Max Horkheimer in the 1930s that claimed there is 'no theory of society...that does not contain political motivations'. Both sentiments emphasize the relation between knowledge and human interests, and yet both formulate two distinct—though allied—ways of approaching 'critical' theorizing. In order to understand the similarities and differences in their approaches, this paper draws out three loci of difference between Cox and Horkheimer regarding the question of emancipation: (i) the epistemological relation between 'critical' and 'Problem-Solving' (Cox) or 'Traditional Theory' (Horkheimer); (ii) the emphasis placed on transformation and historical process; and (iii) the importance of intersubjectivity in how each approach emancipation. It is argued that by actively combining critical (dialectical) approaches across the social sciences, broadening human agency through civilizational dialogue, and retaining a commitment to emancipatory (and visionary) political futures based on human association, that Critical International Theory can maintain ongoing relevance in IR.*

> It's [Critical Theory] goal is man's emancipation from slavery.
>
> (Horkheimer, 1972a, p. 246)
>
> Critical theory allows for a normative choice in favour of a social and political order different from the prevailing order.
>
> (Cox, 1981, p. 128)

The similarities and differences between the thought of Robert W. Cox and Max Horkheimer, two paragons of critical thought, have as yet to be articulated in IR theory. The young Horkheimer (1972a) distinguished Critical Theory (CT)[1] by virtue of its emancipatory interest and viewed this philosophical current as the theoretical arm of *real* social struggle (p. 245). Even before he had named this approach 'critical', Horkheimer anchored it between social philosophy and social science. The tasks of the Institut für Sozialforschung were thoroughly social, that is, its research was to be governed by an overriding concern with the 'vicissitudes of human fate ... not as mere individuals, but as members of a community' (Horkheimer, 1995, p. 1). Developing from Marx, Hegel, and German Idealism, a focus on the cultural life of humanity, the Frankfurt School (FS) came to be defined by its explicit normativity regarding 'the emancipation of humanity from enslaving conditions' (Horkheimer, 1972a, p. 245ff). Freedom, so conceived, was a social achievement in which intersubjectivity, social relations, and human association were the focal point for not merely explaining but rationalizing society: to move from the alienating conditions of 'human fate' to a 'rational determination of goals' (p. 207). From Marcuse's concern with the liberatory 'aims' of humankind, to Habermas' 'deep-seated anthropological interest' in emancipation, to Honneth's ideal of mutual recognition today, CT has maintained a nascent optimism in this emancipatory project first outlined by Horkheimer.[2]

Critical International Theory (CIT) shares in this tradition, part by convention and part by association. The work of Robert W. Cox' has been placed under this umbrella, somewhat problematically, given that he disputes this label, denies that the FS was ever part of his canon, and is uncomfortable with the word 'emancipation' even whilst admitting CT is bound to this concept as the critique of that which *is* (Cox, 2012, pp. 18, 23–24). Nevertheless, through a number of closely shared concerns, not the least of which is the fact that their groundbreaking essays share remarkable thematic and argumentative similarities,[3] Cox's articulation of CT parallels Horkheimer's. They share fundamental concerns, including: the problematization of positivism, the promotion of an historical materialist understanding of social transformation, and the pursuit of normative goals broadly related to an emancipatory politics which they both define as freedom from slavery. And though the question of emancipation is muted in much of Cox's work, it remains a latent presence detectable in his concern for social equity, cultural tolerance, and transcivilizational dialogue and understanding (pp. 20, 21, 24, 32–33).

These synergies lead to the possibility for an evaluative comparison between Cox and Horkheimer, particularly regarding how they distinguish CT from Problem-Solving (PS) or Traditional Theory (TT), respectively. This paper focuses on the form, aims, and purposes Cox and Horkheimer give to CT, that is, the content of critical theorizing, the tasks they direct this theoretical architecture towards, and the 'critical' attitude each takes to the social sciences generally. Rather than pursuing a synopsis of their two essays, the paper draws out three loci of difference regarding this central question of emancipation: (i) the epistemological relation between 'critical' and 'Problem-Solving' (for Cox) or 'Traditional Theory' (for Horkheimer); (ii) the emphasis placed on transformation and historical process; and (iii) the importance of intersubjectivity in how each approach emancipation (which includes questions pertaining to both the agent of emancipation and the addressee of CT). It is argued that by actively combining critical (dialectical) approaches across the social sciences, broadening human agency through civilizational dialogue, and retaining a commitment to emancipatory (and visionary) political futures based on human association, that CIT can maintain ongoing relevance in IR.

Critical Versus PS and TT

In his seminal essay, 'Social forces, states, and world orders' (1981), Cox opens with three suggestions for theoretical inquiry in IR: that it should look at the problem of world order as a whole without reifying the world system; that it must not underrate state power but give proper attention to the social forces contributing to the development of states and the world system; and that theory should be based on changing practices and empirical/historical study. Yet, rather than pursuing the construction of this approach, Cox operationalizes it by examining hegemony and imperialism through social forces, forms of state, global political economy, and world orders, all with a view to how these are related and changing. The main presentation of Cox's version of CT—and the reason for the papers renown—is found only in a few pages under the subheading 'On Perspective and Purposes'. This opens with what is said to be the most-quoted line in IR that 'Theory is always *for* someone and *for* some purpose'—a sentiment that expresses Cox's keen detection for the ideological and normative content within *all* theories. For Cox, all theories have a perspective derived from their position in time and space: a particular *standpoint*. Whilst sophisticated reflexivity may attempt to transcend this condition, the initial perspective is always contained within and must be unconcealed (Cox, 1981, pp. 128–130). If this is the case, then we must ask: who is Cox's theory for? What *purpose* does it serve?

Cox (1980) asserts that theory can serve either of two purposes. The first type, 'problem-solving theory', takes the world as it is with the aim to make it 'work smoothly' (p. 129ff). It assumes the permanence of the prevailing social and political relations that frame its parameters—the acceptance of which belies not only the ahistoricism of such approaches but also how they remain uniquely 'value-bound'. The strength of this approach is to fix a problem through limited variables and precise examination, leading to statements of laws and regularities amenable to generality but which *imply* the very 'institutional and relational parameters *assumed* in the problem-solving approach' (my emphasis added) (Cox, 1981, p. 129). Yet it remains non-reflexive of its own perspective and the social position it mirrors and serves. The exemplar, for Cox, is neorealism that assumes three basic realities as fundamental and unchanging in world politics: the nature of man (as the Hobbesian restless desire for power); the nature of states (as fixed on the pursuit of national interest); and the nature of the state-system (as placing identical rational constraints on the pursuit of the national interests through the balance of power). Within these basic realities that constitute, for neorealism, the permanence of existing relations and institutions, history is merely a recurrent play in which 'the future will always be like the past'. The result is the tragedy of a 'continuing present' (pp. 131, 129). Such methods however lead only to a fragmentary, one-sided, and partial aspect of the whole. Neorealism is built on a 'false premise' because world order is not fixed in the way it assumes, not only because of the relation between all things that eludes this theory, but because all things are also undergoing complex transformations. Neorealism's 'fixity' is exposed not only as the ideological bias of, and for, those 'comfortable' with the given order (pp. 127, 129) but a methodological error, and, I would add, an ontological one regarding what there *is* in world politics.

The second purpose theory can serve is named 'critical theory': it serves to expose PS as an identifiable ideology with conservative consequences. It questions the very framework assumed by PS, instead calling for theory to 'stand apart from the prevailing order of the world and ask how that order came about ... [its] origins and how and whether they might be in the process of changing' (Cox, 1981, p. 129). Cox later ties this emphasis on historicism in CT to Braudel's (1995) approach to the *longue durée* (the examination of how an existing order came into being, its contradictions, and how it may be changed) (p. 21). Cox's version of CT presents a continuously changing social world order with theory as a series of interconnected hypothesis of social transformation (Cox, 1981, p. 139). Yet the capacity of the theory to reason on *possible* futures requires a keen analysis on processes of social forces, forms of state, and global political economy (particularly those forces generated by the changes in production), all of which are seen as configurations of material capabilities, ideas, and institutions, that are in relation and impact each other (Cox, 1981, pp. 130, 138, 1987). Rather than separation and fixity, Cox's CT directs itself to the social and political complex as a process of change in which *both* parts and the whole are involved (Cox, 1981, p. 129). Moreover, it does not regard historical structures as determinative but as a pressure on human agency. This structure, Cox insists, should be viewed from the 'bottom' or the 'outside' for it is only this view that allows CT to be open to possibilities of transformation by looking for the emergence of 'rival structures' that express 'alternative possibilities of development' (pp. 135, 137). Whereas conflict is an inherent condition for systemic reproduction in neorealism, for Cox's CT, conflicts are viewed dialectically as 'possible cause[s] of structural change' (p. 134). Accordingly, whilst the existing social order as a 'framework of action' may *seem* durable or permanent, CT's task is to trace their origins and detect their weakening. Just as material power shifts, so do the shared understandings of social relations and the collective images of social order. Amidst these processes, Cox's CT aims for what he calls 'normative choice' in social order and, through its historicist methods, defends this aim as practical in the sense of transcending existing order within the range of what is feasible within existing conditions (pp. 136–137, 130).

We could operationalize this Coxian methodology of critical theorizing through five steps. As action is never free but takes place within a 'framework for action', so we must start with a historical enquiry into human experience of this framework. Theory is also, necessarily, shaped by this 'framework for action' and as it is therefore relative so too must it be reflexive, aim at a broader time-perspective, and always begin anew. As the 'framework of action' itself changes over time, the 'principal goal' of CT is to understand these changes immanently. This 'framework of action' is a historical structure—a combination of thought patterns, material conditions, and human institutions—that does not determine actions mechanistically but provides a context ('habits, pressures, expectations, and constraints') in which action takes place. The 'framework of action' should therefore be analysed through the conflicts within it that open the *possibilities* for social transformation (Cox, 1981, p. 135). As such, the purpose of Cox's CT is to serve our understanding of the historical situation in which the possibilities of human agency for transforming world politics are located—a view that can have strong to weak interpretations regarding the role of theory, the capacities of agency, and the constrictions of structure.

How Cox sets up the 'critical' and PS divide is compelling and continues to challenge orthodox IR. Yet Cox's articulation has also had two unfortunate, if unintended, consequences: firstly, a tendency to bifurcate PS and CT by positing them as a binary, and secondly, towards privileging a critical historicism rather than a reflexive theory of emancipatory transformations. In regard to the former, as Booth describes it, the Coxian framework sought to shift PS *within* the status quo, to a CT with the problem *of* the status quo. That is, whereas PS 'replicates', CT was to 'emancipate'. Yet Cox's articulation played into those who wanted to dismiss CT as something idealist rather than interested in solving real problems (Booth, 2007, p. 242ff). Through Cox's formulation, CT was easily depicted by its detractors as some extraneous moral critique on social order rather than as a philosophical and scientific examination of overcoming the limits (the suffering and injustices) within the status quo.[4] Without adding in the qualitative dimension to change (i.e. its emancipatory content), Cox's work could lead to the nonsensical assertion that, for example, liberalism is 'critical', given the revolutionary transformations wrought under neoliberalism. Similarly, Jahn has posited that Cox's conceptualization implied that other approaches were not 'critical', or at least not critical in the same way, thus proliferating any number of 'critical' subfields and increasing the compartmentalization of IR. More problematic was that it made declaring one's normative standard an act of placing one's proverbial 'flag in the sand', rather than urging constant reflection (Jahn, 2014). As Booth and Neufeld have argued, as *all* theories are normative, what is unique about CT is not its normativity but how it is reflective upon its commitments—such reflexivity is not a contamination of critical research but constitutive of it (see Booth, 2007, pp. 242–244; Neufeld, 1995, pp. 138, fn 11). As such, Cox's resistance to engage the question of emancipation seems contradictory to his insistence on reflexivity. It is also at variance with Horkheimer's insistence that CT is to be, above all, reflective on the social origins and consequences of all knowledge—*especially* its own. The question, for Horkheimer, was how to combine philosophy and science without either dominating the other.

In distinction to Cox, Horkheimer (1995, p. 1, 1972a, p. 210) articulates CT's emancipatory interest in a way that is to be both practical and wedded to so-called Traditional approaches. For him, the great challenge for CT (and social philosophy generally) was that modern thought had replaced the dialectic of social conflict with the individualist notion of a harmony of individual interests. Whether Kantian philosophy or rational choice theory, today, the rootedness of such approaches in the isolated subject (*Einzelpersönlichkeit*) reified the particular: such approaches see only the individual in society and relations between such individuals. The atomized subject was reflected in the dominant view of scientific method in which the 'mediation between empirical experience and the consciousness of one's freedom in the social whole no longer required a philosophy, but simply linear progress in positive science, technology, and industry'. The dilemma for CT was how to speak of its object—the 'cultural life of humanity'—in ways that did not seem ideological and sectarian to those who only believed in *facts*. For Horkheimer (1995), the point was not to conceive of theory as if it were constructed *beyond* empirical science, but to explore the complicated psychical links between the material and ideational through the 'dialectical penetration and development of philosophical theory *and* specialized scientific praxis' (my emphasis added) (pp. 8–12). This involved the development of a research programme in which TT and CT were 'brought together' in order to pursue 'larger philosophical questions on the basis of the most precise scientific methods ... without losing sight of the larger context' (pp. 9–10). Hence, Horkheimer's use of statistics, surveys, reports, public agencies, specialists, and various methods serves as the basis for philosophically oriented social inquiry. This was not the blind enlistment of empirics but their sublation through CT by mediating *how* and *what* we observe through a perspective sensitive to the social, historical, and dialectical whole, and guided by an emancipatory interest to reduce human suffering. In this way, the epistemological relation between CT and TT was to be placed in the service of a *practical* interest in emancipation.

Transformation and Emancipation

This relates directly to the second consequence of Cox's formulation of CT regarding its understated emancipatory content. In his essay, and indeed throughout the middle part of his writing career,[5] Cox's emphasis on historicism was directed towards developing a more full account of the changing social totality of IR, and only secondarily with the content of the normative choice within this social transformation. Whilst a more sustained engagement with emancipatory concerns would resurface in his later civilizational 'turn', in his groundbreaking essay, Cox (1980) made it quite clear that the 'principal goal' of CT was to *understand change* and explain *historical processes* rather than act as participants in this struggle, though he did suggest it could be a 'guide' to such action (pp. 131, 135), and later stated that CT is interested in 'how change may be influenced or channeled' (Cox, 1996a, p. 525). So, it is not the emancipatory aims within Cox's preferred historical materialist tradition that are emphasized but its methodological benefits: the dialectical exposition of contradictions; the vertical dimensions of power (imperialism); the reciprocal relation between state and civil society complex; and the contradictions of production (Cox, 1981, pp. 133–135).

Whilst Cox rarely engages directly with emancipatory themes—notions of freedom, ethics, and normativity—this is not to say they are absent. In fact, their presence pervades his entire work, appearing in notions of social justice (Cox, 1981, p. 128), new democratic ('consensual') multilateralism (Cox, 1996a, p. 533), 'coexistence in diversity' (Cox, 2007, p. 513), his hopes for a Polanyian 'double movement' against hyperliberalism (Cox, 1996b, p. 32), his insistence on a new world order 'built from the bottom up' (p. 35), and perhaps most openly in his description of the need for subordinate classes and the periphery to form counter-hegemonic relations in a new historic bloc (Cox, 1983, pp. 162–175, 1977, p. 387). Indeed, it is these emancipatory concerns that animate social transformation because, as he writes, our world is seen from a standpoint that includes 'hopes and expectations for the future' (Cox, 1981, p. 128). The point is not the absence of these ethico-normative considerations in Cox's thought but rather his reticence to discuss these openly that, arguably, restricts the reflexivity of his version of CT. For *if* the purpose of CT is to become aware of its own perspective, then this must involve placing up for contestation its own normative ideals. As Hamati-Ataya (2013) has recently posited, Cox (2012) showed that CT must give an account of its own existence so as to not fall to unconscious ideology (p. 675).

Cox's reticence is only partly explained by his uncomfortability with the subjective vagaries of the term 'emancipation'. Another explanation stems from the historicist tradition he draws from. As he has stated on many occasions, rather than the FS, Hegel, or German Idealism, the influences on his work were comprehensively historical: Vico, Sorel, Braudel, Collingwood, Carr, and Gramsci (Cox, 2012, pp. 24–25, 1996b). In this approach, man and its institutions are viewed as genetic, 'a continuing creation of new forms', rather than something essentialist or teleological (Cox, 1981, p. 132). So too does it approach the international in an 'evolutionary way' (Cox, 2007, pp. 513, 516), that is, examining the sequence of changes within history, how a particular 'fit' has come about and comes 'apart' (Cox, 1981, pp. 141–142). As argued by Devetak (2014), Cox appeals to a secular political historicism rather than metaphysical and moral philosophies, on the basis of which Devetak argues that this 'historical mode' of CT could rival PS theories (p. 417). Despite the advantages of such a reading, it leads us back to the problem of bifurcating 'critical' from other theories (discussed above). Moreover, it leaves unanswered the question of how CT could move from mere history (albeit a history with a more detailed understanding of change) to a theory of social transformation that is a guide for 'normative choice in favour of a social and political order' that Cox places as the penultimate aim of CT. One cannot just gesture to normativity; it must be confronted with the greatest possible analysis.

Horkheimer's set-up of the relation between CT and TT provides a means to address such a question. Horkheimer (1995) notes, in a similar refrain to Cox, that all scholarly work is derived from the impulses of one's own world-views (p. 14). At the same time, whilst theory corresponds to the tasks set by researchers themselves, bringing theoretical hypotheses to bear on the facts is not something done by the researcher but by industry, the needs of capital broadly defined. New ideas win out due to historical circumstances and social conditions rather than genius or accident, and in the conditions of late capitalism, the sole purpose of knowledge is its instrumentality. It is in this way that science falls to the '[c]onservation and continuous renewal of the existing state of affairs' (Horkheimer, 1972a, p. 196). And yet, at the same time, this real function served by science is *obscured* (p. 198). Horkheimer's (1972a) conception of CT was, in part, intended to overcome the one-sidedness and limited nature of such intellectual processes when detached 'from their matrix in the total activity society' (p. 199). Rather, CT sought a developing picture of society as a whole rather than as a static snapshot of a part abstracted from its context and historical development (p. 240). On this point the historical and dialectical methods of Cox and Horkheimer parallel: All things in the social process, the 'parts' and the 'whole', are seen to be in the process of movement and the strength of CT is its ability to abstract these particulars whilst integrating such analysis back within the totality. This method of immanent critique enables CT to expose the difference between a *reality* and its *potential*—a task accomplished 'by relating social institutions and activities to the values they themselves set forth as their standards and ideals ...' (Horkheimer, 1975, p. 234).

So Horkheimer shares with Cox the exposition of the hidden purposes and aims served by theory. In Horkheimer's (1972a) words: 'There is ... no theory of society ... that does not contain political motivations' (p. 222). Of crucial importance however is that Horkheimer, in distinction to Cox, does not end with this exposition of the knowledge constitutive interests of TT, nor exclude such approaches because of their buttressing of the status quo and fundamental lack of reflexivity. Rather, Horkheimer seeks to *conjoin* CT and TT in order to reveal the 'problem constellation' in the present through not only *facts* (social empirics) but *values* (social philosophy). This combination of facts and values is to overcome the reification (forgetting) of human-made conditions so that the everyday 'humiliation' and 'horror of history', the 'suffering' and 'death', that are taken as the 'ultimate facts in an age that believe[s] naively in facts' that humankind can allegedly do 'nothing about it', can once again be evaluated (Horkheimer, 1995, pp. 5–7). With the deepening of the contradiction between individual happiness and their *real situation* in modernity, this critical task becomes ever more urgent (pp. 7–11).

Within this broad appeal for an emancipatory social science, Horkheimer outlines two forms of knowing: TT, premised on Descartes *Discourse on Method*, and, CT, based on Marx's political economy. The former shares many similarities to Cox's notion of PS: it organizes experience through questions from present-day society, separating theory from science, and leaves unreflected the historical goals, purposes, and tendencies such knowledge serves and is a part of. The other proffers a theory of society that is concerned for the 'reasonable conditions of life' (Horkheimer, 1972a, pp. 198–199). Accordingly it calls for 'the rational organisation of human activity' or the 'rational constitution of society' which Horkheimer (1972a) defines as the fulfillment of humankind 'and all their potentialities' or the 'free development of individuals' (pp. 244–246, 249). In present conditions, this means a through-going critique of the 'cause of wretchedness', namely political economy, and the potential within these deformed conditions for a 'free, self-determining society' (pp. 249, 248). Accordingly, CT takes an active posture to history: not only is humankind the producer of its history and way of life, the necessary conditions for its emancipation from suffering *already* exist (p. 227 Note 20, pp. 244–245). Moreover, it places this actualization of freedom as a social achievement wherein Horkheimer's notion of 'rational' hinges on the conditions of human association. Even though this rational society seems to exist only in fantasy, Horkheimer (1972a) affirms that it 'is really innate in every man', bringing to the fore the intersubjective basis of individual freedom and equally so, the notion of social struggle in which the actualization of this rational society is dependent on 'historical conflicts' (pp. 251, 200). Horkheimer describes the world of capital, the world experienced as a natural process, as a 'pure' mechanism, a 'supra-historical eternal category', a world that 'is not [our] own', a form of 'deadened existence from which society must emancipate itself'. The suffering inherent to these pathological social conditions may override the co-optation of the oppressed in the cultural and psychical bonds of capital. The oppressed's 'despair' at the void between their individual actualization and their real situation can become a 'decisive factor' pushing towards emancipation (p. 212).

Yet such awareness of social injustice does not, of itself, lead to emancipatory change. Horkheimer (1972a) rejects the idea that the working-class (and other oppressed groups, one should add) have some 'guarantee of correct knowledge' either of their predicament or their power (pp. 240, 213). What is guaranteed however is a 'circle of transmitters' who will necessarily be aroused by 'prevailing injustice'. But, Horkheimer warns, this guarantees only a contemporary—not a *future*—community of transmitters. We may arrive in conditions where such awareness has become impossible (indeed this is what Horkheimer and Adorno would later presume in the *Dialectic of enlightenment* thesis). But well before his pessimistic turn, Horkheimer, like Cox, gave CT a guiding role to the emancipatory project. Here, echoing Marx, Horkheimer asserts that the 'social function' of CT is to form a dynamic unity with the oppressed to become an 'expression of the concrete historical situation and a force within it to stimulate change' (p. 215).

Yet this aspirational quality of theory as an active social participant results in an unresolved political tension at the heart of CT. For whilst suffering provides the materialist content for a critical reason (Horkheimer, 1972a, pp. 242–243), the potential for emancipation is reduced to a weak entreatment based on the awareness of one's suffering *and* the rational understanding of a way out of it. The impetus towards reasonable conditions of life—'from a blind to a meaningful necessity' (p. 229)—is deemed to be the self-knowledge of all and, as we have seen, the conditions necessary for this rational, consciously directed form of self-determination are deemed to be already present. And yet, this relies on a type of social individual that possesses an awareness of, and ability to act on, this concern with attaining the 'reasonable conditions of life'. Against the dominance of 'traditional' thinking that Horkheimer (1972a) admits would view such aims as purely subjective, speculative, and useless against a reason thoroughly determined by instrumentality, the ground seems to be taken-out from underneath the emancipatory possibility of CT (pp. 217–219, 233). Against the dominance of such thinking, Horkheimer's admission that CT has no influence on its side *except* the abolition of injustice seems to lack the social conditions to make it actual. Horkheimer has one way out of this theoretical cul-de-sac, however, something emphasized also by Cox, particularly in his later work. This is the importance attached to human 'association', basic forms of intersubjectivity, through which emancipation is re-cast not as some abstract utopia but a real possibility within present conditions and productive forces (pp. 217–219).

Association and Intersubjectivity

As we have seen, in Horkheimer's conception, CT does not seek merely an increase in knowledge but humankind's emancipation. The most frequent description of this emancipatory interest centres on the rational construction of society in which self-determination equates to the meaningful direction of individual and social life. The rational society is that which overcomes the accidental, frictive, and blind mechanism of conflicting forces within bourgeois society to instead take into account the 'life' of the entire community. The basic exchange relation—alongside the juridical, political, and cultural aspects of bourgeois society—is regarded as the 'straitjacket' inhibiting the further development of human association (Horkheimer, 1972a, pp. 213, 229, 23). However, bringing together CT and the empirical insights of the social sciences leads to understanding how the exchange economy must, necessarily, lead to a heightening of social tensions: restrictions on individual free development, growing inequality, and increasing toil (pp. 226–227). It is humankind's striving against this restriction under capitalism that generates the constant 'potential' for emancipatory transformation of which CT can help guide (see esp. Horkheimer, 1971). Emancipation is defined by this struggle for the 'general interest' inclusive of the free development of all individuals, the just allocation of scarcity, and equality in community (Horkheimer, 1972a, p. 246; see Held, 1980, p. 197).

Horkheimer's 'rational society' therefore places intersubjectivity—how we associate at the centre of the emancipatory project, and explains why CT has privileged access into this form of social inquiry. This is because Horkheimer cast CT as part of the philosophical line of thought that sought to overcome the tendency, so pronounced in late modernity, of being rooted in the isolated subject (*Einzelpersönlichkeit*). Instead of an autonomous creature, the Hegelian tradition saw the overarching structures of the socio-historical totality that gives (or conditions) the subject, giving it 'objective form' (Horkheimer, 1995, pp. 1–2). The notion of positive and social freedom upheld by the FS was grounded in Hegel's search for the unification of the universal and particular in ethical community (see Jay, 1996, p. 276). As such, Horkheimer's CT opposed the illusion of both an individual atomized from society (as in liberalism) and an individual subsumed under a false collectivity (nationalism) but instead sought to focus on the subject as a relation. As Horkheimer describes it, CT deals with the human subject as 'a definite individual and his real relation to other individuals and groups', one in conflict with other classes, and one immersed in a 'web' of relationships with the social totality and nature (Horkheimer, 1972a, p. 211). In his opening address for the *Institute*, its research programme was said to be directed to explore the relations of intersubjectivity, specifically, between the economic life of society, the psychical development of individuals, and the changes in culture (Horkheimer, 1995, p. 12). Moreover, Horkheimer (1972b) concluded that the attainment of individual happiness is a 'social achievement', echoing the Hegelian notion that one cannot be free alone and that the social conditions of happiness can be rendered pathological, given deformations in human association within bourgeois society (p. 252). Though Horkheimer (1972a) regarded the 'circle of solidarity' to be narrow for this transition towards emancipation, his musing that even in a gang of thieves may have positive traits of human community both exposes the relational deficiencies of our time and the potentials within it (pp. 241–242).

Horkheimer suggested that education, rather than social position or income, provided the best possibility for developing 'a wider vision' regarding human association (p. 221). Yet the limit of Horkheimer's analysis—and the FS generally—was the myopic focus on the Western subject from which this vision was to emanate. CT was to be guided by a search for the praxis of emancipation, a generalizable interest (*Allgemeinheit*), and yet, despite sporadic references to social struggles in the global periphery and colonially subjugated peoples, it looked only inwardly to the West. Part of this is evident in Horkheimer's (1995) emphasis on Hegel's *Philosophy of History* in his foundational comments on CT, made with little problematization of its core tenants. Moreover, he sought to initially apply CT to 'skilled craftspeople and white collars workers in Germany', and whilst he intimated an intention to examine other developed European countries, this Eurocentric and modernist narrative came to pollute the entire endeavour (pp. 11–12). Viewed in this light, Horkheimer's late retreat to theology as the expression of humanity's longing to establish a free and just community can be seen as a response of his own failure to engage with global sociology and the possibilities within humanity taken as a whole. As such, it is by broadening the notion of intersubjectivity that the thought of Cox is most effective in overcoming the methodological nationalism and Eurocentrism of CT by giving it new categories.[6] Indeed, one could borrow from Cox's comments on Spengler that the Copernican Revolution that must take place within CT is that the West is *not* the centre to which all other societies revolve—and that there exist multiple emancipatory currents outside this socio-cultural sphere (Cox, 2001, pp. 105, 108).

Intersubjectivity: Human Association as Civilizational Coexistence

Even in interviews, Cox (1981) has remained guarded on his own normative position regarding the social 'choices' that he considers feasible in the 'range' of alternatives to existing order (p. 130). On the strategic role CT can play in social transformation, Cox (1981) is far more comfortable with using indicative terms such as 'directed towards' or 'leads towards' or 'concerned', consistently emphasizing a more accurate historicism rather than the desired aim or purpose such transformation should be directed towards. Whilst this importance attached to historical process continues throughout his work, in his later conceptual refinements of CT, 'theory' begins to become expressed more actively—he even quotes Marx's dictum favorably that the study of society is made in order to *change* it (Cox, 1996b, p. 28). At this point, a discernable interest in 'how people can participate in creating new forms' becomes of equal concern to the actual process of transformation (Cox, 2007, p. 516)—a point at which we come full-circle to his ideal of 'normative choice' in socio-political orders made in 1981. In particular, a 'new form' of human association becomes a focal point of Cox's hopes—what he refers to broadly as 'civilizational co-existence'—the normative commitments of which offer the most clear illustration of the emancipatory content of Cox's thought. Moreover, it is through this development that Cox contributes towards a massive and necessary shift in the tradition of CT as a whole by emphasizing social relations at the local *and* global levels. This pushes the typical analytical categories of 'intersubjectivity' through what Cox (1992a) calls an 'enlarged conception of global society' (pp. 162–163), which, when coupled with his work on the internationalization of the state and globalization, offers a research programme for CT that overcomes many of the limits of the Western-centric FS. As is well known, Ruggie and Wendt popularized the term 'intersubjectivity' in IR, deploying it as a corrective to positivism in which social facts are said to not be objectively given but agreed upon by subjects. Yet this notion of intersubjectivity does not penetrate below the level of states to human-beings to which the term has been alternatively used in FS, particularly the work of its later generations (see Honneth, 1995: esp. Chapter 5).[7] The benefit of Cox's account of intersubjectivity is that it reaches into these concrete relations between subjects but also such historical processes and engagements at the civilizational level. Cox's use of Khaldun's historical thought is the key example. This demonstrates the possibility of a non-orthodox IR that deploys a critical method with an 'accent' of historical materialism in such a way that can draw out the *longue durée* of civilizational relations alongside the examination of the constraints on human action to long-term change (Cox, 1995, p. 24 citing Khaldun, 1967).

Following from Khaldun, Sorel, and Collingwood, Cox posits that throughout history peoples collectively confront challenges in which their social practices embrace different rationalities and normative orders. Based on this insight, the central issue for politics is that communities are *formed* by such struggles (Cox, 1996b, p. 28). Here, intersubjective relations between individuals and groups are assumed to be inherent to, and properly formative of, the internal processes of societies *and* of civilizational encounters through the 'recognition of the ontological equality of other civilisations' (Cox, 2001, p. 109). It is the possibilities contained in this latter form of recognition that interests Cox most and he begins with dimensions of intersubjectivity that frame the understandings of difference between civilizations, their relations, and their transformation (p. 105). Cox inquires into civilizations as complex webs of intersubjectivity, looking for processes that may lead to what he describes as 'mutual and pacific recognition of differences among peoples' (Cox, 1995, p. 11). Consistent with his historicist form of CT, the point of access is in understanding these historical processes. Developing from Braudel and Kuhn, the ideas of the mutual borrowings across civilizations, Cox focuses on those tendencies towards the recognition of difference in community and *amongst* cultures and civilizations (p. 14). Thus, any commitment to universalism is tempered by relativism through the 'mutual recognition of difference in value systems among cultures and civilizations' (Cox, 1996b, p. 22). In this way, recognition functions as a regulative ethic across the global community in that its principles preclude the imposition of particular concepts of emancipation *on* civilizations but not, of course, the possibility of mutual supports *across* civilizations.[8] As Cox (1995) writes: '[t]he prospects of compatibility in world order depend very largely upon the strengthening of this recognition and the acceptance of difference through internal developments in each civilization' (p. 14).

In what I would describe as an outline framework for an intercivilizational process of recognition, Cox focuses on the 'bonds of solidarity'—the institutions and practices—that he believes could be the basis of 'an alternative vision of society'. Regarding his normative choice of an alternate vision of society, Cox is at his most speculative when he pleads for such a vision of a 'real creative alternative' to come about. What shifts this from a mere longing to a feasible process however, relates to the problem of *asabiya*—the moral quality or sense of group solidarity—that Cox upholds as essential to the creation (or decay) of a community (Cox, 1995, pp. 23–24). Processes contributing towards intercivilizational learning—those leading to the strengthening of a *global asabiya* as a 'new social and political solidarity' (Cox, 2007, p. 35, 1992b)—become of key importance (Cox, 1996b, p. 35, 1992b). The basis for a consciousness towards such a new global order is self-knowledge that relativizes and challenges the commonsensical views of one's own society and is considered an important starting point for a knowledge of others (see Cox, 2007, p. 517).[9] As such, for civilizational coexistence, 'mutual comprehension' or the 'ability to enter into the mental framework of the Other' is essential for this vision of peaceful coexistence (Cox, 2001, p. 105). Alamuti discusses Cox's argument on the coexistence of civilizations and the problem of mutual comprehension, positing a defense of openness to individual and collective learning as being the key to a just order (Alamuti, 2015, p. 244, note 1). Cox (2001) links this sentiment to Collingwood's notion of 'generating civility' and Bakhtin's notion of the condition of dialogue as the mutual recognition of self-conscious beings (pp. 121–125). Decentration (Habermas) or detachment (Elias) provides similar ideas towards this necessary openness to the Other as fundamental to moral learning.

Whilst Cox seems pessimistic about the prospects for the emergence of such solidarity (much like Horkheimer regarding the future 'circle of transmitters'), we can see in his stated hopes for such a possibility a clear connection to his earliest influences—Burkeian conservatism and socialist ideals—that tether his understanding of society, whether local or global, as organic and solidaristic (Cox, 1996b, p. 20, 2012, p. 16). Here, Cox's (2001) key achievement has been his ability to re-capture the possibilities for *coexistence in the plurality of civilizations* (pp. 108–109), a possibility obscured and lost to those that have depicted civilizational encounters under Americanized (Luce), teleological (Fukuyama), or conflictual (Huntington) models, rather than in dynamic, relational terms. Tehranian takes up such a historical approach, anticipating some of the arguments here, as consistent with a Coxian framework that rejects the false choice between the end of history or the clash of civilizations that dominate so much thinking in IR (Tehranian, 2016, p. 41). Cox (2007) speculates on the conditions for the mutual recognition of distinct civilizations to emerge—or what he calls the 'material basis for coexistence in diversity' (p. 513)—as including: elements of shared consciousness that can bridge the distinct traditions and sources of intersubjective meanings; the maintenance of the biosphere; and the governance of a plural world through social solidarity, equality, restraints on violence, and human rights (see Cox, 2007, p. 523, pp. 526–527, 2001, p. 126). Whilst these conditions are immanent, they remain in contradiction in power, production, and social forces.

Accordingly, it is important to note that Cox does restrict the possibilities in this relational/recognitive process. Specifically, Cox limits such recognition to the enhancement of one's subjective understanding regarding the different perspectives, understandings, and perceptions of the world of the 'other'. It functions more as a form of reflexivity on the conditioning of our own thoughts/perspective—a self-awareness of the cultural situatedness of our own mind—and thereby contributing to the possibility of mutual recognition. This downplays the *relational* aspect of intersubjectivity in favour of the *subjective*. For one could contend that intersubjectivity is formative of the very perspectives, understandings, and perceptions of the subject. These are not created by the subject and related outwardly but are intersubjectively mediated all the way down. This means that social relations remain fundamental. Whilst Cox (2001) does give some indication that changes in intersubjectivity emanate from the 'bottom', that is, from injustices in civil society and the generation of new social norms through social struggle (p. 125), this does not yet equate to a full theory of intersubjectivity for IR but gestures towards it. Moreover, if such corrective work could be achieved, Cox's (2001) intercivilizational approach to intersubjectivity (p. 110) would then overlap with the empirical and normative conditions of central concern to more recent developments in the FS, specifically, Axel Honneth's theory of recognition that looks to the forms of 'intersubjective understanding' that make possible politically significant emancipatory practices through domination-free networks of interaction (see Honneth, 1995, pp. 97, 106). Such shared interests could form the basis of a productive research endeavour combining forms of CT in social theory and CIT in IR—a question beyond the scope of this paper to address, however. Whilst Cox's connection to a fully fleshed recognition theoretic should not be over-played, the remarkable synergies with Honneth lend impetus for further research into recognition in the cosmopolitan or intercivilizational sphere—and support Cox's ongoing association with the label CT.

Conclusion

Cox's meaning of 'critical' in his own approach has been always *sui generis* and yet bears a number of synergies with Horkheimer. As we have seen, Horkheimer's set-up of the critical divide actively combined CT with other theoretical and empirical approaches as a means to ground practical, social inquiry into emancipation. He saw freedom as a social achievement, with the liberation of the individual as possible only in a rational society. Yet the application of this radical method was limited by the FS's myopic focus on the West that curtailed its understanding of the social totality. In distinction, Cox's set-up of the critical divide tended towards separating CT from other approaches—particularly positivist and neorealist accounts. His work was less normatively driven by emancipation but which, nevertheless, remained a consistent theme, albeit one under-theorized. In particular, Cox's critical historicism contributed significantly to the opening up of CT towards the emancipatory possibilities located in civilizational coexistence, something that promises the radical extension of intersubjectivity to the human community taken as a totality. This refined intersubjective ontology promises much for the future of a 'critical' theory that holds to an emancipatory interest.

But this reading cuts against many of Cox's interlocutors. For some, like Persuaud, Cox provides first and foremost a theory of domination and resistance. This is patently true in terms of what it primarily addresses: the existing composition of social forces and the forms of domination within this status quo. But to linger here is to risk remaining one-sided. For Cox is above all a dialectician and, as such, we must give equal consideration to the affinity or the 'other-side' of this form of domination: emancipation. Of course, the positivity of socio-political order must be our principal concern, given that we as humans experience it as suffering. But resistance is always purposive, it is not intended to preserve domination, but to remove or alter the conditions of suffering. Sublation, or the possibility of sublation, must be given its due lest we fall to the illusion of that which *is*. For others, like Kubalkova, my reading is too much of an attempt to mainstream a 'critical theory' of IR as a generic term, much less as a movement, as the differences between Cox and others associated with CIT are too vast.[10] Yet, at its core, and particularly so in his later work that actively seeks the extension of solidarism between civilizations, Cox presents a distinct, normative choice for an alternative vision of the human future that is open, just, and dialogic. Here, his work is less in the 'philosophical mode' of CT that is endangered by its own cultural insignificance, towards one concerned in concrete terms with the real, historical world, and the question of how humans can continue to relate with each other, presenting this as problem of *our* moral and social choices on a world-scale. This is Cox's greatest lesson to us—but it is also a theme shared with the emancipatory commitments of the FS. To separate them would be an artifice based on the intellectual development of a discipline, rather than seeking out shared theoretical and political commitments that are far more important.

And it is on his question of politics that answers why Cox's work is not read widely in the North American academy. This field prefers the safe *a*politicism of constructivism that serves the status quo that seeks to explain through elite politics like norms entrepreneurs and cascades, rather than the critical and emancipatory content of Cox's (and Horkheimer's) thought that is immersed in real social relations and the possibilities for change contained within them. It is because of the critical content of Cox's ideas—his implicit emancipatory commitments—that he remains a 'fugitive' in the academy (see Leysens, 2008) and which, more than anything else, proves my argument regarding the 'critical' content of his thought and the appropriateness of the label accordingly. It is because of this critical content of Cox's ideas-his implicit emancipatory commitments-that he remains not only a 'fugitive' in the academy (see Leysens 2008) or an 'eccentric' (this is Susan Strange's label, see Cox, 2012: 18, 23-24), but why he must be considered a 'critical' theorist. For even though the FS did not form a significant part of his canon, Cox shares the content of their concerns as the main purpose to which his theory is to serve. Cox therefore can be seen—as Susan Strange would have said—a 'Critical Theorist' in the *best* sense of the term.

Disclosure Statement

No potential conflict of interest was reported by the author.

Notes

1 In this article I use CT to designate Horkheimer's approach and the theoretical programme as developed by the Frankfurt School FS. This has become customary in the literature, even though in his essay 'Traditional and

Critical Theory' Horkheimer (1972) uses lower cases when expressing this term and frequently describes it not just as a theory but also as an 'attitude' or 'thought'.
2. On the FS, see generally Dubiel (1985). On Horkheimer's influence in IR, much less has been explored. For exceptions, see Hoffman (1987) and Brincat (2012).
3. As the article focuses on these two essays and for reasons of length, wider reflections on Cox and Horkheimer's corpus of work are made only to shed light on aspects of how each sets up the 'critical' divide.
4. Nevertheless, despite this 'unhelpful choice of words', Booth (2007) sees in Cox an attempt to infuse theory and practice with the idea of struggling to make a better world, in which CT becomes a tactical and strategic action for emancipatory purposes (pp. 48, 198, 264, 242–244).
5. The period where Cox was primarily concerned with Gramsci, history and globalization. For a periodization of Cox's work, see Cox and Sinclair (1996, pp. 537–544).
6. For an exemplary critique of CIT on the grounds of its Eurocentrism, see Hobson (2007).
7. I thank Vendulka Kubalkova for a discussion on this point.
8. While Cox is discussing gender in this particular reference, the point can also be generalized concerning the respect of difference (see Cox, 1995, p. 14).
9. Note the overlap with Horkheimer's emphasis on the importance of education for developing such a 'vision', explored above.
10. Both Persaud and Kubalkova's readings were based on lively discussions at 'On Robert W. Cox's Contribution to IR, IPE and IS', at the ISA 56th Annual Convention, 19 February 2015, New Orleans.

References

Alamuti, M. M. (2015). *Critical rationalism and globalization: Towards the sociology of the open global society*. London: Routledge.

Booth, K. (2007). *Theory of world security*. Cambridge: Cambridge University Press.

Brincat, S. (2012). On the methods of critical theory: How CIRT has advanced the project of emancipation in the early Frankfurt School. *International Relations*, *26*(2), 218–245.

Cox, R. W. (1977). Labour and hegemony. *International Organization*, *31*(3), 385–424.

Cox, R. W. (1981). Social forces, states, and world orders: Beyond international relations theory. *Millennium*, *10*(2), 126–155.

Cox, R. W. (1983). Gramsci, hegemony and international relations. *Millennium – Journal of International Studies*, *12*(2), 162–175.

Cox, R. W. (1987). *Production, power, and world order: Social forces in the making of history*. New York, NY: Columbia University Press.

Cox, R. W. (1992a). Multilateralism and world order. *Review of International Studies*, *18*(2), 161–180.

Cox, R. W. (1992b). Towards a posthegemonic conceptualisation of world order: Reflections on the relevancy of Ibn Khaldun. In J. N. Rosenau & E.-O. Czempiel (Eds.), *Governance without government* (pp. 132–159). Cambridge: CUP.

Cox, R. W. (1995). Civilizations: Encounters and transformations. *Studies in Political Economy*, *47*, 1–31.

Cox, R. W. (1996a). Globalization, multilateralism, and democracy. In T. Sinclair (Ed.), *Approaches to world order* (pp. 524–536). Cambridge: CUP.

Cox, R. W. (1996b). *Influences and commitments*. In T. Sinclair (Ed.), *Approaches to world order* (pp. 19–38). Cambridge: CUP.

Cox, R. W. (2001). Civilizations and the twenty-first century: Some theoretical considerations. *International Relations of the Asia-Pacific*, *1*(1), 105–130.

Cox, R. W. (2007). 'The International' in Evolution. *Millennium – Journal of International Studies*, *35*(3), 513–527.

Cox, R. W. (2012). *For* someone, and *for* some purpose. In S. Brincat, L. Lima, & J. Nunes (Eds.), *Critical international relations theory and security studies: Interviews and reflections* (pp. 18, 23–24). London: Routledge.

Cox, R. W., & Sinclair, T. (1996). *Complete bibliography of works by Robert W. Cox to 1995, approaches to world order*. Cambridge: CUP.

Devetak, R. (2014). A rival enlightenment? Critical international theory in historical mode. *International Theory*, *6*(3), 417–453.

Dubiel, H. (1985). *Theory and politics*. Cambridge, MA: MIT Press.

Hamati-Ataya, I. (2013). Reflectivity, reflexivity, reflexivism: IR's 'reflexive turn' – And beyond. *European Journal of International Relations*, *19*(4), 669–694.

Held, D. (1980). *Introduction to critical theory*. Berkley: University of California Press.

Hobson, J. M. (2007). Is critical theory always for the white west and for western imperialism? Beyond Westphilian towards a post-racist critical IR. *Critical International Relations Theory after 25 Years*, special issue of *Review of International Studies, 33*(S1), 91–116.

Hoffman, M. (1987). Critical theory and the inter-paradigm debate. *Millennium – Journal of International Studies, 16*(2), 231–250.

Honneth, A. (1995). *The struggle for recognition*. Cambridge: Polity Press.

Horkheimer, M. (1971). *Montaigne und die funktion der skepsis*. Frankfurt am Main: Fischer Bucherel.

Horkheimer, M. (1972a). Traditional and critical theory. In M. T. O'Connell and others (Eds), *Critical theory* (pp. 188–243). New York, NY: Herder and Herder.

Horkheimer, M. (1972b). Postscript. In M. T. O'Connell and others (Eds.), *Critical theory* (pp. 244–252). New York, NY: Herder and Herder.

Horkheimer, M. (1975). Notes on institute activities. *Studies in Philosophy and Social Science, 9*(2), 121–123.

Horkheimer, M. (1995). The present situation of social philosophy and the tasks of an institute for social research. In M. S. Kramer, J. Torpey, G. F. Hunter (Eds.), *Between philosophy and social science: Selected early writings* (pp. 1–14). Cambridge, MA: MIT Press.

Jahn, B. (2014, August 8). Comments in "Semiplenary 2: Frankfurt, critical theory and international relations". In *4th WISC*. Frankfurt: Goethe University.

Jay, M. (1996). *The dialectical imagination*. Berkley: University of California Press.

Khaldun, I. (1967) *The muqaddimah*. (F. Rosenthal, Trans.). Princeton, NJ: Princeton University Press.

Leysens, A. (2008). *The critical theory of Robert W. Cox*. New York, NY: Palgrave & Macmillan.

Neufeld, M. (1995). *The restructuring of international relations theory*. Cambridge: CUP.

Tehranian, M. (2016). Where is the new world order? At the end of history or a clash of civilizations. In R. C. Vincent, & K. Nordenstreng (Eds.), *Towards equity in global communication* (pp. 17–46). New York, NY: Hampton Press.

Framing Robert W. Cox, Framing International Relations

VENDULKA KUBÁLKOVÁ

University of Miami, Coral Gables, FL, USA

ABSTRACT *In the recent years, R.W. Cox has distanced himself from some genealogical connections made by his followers in regard to what he meant in his famous 1981 article. Was he mischaracterized, framed? This paper focuses on how Cox has been 'framed', a concept elaborated and used across social sciences in different contexts. Here, it is used to look at different mechanisms by which ideas, such as those of Cox, can be connected, 'framed' to other ideas, not only to advance knowledge but to strengthen individual careers, to strengthen and construct approaches and disciplines. Framing highlights and creates a space but also constrains and obscures. Cox deserves to be seen outside any frames other than the one he creates for himself, one which is changing and developing as does the real world, not captive to any approach, paradigm, discipline, or any other frame.*

Over three decades ago, R.W. Cox caused a major stir in the discipline of international relations (IR) on both sides of the Atlantic. His paper 'Social Forces, States and World Orders: Beyond International Relations Theory' first published in 1981 by *Millennium: Journal of International Studies* is to this day referred to on the website of the journal as one of the most cited papers in the journal's history (Cox, 1981). That article made Cox virtually overnight into an IR celebrity with decades of his further prolific contributions to follow. What exactly Cox meant and what others thought he meant, in his 1981 article, remain controversial. The ambiguity has affected his stature as an IR scholar. The ramifications of the ambiguity open a door to the exploration of what has been in social sciences called 'framing': more broadly, what we regard as knowledge and what do we do with it. Cox never used the term 'frame'; it was, at that time, outside the bounds of the IR discourse. However, 'frame' and 'framing' are now terms used in the IR discipline, in the positivist mainstream (also known as soft) form of constructivism. Frames and framing are tools used by 'norm-entrepreneurs'. A 'norm-entrepreneur' (a term coined by American legal scholar, Cass Sunstein in 1996) is someone interested in changing social norms, reflecting 'legitimate social purpose', and doing so by manipulating, 'framing' messages. Norm-entrepreneurs are now a new topic of IR, studied by one of the three main US IR approaches as described for example in an authoritative article by Walt (1998).

This essay is not about norm-entrepreneurs, although we refer briefly to what they do; here we look at what 'academic entrepreneurs' do via their approaches, paradigms, and disciplines—that is to say, via different frames, delimiting both space for and constraints on the creation and dissemination of knowledge. In these processes, we as academics assign places to other scholars in approaches and paradigms, and thus, if it is without their nod, frame them. Cox did not use the term 'frame' in his 1981 article. In essence however, he talked about frames; in his view the frame of the IR discipline was flawed regarding what it included, what it excluded, and what it acknowledged including and excluding. The real social world, said Cox, is divided by academic conventions into separate spheres/ disciplines, which scholars have delimited among themselves, as if these subjects were the natural and inevitable way to arrange the production and dissemination of knowledge. The subtitle of Cox's essay 'Beyond International Relations Theory' is a call for radical re-framing of the study of the world. In his most memorable line, which became something of a war cry, he argued that 'theory is always for someone and for a purpose', with ideology always hidden in the frame. Every theory has what Cox calls a 'concealed' ideology. Ironically, this is no longer that outlandish, either: 30 years after Cox, Bryan Rathbun argued in a mainstream US IR journal that all theories have *implicit* ideologies (Rathbun, 2012), not just *concealed*—a term Cox used. Cox does not stop there, however. He argues that the world is different from what IR sees, how it frames the world, excluding historical perspective, social forces, and world orders. He points away from the state-centric, ahistorical realist approach, away from realism, its new form at that time, for which Cox coined the name neorealism. Then Cox—and this is the nub—makes a distinction between two ways of seeing the world and names one of them 'critical'.

His choice of the word 'critical' has triggered yet another frame associated with Cox but one not quite of Cox's making. In one of its meaning the term 'critical' has undeniable Marxist roots, and Cox's 'critical' has become associated with, framed together with, subsumed into the Marxist-derived term. To follow the maze of frames all somehow touching on R.W. Cox, we begin with the question (i) what are frames, historically speaking and on their path to IR via social sciences, (ii) was R.W. Cox mischaracterized/framed, (iii) how was he framed, and (iv) why? To answer why he was framed in IR discipline we look into the dynamics of the academic enterprise: Framing International Relations. Approaches/paradigms and academic disciplines too could be seen as framing, 'disciplining'—to use Foucault's term. (v) Finally, it is not particularly new to say that Cox eschews frames, approaches, or indeed disciplines. The initial mischaracterization that stuck distracted from seeing other aspects of his contribution—he deserves a different place in the IR discipline and beyond it, a point made in the conclusion.

1. About Frames

Historically speaking, frame as a word was seen as having essentially two meanings: in its first sense, in the physical, material world, 'frame' described objects, as in 'border or case for a picture of a pane of glass'; also, human bodies, bicycles, motor cars, and other structures, or separate pictures in films had frames. In its second sense referring to ideas, 'frame' initially had a very limited place, only in detective stories and criminal investigations denoting devising criminal charges to blame or to incriminate an innocent person through the use of false evidence. Etymological studies claim that the use of the word 'frame' as 'plotting in secret' or fabricating stories 'with evil intent' has existed since at least the sixteenth century.

In a broader sense, 'framing' has many ancestors. Its history goes back to the ancient Greek and Roman rhetoric, the art of effective or persuasive speaking or writing. In social sciences, the word's pedigree goes back to one of its magisterial figures, Kenneth Boulding, his book entitled *The image* (1956), which was followed by his essay *National images and international systems* (1959). The pedigree includes the work of Amos Nathan Tversky, a cognitive and mathematical psychologist and a student of cognitive science, the collaborator of the 2002 Nobel Prize winner, Daniel Kahneman, who defined systematic human cognitive bias (Tversky & Kahneman, 1986). Framing processes as an *analytical* category have proliferated in psychology, particularly cognitive psychology, linguistics and discourse analysis, communication and media studies, political science, and policy studies. The framing and kindred processes have been applied analytically and *explored empirically* particularly in sociology, probably because of the influence of Goffman's *Frame analysis: An essay on the organization of experience* (1974), developing his earlier work, *The presentation of self in everyday life* (1959). The study of framing has been extended to politics—particularly electoral politics—as well as in relation to the manipulation of opinion, the mobilization of social movements, deriving from the much-quoted work of Snow and Benford 'Ideology, frame resonance, and participant mobilization' (1988).

Thus, having developed since the 1970s across social sciences, psychology, particularly cognitive psychology, linguistics and discourse analysis, communication and media studies, political science, and policy studies, the concept of frame found its way into IR. International relations, in so far as it has been based on positivism, has dealt only with objective reality ascribing causal force only to material forces and power. The idea that frames somehow influence choices, that they contain subjective biases, would be antithetical to the very core of IR discipline. In rational choice theory, still important in IR, people always strive to make rational choices; rational choosers are always assumed to make the same decisions when given the same data. In contrast, framing implies normative content; it highlights the importance of language, of words, left out ostensibly from the mainstream US IR theories. Framing describes an active processual phenomenon that draws attention to an agency, to the role of subjective factors that are always in contention at the level of social reality and its construction.

These ideas are not compatible with how IR was traditionally studied in the US. Nobody would seriously consider that academic disciplines, such as IR, are anything but somehow given; only the staunchest critics of the IR discipline would ever imply that the IR discipline with its delimited (and vigorously defended) subject matter is mere arbitrary convention, that it is 'framed'. Nor would anybody insult scholars that their 'debates', their 'turns', and their different 'approaches' and 'paradigms' are anything other than given, albeit arrived at after contestations and empirical confirmations, but always reflecting the reality of their field of studies, the world. The use of 'framing' in the title of this paper, framing both Cox and IR, would be an affront to many scholars.

However, the concept of a frame has arrived into IR as a part of constructivism, one of the three mainstream positivist approaches, referred to as soft constructivism, it became very popular. The change required that objective facts, hitherto the only subject of inquiry, have been supplemented by 'social facts', a result of inter-subjective understanding. In a major shift, inter-subjective understanding became seen as the constructing and re-constructing social facts. In addition—in an incredible move in the history of IR discipline—subjective became inter-subjective, inter-subjectively agreed upon, and no longer out of bounds of scholarly pursuits in IR discipline, at least in one of its approaches.

It is important to reiterate that none of these ideas were invented in IR: they were imported, selectively, from a range of social science sources and also selectively applied only to some aspects of what is going on in the world. Most of the imported ideas came from sociology, the study of social movements in particular. Frames arrived in tandem and as a necessary adjunct of 'norms', reflecting 'legitimate social purpose'. There developed a new narrative, a new vocabulary, and new things to study: occupying the central stage are the 'norms-entrepreneurs', the agents crafting norms, 'shared understanding' reflecting 'legitimate social purpose'. And norms-entrepreneurs craft norms via frames which they devise. This shift brought with it a stress on ideological building blocks that undergird community's shared understandings—rather than only material forces.

A large and rapidly growing literature (see Payne, 2001) tells us that frames differ in kind and perform different roles. Frames are crafted; they are strategically manipulated to resonate with audiences. There are multiple coexisting frames, distorted frames, master frames, strategic frames, interpretive frames, and cognitive frames. Once extended to IR, the constructivist scholars discover that in the worldwide new setting, there are many competing normative claims that 'targeted' states and especially their domestic populations have to be persuaded so that they embrace the normative ideas their framers support. Much attention is then paid to how political actors communicate, how persuasive frames change actors' preferences since frames are now seen as prominent means in the process of imputing social knowledge by their framers and advocates. Frames are normative—they work just as any norm does. They tend to become fixed, and yet they are always open to challenge. Thus, there are frame contests; there are frames and counter-frames, and this is vital since it is argued that the targets then 'see different things, make different interpretations, and propose different courses of actions'. But the change—and it has taken place only in one of the three IR approaches—is still only on the surface; positivism still looms large. Empirical evaluations and evidence continue to be central; norm-entrepreneurs employ sophisticated means-ends calculations to overcome the criticism that frames and counter-frames cannot be calculated and that they indeed evade empirical tests.

Constructivism, aka 'soft' constructivism, which is recognized as one of the three mainstream approaches of the IR in the US, has met with diametrically opposite reactions. On one hand, in the IR discipline in the US, it is criticized for departing too much from positivism. On the other hand, to Nicholas Onuf, who first introduced constructivism to IR as a social theory, the mainstream form of constructivism does not depart from positivism at all (e.g. Onuf, 1989, 1998, 2002, 2014b, 2015). Onuf regards its followers as 'self-described constructivists', 'faux constructivists', or liberal internationalists who are misusing the label 'constructivism'. The IR discipline, which has been 'long dominated by political realists', has not changed at all (Onuf, 2014a, p. 2). The three approaches of IR in the US, neorealism, neoliberalism and the soft constructivism, share 'the ontological and epistemological hegemony of the "neo-neo consensus" ... with the soft constructivism, the main form of constructivism in the US, too ending up adopting the neo-neo infused direction' (Hoffman, 2003). In Onuf's view, there is not much 'constructing' in this constructivism. The norms central to this type of constructivism are, according to Onuf, 'rules by another name' but are, in Onuf's view, conceptually unexplained, the source of their normativity under theorized. 'Norms-entrepreneurs' are singled out as if, somehow, they were the only agents 'constructing' the social world. As far as 'framing' is concerned, in Onuf's form of constructivism, known as rule-oriented or linguistic constructivism, agents and social arrangements (structures) mutually co-construct each other via rules that are ubiquitous in the social world. The terms 'frame' and 'framing' are, then, nearly redundant and subsumed in the social construction and co-construction of which they are a form. Frames, in fact, imply only a one-way, one-sided process; the use of the term per se would make sense if it refers to 'plotting' or 'fabricating associations'. However, whether created spuriously or not, frames do construct social arrangements of social consequences.

Thus, unsurprisingly, because of the prevailing positivism in IR, importing ideas by the mainstream form of constructivism stop short of borrowing from cognitive scientists. The latter go further in their theories, making the understanding much broader and more generally applicable and not just to norms construction. Neuroscientists and cognitive scientists argue that frames and their 'filters' have not only social roots but also biological roots (e.g. see Lakoff, 2004; Lakoff & Johnson, 1980). After conducting laboratory experiments, cognitive scientists claim to have 'linked framing effect to neural activity', which means that a frame is realized by neural circuitry. Every time a neural circuit is activated by a certain word, the frame is strengthened, and associations between words and concepts are created. Certain words, then, recall their distinct associations more or less automatically. 'Frames' create reference-dependent perceptions and strategic terms that activate connections. The word 'frame' itself is an example: it has now new associations—no longer related to physical objects such as pictures on the wall or shady activities implicating innocent people in wrongdoing.

Nothing prevents the broadening of the relevance of frames. Academic institutions also filter, frame, 'generate, diffuse, and contest ideas and meanings' just as much and not only as norms according to soft constructivism. Framing, we argue, has widespread consequences for the formulation and furthering of knowledge. That brings us to R.W. Cox. We will turn now, first of all, to his mischaracterization: it was not done by norm-entrepreneurs but by fellow scholars.

2. Was Cox Framed?

In his Preface to a book-length study of R.W. Cox by Leysens (2008), Craig Murphy sees R.W. Cox as one of the very few IR scholars who will still continue to be relevant in the mid-twenty-first century. Murphy compares Cox's oeuvre to E.H. Carr's canonic text *Twenty Years Crisis* describing Carr's book as 'probably the only mid-20th century book which is read by most international relations graduate students today'. Murphy argues that R.W. Cox is one of very few who will not lose relevance and will be sending messages in the mid-twenty-first century where 'the future' is highly unlikely (contrary to 'realist' precepts) to 'look like the past'. There could be no greater compliment to Cox than Murphy's comparison with E.H. Carr, which is why it is fitting to highlight it in a Festschrift.

In the same Preface, however, Murphy makes a troubling observation, namely that many of Cox's admirers—including some who, says Murphy ... have read him carefully and understood him well—but they have:

> very deliberately lumped his views together with a wide range of theories with which Cox's ideas ... [are] only marginally connected ... Cox's self-described 'critical' theory ... [is] lumped together with a range of work that ... [leans] heavily on the 'Critical Theory' of the Frankfurt School ... Clarity—and some might argue, a degree of intellectual integrity— ... [has been] sacrificed to the more pressing goal of creating and preserving space in the academy for the whole range of what ... [is] called 'dissident' scholarship in international relations. (Murphy, 2008)

Murphy is not the only one making a similar comment. After a meticulously researched 300-page work that examines not just Cox but those who claim to be his followers, the South African scholar Anthony Leysens concludes unequivocally that Cox is incorrectly placed or associated with the Frankfurt School of critical theory and the Habermasian 'critical turn' in the field of International Relations [and that seeing] ... the identification of Cox as the head (guru) of a neo-Marxist or neo-Gramscian school [is] problematic ... (Leysens, 2008)

There is also more than 'circumstantial evidence' for this conclusion. There is what Cox himself has said. There is, in other words, his own testimony. In 2012 an Australian, Shannon Brincat, put to Cox a series of questions designed to dispel the doubts articulated by Murphy and Leysens, such as: Was he a Marxist or a Gramscian or a neo-Gramscian? Did he follow the work of the Frankfurt School? Did he paraphrase, or was he otherwise influenced by, a piece written in 1937 by Max Horkheimer, the then-Director of the Frankfurt School, who made a distinction between 'critical' and 'traditional' theory (a distinction notably similar to the one Cox made 40 years later between 'critical' and 'problem–solving' theory) thus denying Cox any originality? Brincat asked other questions and all were answered in the negative or with important qualifications: Was Cox a 'historical materialist'? Did he subscribe to the goal of 'emancipation' and what did he understand by it? Did he believe in 'progress' (both of these concepts being central to 'critical' IR approaches? Others also question whether he rejects 'positivism'— a move central also to all 'critical' IR approaches (Kurki & Colin, 2010, p. 28).

The key point made by Leysens (2008), Murphy (2008), and Brincat, Lima, and Nunes (2012) is that Cox is mischaracterized. He has been 'lumped together', as Murphy puts it, by those who speak in his name. This leads to a number of questions: Why do the incorrect assertions that Leysens and Murphy note continue to be made? How do those who make them succeed in doing so when in recent interviews Cox himself denies the role he is supposed to play? Why the mischaracterization? What stature do they achieve by standing on his shoulders? What does this cost Cox? What does it say about the discipline of IR?

In short, Cox's followers 'framed' him in the old colloquial sense of the term. They convicted him of being a critical theorist, of the variety they defined, and they sentenced him to a prison-house of words not of his choosing. In this essay, I hope to expose the framers and perhaps undo some of the damage they have done. The damage is not to Cox's reputation, which in some regard may have benefitted from his having been 'framed'. The damage is to his scholarship and, behind it, his intentions, his normative concerns. This is no doubt that fate of every scholar—everything any of us writes is susceptible to being ripped from its frame and reframed or, to use a cliché of the moment, re-purposed. In Cox's case, however, the (re)framing is excessive, gratuitous, disrespectful.

3. How Cox Was Framed

To summarize, what then do scholars do when they 'frame'? Simply put, framing means fastening on a specific term by adding to it, subtracting from it, suppressing some aspect of it, or genuinely failing to notice part of it. When the process is finished, what is 'framed' is something else. It is a different idea, a different concept, with a different meaning (though the original idea may remain intact inside it).

'Framing' is often justified by referring to the 'spirit' that is 'divined' in the process and that is said to make such 'framing' possible. Inside the new 'frame', the new meaning of the subject is accepted, often on the authority of the 'framer' alone. Other components of the 'frame' are not examined. The author and the new 'frame' are seen in the different light that it manifests. It then eventually becomes disseminated like a game of Chinese whispers where new understandings are repeated and passed on and on and on. The word and its meaning are different from what they were before they were 'whispered'. With the word 'critical', at least four particular associations come to mind. Changing from one to another changes the 'frame' as well as meanings. The multiple meanings of the word open the door to distortions.

First of all, there is the common dictionary usage. This 'critical' means essentially 'finding fault' or 'tending to point out errors' or 'expressing adverse or disapproving comments or judgments'. Second, there is the commitment to being 'critical' enshrined in the foundational documents of most educational institutions. These make a commitment to instilling 'critical and analytical' skills in their students and to advancing knowledge with their use. Third, there is 'critical' as Cox used the term in his famous 1981 article, juxtaposing 'critical' with 'problem-solving'. The latter concept, problem-solving, he said, deliberately hides the ideologies all theories promote. This is why the juxtaposition he highlighted was not a 'critical' versus 'non-critical' but a 'critical' versus 'problem-solving'. He did this to highlight how theories are used to maintain the status quo and present it as objectively given. He argued that in IR, all theories are ideologies, by which he meant that any theory is in effect 'framed' by an ideology and by the values the particular ideology promotes and protects. According to him, even a 'critical' theory is ideological. Or to repeat and paraphrase his most famous observation, every theory is always 'for somebody and for a purpose' where 'somebody' and 'purpose' are in the frame, concealed. This particular juxtaposition was a challenge to 'positivist' scholars who insisted that their kind of theorizing is value-free. Cox's challenge came as a surprise to its IR mainstream proponents. Indeed, it came as an eye-opening—even heretical—shock.

There is another meaning of the word critical and another dichotomy in addition to the three already discussed. Six years after Cox introduced his 'critical/problem–solving' dichotomy, 'critical' was introduced to IR in a different 'frame'. Although Cox did refer to 'critical' in 1981, it was Mark Hoffman who instigated its current usage in 'critical IR studies' or 'Critical International Relations theory' with the frequently used acronym CIRT or CIT (1987). He made a fourth connection to the term 'critical' and thus another 'frame'. His frame subsumed Cox's version of critical to his.

While a student at LSE, Hoffman seemed to have been familiar with the literature outside IR, and because of Cox's established reputation, his academic publications, and the famous 1981 article, it must have seemed that adding Cox to this fourth 'frame' was a good idea. There was a different, the fourth, usage of 'critical' before Cox. By doing so, it could be argued that Cox was not the first one to introduce the term. Giving Hoffman credit for introducing the term in this sense to IR rather than to Cox should be seen in this context.

As far back as Immanuel Kant, it is possible to find 'critical' being used analytically. Hoffman saw it as having a more recent ancestry, highlighted its use by the Frankfurt School, and identified Cox as a member or follower of this school. What Hoffman did was, in essence, making a connection with the term 'critical theory' as used by some of the Western scions of Karl Marx although Cox himself never once made a reference to the Frankfurt School and those who pointed it out were very harshly criticized.[1] Few IR scholars were familiar with this lineage. International Relations did not have a left wing until the 1980s (Kubálková and Cruickshank, 1985/1989). Even if the connection was neither noticed nor understood the term critical sounded right. Who did not want to be 'critical', much less contravene their university's mandate to be analytically so? What Hoffman (or any of the 'gurus' of the newly formed 'critical' IR approach) did not do was highlight how 'critical theory' was first created as a code word for Marxism. It was glossed over that it was inspired initially by the subtitle to Marx's *Grundrisse* (which was *the Critique of Political Economy*). It was in this sense that the concept of 'critical theory' was coined in 1937 by Max Horkheimer, one of the first directors of the Institute for Social Research (aka the Frankfurt School). The Frankfurt School played a key role in what was left of Marxism in the West after all the attempts at proletarian revolution had failed. It carried on (though not alone) to what was referred as Western Marxism, a term coined by Merleau-Ponty.

The reframing of the philosophy of the Institute for Social Research away from any connection to Marxism and renaming its research orientation as critical theory was necessary at that time since visible connections to Marxism could not be made in the Weimar Republic, particularly after Hitler's ascension to power. Most members of the Frankfurt School had already rejected the 'classical' Marxism of Marx and Engels, with its economic determinism and also Marxism–Leninism (the doctrine on which the Soviet Union was founded). Members of the Frankfurt School had no sympathy for the Soviet Union. If they did, they soon lost it. 'Classical' Marxism, with its contending classes, seemed no longer practical and applicable, and with the proletarian revolution out of the picture, so was any connection to any political party or movement. The approach subsequently became philosophically erudite, largely intellectual not written in an easy to comprehend language by mass movement.

The detailed story of the Frankfurt School is well documented (e.g. by Anderson, 1976 and by Jay, 1973), but it is rarely quoted—except selectively—by most of those who think of themselves as 'critical' in IR. They may not even know where the concept comes from and the historical part it has played. A mere glance at any biography of the Frankfurt School shows that saying 'follow the Frankfurt School' also makes little sense, given how highly variegated in its interests and contributions the Frankfurt School became. A couple of its members and their ideas were cherry-picked by IR analysts, but the Frankfurt School, as an integrated whole (which it never was), was rarely considered. Martin Jay, in his germinal study (Jay, 1973), demonstrates how it consisted of a large number of individuals whose interests ranged from art to literary criticism to economics. None focused on 'IR'—relations among states worldwide. This had barely begun as an academic discipline of IR in the UK and the US when, in the early 1920s, the Frankfurt School came into existence; the interest of its members in the issues involved in IR was minimal or non-existent. Perry Anderson has argued that the Frankfurt School drew on two sources equally: Karl Marx and Sigmund Freud. Knowledge emancipates the mind, and it is this emancipation that is all that can be hoped for when there is no chance for a revolution, that is, an energetic political action through such as the 1917 successful October revolution in Russia (Anderson, 1976).

Similarly problematic is the inclusion of Jürgen Habermas, a generation later. Habermas—a 'critical' sociologist—followed his own path. Only one or two of his earlier works attracted the attention of 'critical' IR analysts, and he now champions different ideas such as that of 'post-secularity', 'a post-secular age', a phrase he coined. He does not shy away from exploring what is now referred to as the 'return of religion to IR' either—something few 'critical' IR theorists heed.

4. Why Was Cox Framed? Framing IR

The 'framing' of Cox so far discussed is only one part of the story. It would be simple enough just to label, to place somebody's work into an approach or a paradigm, or to figure out the author's intellectual pedigree. A few might even notice. It is more complicated to make the associations triggered and activated automatically, make them stick, repeated—and institutionalized. To put it differently, the question is how the dominant discourses of IR are constructed, maintained, resisted, or made to disappear: for that we have to look into the dynamics of academic pursuits.

There is no need to repeat here the well-known narrative of the history of the IR discipline, its various debates, grand debates, and 'turns'. What is relevant to us here is to recall, first of all, that the Anglo-American discipline of IR originally started in 1919 as one but split into two: an 'Anglo' and an 'American' part (Section 4.1). It is relevant here since, in these two parts, 'critical' approaches and Cox's work have been received and fared differently. The academic following of Cox is mainly to be found in the 'Anglo' part—the UK, Australia, and Canada. It is much less visible in the 'American' part, the US/IR. Second (Section 4.2), we examine specific organizational principles on which academic disciplines are based and which have played a role.

4.1. *The Anglo-American IR Split*

Available figures confirm that the Anglo part is small, while the American part, US/IR, as befits its geopolitical significance as a superpower, is huge. As Steve Smith, the leading British IR scholar, once put it in a conversation, the British International Studies Association could fit in a bus. To complete the comparison, the US IR Academy would need a football field.

It is not just the staggering difference in size to highlight the differences in the numbers of universities, IR faculty, and different foci of study[2] but the hubris of those identifying with and speaking on behalf of a superpower. In the liberal tradition, academics and practitioners have been regarded as two distinct ethnic groups with only limited intermingling, with the exception of a few Kissingers defecting to diplomacy and lapsed diplomats seeking careers in the academe. The 4400 IR scholars in the US registered and surveyed by the Institute for the Theory & Practice of International Relations and its Teaching, Research, and International Policy (TRIP) Project (TRIP https://trip.wm.edu/home/) is by no means the sum total of those who teach IR in the US at the more than 5000 plus tertiary outfits. They are presumably engaged full time in research and teaching. Thus, in terms of linguistic (of the Onuf's variety) constructivism, they have agency granted to them by the society, by its educational system, to act as guardians of the knowledge and culture of which, in turn, they are products and whose culture they reproduce. IR's scholars in the 'American' part of the discipline have acted on the assumption that their theories and practices have been globally valid and globally accepted, promoted worldwide by the flood of American publications and presses. They reassure themselves they have been doing well by the world. By teaching a realist, state-centric perspective, they have seen themselves as describing and explaining what globally obtains. Underscoring its claim at universal validity, the American IR discipline sees itself as practicing 'science', being scientific, a mere subfield of political science.[3] In practical terms, this has meant promoting those analyses that are implicitly based on axiomatically postulated 'positivism'. Thus (perhaps subconsciously), the admonition that 'philosophy ... [should be] left to philosophers' is followed, and any serious questioning of the philosophical basis of the IR discipline is out of bounds. Indeed, according to regular surveys made by TRIP, most IR scholars in the US plead allegiance to 'positivism' with their numbers growing despite the philosophical critiques of positivism outside IR. The US/IR discipline continues to remain firmly ensconced in the modernist project.

The problem is that US views of IR have not been necessarily globally shared. Scholars outside the US saw the proliferation of US views as cultural imperialism, an attempt to assert intellectual hegemony, and have seen evidence at the same time of US parochialism (cf Biersteker, 2009; Cox & Nossal, 2009; Messari, Tickner, & Ling, 2012; Tickner & Weaver, 2009; Weaver & Tickner, 2009). Late modernity brought into sharp relief the existence of cultural premises and traditions questioning the US hegemony. The popularity of 'critical' approaches is one component of the questioning process. Cox's pointing in his 1981 article to the US neorealism as an ideology of the US superpower fueled such questioning. The ontological and epistemological hegemony of the 'neo–neo consensus' of the US/IR, as it has been referred to, has been challenged in the counter-discourse by the approaches using the prefix critical coming into full bloom a few years after Cox's 1981 article and citing him as an inspiration and anointing him as the leader.

There were other, less obvious attempts to challenge the US/IR hegemony, more subtle, eventually not successful, and by now the circumstances of their entry into IR forgotten. We mention here only one, the idea of a paradigm, a form of a frame. It arrived into IR with a delay from philosophy and sociology of knowledge, brought on in those fields by major debates over the status of positivism, in light of the work of Karl Popper and Thomas Kuhn. Its introduction to IR seemed to be an easy fix. Those, who had been impatient with the objectivism of positivist science, realism, and their apparent and unshakeable staying power, found solace in the idea of the 'paradigm', hoping that it would work as Kuhn saw it working in the physical sciences. Kuhn's term, 'paradigm', (1962) conveys that any theoretical effort is only of temporary nature. Thus, there can be no continuity of knowledge but, instead, a succession of paradigms, offering different ways of viewing the world. There is an element of contingency in the creation of a paradigm (via consensus in the discipline) and, of course, doubt on the proclaimed goal of an objective search for the truth. When the change happens, there is no continuity, in what Kuhn had called a scientific revolution: instead, a paradigm change or shift takes place; the old paradigm is rejected as incommensurable with the old one. The term runs counter to the basic premises of positivism. Thus, as soon as the word paradigm was used, those who had understood its meaning knew that it was an attack on positivism and its belief in the value-free knowledge and the monopoly of one approach. Out went the idea that the knowledge of IR has been cumulating since Thucydides. Kuhn made a caveat: his concept of paradigm applies to natural sciences, specifically shifts between Newton and Einstein physics, and recognized that less-advanced fields might go through what he called the inter-paradigmatic stage.

In IR, Michael Banks of the London School of Economics had become one of the main advocates of developing theoretical positions that would constitute a counter-weight to the intellectual dominance of political realism (Banks, 1985). In developing these ideas, Banks was one of the first individuals within the discipline to 'latch on to Kuhn's arguments' (Hoffman, 2003) and in particular his notion of 'paradigms' and to use this as the basis for arguing that IR had now entered its third 'great debate'—what Banks would characterize too, following Kuhn, as an 'inter-paradigm debate'. The inter-paradigmatic debate would involve suspending epistemological judgments and granting the validity, integrity, and autonomy of diverse views in continuous reflexive discourse. It would institutionalize an acceptance of a plurality of approaches if a replacement of one by another turned out to be out of reach.

It has not happened or happened differently: the three main US/IR approaches are referred to as three paradigms, based on the neo–neo consensus not significantly differing from each other with the soft constructivism, the third of the three pillars sharing their rationalist positivist foundation. The term 'paradigm' has become but a synonym to 'approach'. If there was an inter-paradigm debate it turned out to be between the US/IR mainstream and those styling themselves as critical. It should come as no surprise that US/IR does not really encourage 'critical' approaches. It does not want them in its midst. Thus, the US/IR discipline chugs along in its 'problem-solving', 'positivist' mode. How is this done? How have so many IR scholars managed to keep 'critical' approaches at arm's length? Why don't more of US/IR scholars adopt them? Why do British 'critical' IR theorists declare so confidently (despite the hubris also on their part) that their 'critical' approaches are the 'next stage' in the IR discipline in the UK and in the US?

To put it in a nutshell, in the UK, Australia, and Canada, Cox was celebrated and put in an important place of IR, 'disciplined' for having articulated a pivotal approach, the critical IR theory (CRIT). Those defining the subject insisted that he belonged where they put him, not where he put himself. In the US, it was not so much Cox but 'critical' IR approaches in general, and thus Cox with them, that were 'disciplined' out of the mainstream IR. Celebrated in the UK and Australia, Cox was consigned to the margins of the subject in the US. This is where a deeper understanding of the mechanism of 'disciplining' as a special form of framing what is studied in academic disciplines—and how—comes in. This is where it is necessary to see how the 'knowledge industry' (as it is pejoratively called) works and how conformity to its main approaches is accomplished.

4.2. *Disciplines Discipline*

The modern US university as we know it took shape in Germany in the eighteenth and nineteenth centuries, developing the medieval European model. The main building block of the modern university in the US is discipline, the feature emphasized when the German model was imported to the US. 'Discipline', as the term was used in the earliest medieval universities, referred to groups of *discipli* (the plural of *disciplus*), the 'followers' of a field of inquiry. The word did not refer to the practice of training people to obey rules or codes of behavior, nor did it refer to the use of punishment to enforce obedience—a meaning that presumes that there is someone or something who will do the enforcing. An academic 'discipline' does not have such an entity in any obvious sense. However, the enforcement that takes place in universities is not merely metaphorical. It is the 'discipline' as a particular form of organization, which is the enforcer.

Teti (n.d., 2007) proposes that we look at 'disciplines' in the late modern university from the post-modern perspective: a combination of Michel Foucault's 'panopticon' and Jacques Lacan's concept of the 'gaze' inspired, in turn, by Jeremy Bentham's (1748–1832) architectural design for a prison. The 'gaze' here is not just people looking at each other or the world. It means that people modify their behavior because they believe they are being constantly watched. The 'gaze' under these circumstances becomes a property of the object and not of the subject doing the gazing. The 'gaze' is the process whereby the object makes the subject look. In any prison built like a 'panopticon', it only takes a few guards to oversee the prisoners. Standing in the center of a circular building with cells radiating out to its perimeter, the guards can see inside every cell—not at the same time, but potentially so. The inmates know this. They know they are under surveillance. They are more likely, therefore, to 'behave'. Economically speaking, the 'panopticon' is cheap. Politically, it is barely visible. It is also unlikely to result in objections. It generates docility, and if it works properly, there is not likely to be much need for those who guard the prisoners to use overt, coercive power or even threats. The outcome is the systematic ordering and control of people by subtle, largely unseen means. People discipline themselves when they know that they are under surveillance (the 'gaze') and that this is upon them at all times. They internalize the 'disciplining' process. Contemporary advances in technology, together with the requisite technology, are making Lacan's and Foucault's concepts not a last-century post-modernist fantasy but a post-modernist reality today.

How does this pertain to universities? Though universities do not seem like prisons, the concept of self-policing self-surveillance, argues Teti, is relevant regardless. There are certainly no prison guards and no prison cells, but there is still a parallel to the way academic careers take place in what he thinks are highly policed camps. They make it unnecessary for any particular 'agent' to impose order. No department chair, university president, or board of trustees is needed to 'look down' on them since 'disciplines', in their particular departments in particular universities, are connected to all those departments housing the same 'disciplines' elsewhere, 'disciplines' functioning as networks. These run through all universities, connecting all the departments where specific 'disciplines' are practiced. Particular 'disciplines', as represented by their departments, are connected to all those departments that house the same 'disciplines' elsewhere, however, while the disciplinary 'mainstream' is at the heart of these camps. In them, one finds the discipline's 'heroes'. Once someone is a 'hero', there is no way that this status can be removed (even when further analysis of the hero's work shows it to be radically flawed). A camp's hierarchy, moreover, tends to reproduce itself. It also undermines the possibility of cross-disciplinarity. Cross-disciplinarity becomes high-risk, and despite lip service to the need for it, the lip service remains just that. This is because US/IR scholars (and surveys confirm this) see high 'costs' in making any forays beyond a discipline's boundaries. Few 'converts' manage to learn the language of another camp or field or master the knowledge of its rankings regarding publishing houses and journals. It is this, according to Teti, which constitutes the examining 'gaze' concerning academic activity and which 'normalizes' the organization and production of knowledge there. It is this that sets the knowledge standards by which particular 'disciplines' abide. The net effect, argues Teti, is the 'territorialization' of relations between fields and intellectual inertia within any particular field. This accentuates 'hysteresis' (literally, determinism or lack of dynamism) concerning the willingness to follow developments in cognate fields. As academics adapt to the canons—as observed by 'top' journals, publishing houses and funding institutions—they learn to 'publish or perish' where it 'counts'. Eventually, this works to catalyze the differences between ontological, epistemological, methodological, and theoretical stances concerning other fields as well as those fields that have the same name outside the US. The differences grow to the point where the fields become incommensurable. Explicit rules are formulated by which the faculty and graduate students have to abide if they are to remain within the spaces determined by the paradigms or the approaches within which they do their research, their publishing, and their teaching. The most influential scholars exemplify the discipline's best practices as judged by the standards that they themselves articulate. They groom the best students in order to promote and protect the paradigm/approach of their choice. They systematically ignore the emergence of global and regional IR networks, and they are totally impervious to criticism from beyond the shores of the US. The people within a 'discipline' defined in this way hardly notice the rest of IR, much less take it into account. Indeed, why would they? After all, they are the ones who define what IR 'is', what is worth knowing about the subject, and how it should be known.

The key here, or the glue, is the commitment to positivism/neo-positivism (to which Patrick Thaddeus Jackson adds the word 'science'), which in IR plays the most radical 'disciplinary' role (Jackson, 2011, p. 9). 'Science', as deployed in US/IR (and it should not be forgotten that US/IR has become a subfield of political science), has become something of a trump card. Indeed, it is not too much to note that it has now become a 'substitute for God' (Laitin, 1995, p. 189). It certainly privileges highly particular modes of inquiry with the result that labeling a practice non-'science' is to see it as a 'bad thing'. Jackson points out that there is 'no effective way around' the current situation unless the 'whole field abandons any claims to or aspirations of being scientific' (Jackson, 2011). As long as US/IR is ensconced inside political science and shares its premises, this is not likely to happen.

5. IR and R.W. Cox

This paper started with two panels celebrating R.W. Cox at conventions of the International Studies Association in Toronto and New Orleans. Most panelists demonstrated, and celebrated, in their contributions how Cox goes on inspiring their work as scholars. The daunting question remained hanging in the air. How about the work of others, and what is Cox's impact on a broader audience? Why is the same author read in one country much more than in another, much less so in the US than in the UK? Different explanations came to mind. Cox was cited to have said privately: 'Americans do not understand me.' Benjamin Cohen wrote about 'two cultures' at the two sides of the Atlantic (Cohen 2007, 2008). Cox's friend, the late Susan Strange, called him an 'eccentric' and a 'loner'; these characteristics somehow contributing to Cox's position in the field of studies to which he devoted his entire life. Teti's Foucauldian insight shows that it is not just individual academics but their academic disciplines, with their mechanisms of surveillance and ordering, which can play tricks at first difficult to grasp.

This was all very well until now. Things have changed. The world seems dangerously unmanageable in the twenty-first century: unsettled, diffuse, chaotic with all of the traditional methods of statecraft, diplomacy, and even war, feeble. The world of states is crowded with 'non-state actors'—terrorists, global corporations, religious and ethnic tribes, sovereign wealth funds, and nonprofit charities, weapons of mass destruction capable to destroy humanity, to name a few. Multiple crises are breaking out around the interdependent globe. The waves of immigrants and refugees 'within nations and between them' seem to defy not just traditional diplomatic or military methods or accumulated knowledge of IR but how we understand IR. The traditional frames through which we viewed the world are becoming windowless prison cells.

There is a growing chorus—mainly outside IR—and not just of those 'talking post-modern' who see the great instability of the world, and Cox is one of them. They see evidence that there are 'disjunctures', pointing to the emergence of what Foucault called different spaces of knowledge, in what it is 'possible to know'. In any given culture, he says, and at any given moment, there is a common space in the minds of its members that only a few can transcend (Foucault, 1971, pp. xi, xxii–iii, 168). By this, he—and the others thinking along similar lines—means that humanity is in the process of developing a different 'space of knowledge', something very difficult to imagine.

According to Foucault, each 'space of knowledge'—yet another 'frame'—is putting limits on what human beings within that space are able to make of their experiences. Thus, 'in any given culture at any given moment there is always only one episteme that defines the conditions of [the] possibility of all knowledge, whether expressed in a theory or silently invested in . . . [what people do]' (Foucault, 1971, p. xx). In every culture, that is, there are fundamental 'codes'. These govern a culture's 'language, its schemas of perception, its exchanges, its techniques, its values, [and] the hierarchy of its practices' (Foucault, 1971).[4]

Is Cox one whose work transcends his time? Working all alone, largely oblivious to 'mainstream' disciplinary concerns and thus unconstrained by them, did he see the bigger picture, see beyond? Most importantly, was he capable of moving on from any particular frames and not getting stuck in any of them? The 'critical', the term he used in 1981 which then became attached by others to an entire approach/paradigm, is a case in point. 'Critical' in IR has now become a portmanteau term which includes anything that is 'anti-': even feminists, environmentalists, post-colonials, indigenous peoples, and the very poor. Most of them do not follow the Frankfurt School though there is nothing to stop them from doing so. Most of them do not follow Cox, either, though they are free to do that too. 'Critical' is now the cover-concept for many different paradigms/approaches. Indeed, it is used so promiscuously that it is not analytically meaningful anymore. Cox himself sees 'critical' thinking as asking questions about how an identifiable pattern of world affairs came to be, what are the basic assumptions policy-makers make, and how to understand the contingent character of any particular world configuration (Cox, 2010, 2012). What serious scholar looking at the multifaceted world crisis does not agree that these questions must be asked?

Cox thinks in terms of a mosaic of parallel societies as opposed to a hegemonic or universalizing space since it would consist of many worldviews. It would be a plurality of rationalities, multiple world cultures, or 'world orders' (a term Cox likes to use). Akin to what the late Israeli sociologist, Shmuel Eisenstadt, saw as the advent of 'multiple modernities' (2000), which might result—to quote Jackson—in a 'pluralistic science of IR', a science different from IR as known today and with an emphasis on inter-subjective understandings. There has never been any one paradigm/approach, nor three, as we know them today, into which Cox would have fitted. But none of the approaches or paradigms are likely to exist for much longer. Given that IR as a discipline did not exist 100 years ago, it too may not survive, unless it becomes reframed as 'world affairs', a social theory that articulates social equity, civilizational diversity (or plurality), and environmental sustainability (an issue Cox now sees as being highly significant). Cox's historically informed eclecticism is the kind of thinking in the new 'space of knowledge' likely to last. This is why Murphy predicted that Cox would be read in 2050.

Acknowledgements

I would like to thank Ralph Pettman, who worked with me on an earlier version of this paper, and Nicholas Onuf and Shannon Brincat, the editor of this special issue.

Disclosure statement

No potential conflict of interest was reported by the author.

Notes

1. As noted by Leysens (2008), it was very likely that Kubálková and Cruickshank (1986) were first at pointing out that Cox's 1981 article had no reference to the Frankfurt School and then became criticized for pointing this out (Hoffman, 1987). Others separating Cox from other critical theorists were Falk (1997), Wyn Jones (2001), and Mittleman (1998).
2. Approximate figures of US, UK, Australian, and Canadian universities establishments convey the sense of the enormity of the number of the US universities and their IR faculty: 4400 in the US, 319 in the UK, 228 in Canada, and 106 in Australia
3. Unlike outside US, IR has become downgraded into a subfield of political science, alongside a number of other subfields such as American Politics, Comparative Politics, Public Administration, Local Government, and many others. Thus across the US, IR is being housed and taught in departments of political science. http://www.apsanet.org/; http://www.isanet.org/ISA/About-ISA/History. In the US, International Political Economy introduced as a field of study by Susan Strange and R.W. Cox became a subfield of US IR discipline (Cohen, 2007, 2008).
4. In this reading the Renaissance began by treating things that seem to be alike as indeed alike. Matter and human beings—like everything else—were part of it and the laws of the cosmos applied to both. This led to a certain way of thinking about social concerns, which enables positivists to isolate things—such as human beings and national states—and to measure their properties in space and time. Moreover, it did so with such force that permeates Western thinking to this day. Modernist rationalism spawned new human sciences, namely, political science, sociology, psychology, anthropology, and international relations (Onuf, 2013, p. 201)—though Martin

Wight, one of the founders of IR, says that thinking theoretically about IR was initially manifest only in the West. Rightly or wrongly, Wight claims, thinking about international relations was absent in those parts of the world that lacked Western-style political ideals such as the one of "progress" (Buzan & Amitav, 2010, p. 2).

References

Anderson, P. (1976). *Considerations on Western Marxism*. London: New Left Books.

Banks, Michael. (1985). The inter-paradigm debate. In M. Light & A. J. R. Groom (Eds.), *International relations: A handbook of current theory* (pp. 7–26). London: Frances Pinter.

Biersteker, T. J. (2009). The parochialism of hegemony: Challenges for 'American International Relations'. In A. B. Tickner & O. Weaver (Eds.), *International relations scholarship around the world* (Worlding Beyond the West, pp. 308–327). London: Routledge

Brincat, S., Lima, L., & Nunes, J. (Eds.). (2012). *Critical theory in international relations and security studies*. London: Routledge.

Buzan, B., & Amitav, A. (Eds.). (2010). *Non Western international relations theory: Perspectives on and beyond*. Asia: Routledge.

Cohen, B. J. (2007). The transatlantic divide: Why are American and British IPE so different? *Review of International Political Economy, 14*(2), 197–219.

Cohen, B. J. (2008). The transatlantic divide: A rejoinder. *Review of International Political Economy, 15*(1). Retrieved February 2008, from http://www.polsci.ucsb.edu/faculty/cohen/inpress/pdfs/TD_final_word.pdf

Cox, R. W. (1981). Social forces, states and world orders: Beyond international relations theory. *Millennium – Journal of International Studies, 10*(2), 126–155.

Cox, R. W. (2010). Robert Cox on world orders, historical change, and the purpose of theory in international relations; theory talk #37: Robert Cox. Retrieved March 12, from http://www.theory-talks.org/2010/03/theory-talk-37.html

Cox, R. W. (2012). Lecture (video) at York University Oct.

Cox, W. S., & Nossal, K. R. (2009). The 'crimson world': The Anglo core, the post-Imperial non-core, and the hegemony of American IR. In A. B. Tickner & O. Weaver (Eds.), *International relations scholarship around the world* (Worlding Beyond the West, pp. 287–308). London: Routledge

Eisenstadt, S. (2000). Multiple modernities. *Daedalus, 129*(1), 1–29.

Falk, R. (1997). The critical realist tradition and the demystification of interstate power: E.H.Carr, Hedley Bull and Robert W. Cox. In S. Gill & J. H. Mittleman (Eds.), *Innovation and transformation in international studies* (pp. 39–55). Cambridge: Cambridge University Press.

Foucault, M. (1971). *Order of things: An archaeology of the human sciences*. New York, NY: Pantheon.

Goffman, E. (1974). *Frame analysis: An essay on the organization of experience*. Cambridge, MA: Harvard University Press.

Hoffman, M. (1987). Critical theory and the interparadigm debate. *Millennium: Journal of International Studies, 16*(2), 231–250.

Hoffman, M. (2003). Critical voices in a mainstream local: Millennium, the LSE international relations department and the development of international theory. In H. Bauer & E. Brighi (Eds.), *International relations at LSE: A history of 75 years* (pp. 139–173). London: Millennium Publishing Group.

Jackson, P. T. (2011). *The conduct of inquiry in international relations, philosophy of science and its implications for the study of world politics*. New York, NY: Routledge.

Jay, M. (1973). *The dialectical imagination*. Boston, MA: Little, Brown Jackson.

Kubálková, V. (1998). Reconstructing the discipline: Scholars as agents. In V. Kubálková, N. G. Onuf, & P. Kowert (Eds.).

Kubálková, V., & Cruickshank, A. A. (1980). *Marxism-Leninism and theory of international relations*. London: Routledge and Kegan Paul. Re-issued in 2015, Taylor & Francis Group.

Kubálková, V., & Cruickshank, A. A. (1985/1989). *Marxism and international relations*. Oxford, NY: Oxford University Press. Revised edition with two new chapters, Oxford Paperback, Oxford University Press.

Kubálková, V., & Cruickshank, A. A. (1986). The 'New Cold War' in 'critical international relations studies'. *Review of International Studies, 12*(3), 163–185.

Kubálková, V., Onuf, N. G., & Kowert, P. (Eds.). (1998). *International relations in a constructed world*. Armonk, NY: M.E. Sharpe.

Kuhn, T. S. (1962). *The structure of scientific revolutions*. Chicago, IL: Chicago University Press.

Kurki, M., & Colin, W. (2010). International relations and social science. In D. Tim, K. Milja, & S. Smith (Eds.), *International relations theories: Discipline and diversity* (2nd ed., pp. 14–33). Oxford: Oxford University Press.

Laitin, D. D. (1995). Disciplining political science. *The American Political Science Review, 89*(2), 168–173.

Lakoff, G. (2004). *Don't think of an elephant!: Know your values and frame the debate.* White River Junction, VT: Chelsea Green Publishing.

Lakoff, G., & Johnson, M. (1980). *Metaphors we live by.* Chicago, IL: University of Chicago Press.

Leysens, A. (2008). *The critical theory of Robert W. Cox: Fugitive or Guru?* New York, NY: Palgrave Macmillan.

Messari, N., Tickner, A. B., & Ling, L. H. M. (Eds.). (2012). *International Relations theory: Views beyond the west.* London: Routledge.

Mittleman, J. H. (1998). Coxian historicism as an alternative perspective in international studies. *Alternatives, 23*(1), 63–92.

Murphy, C. (2008). Preface in *The critical theory of Robert W. Cox: Fugitive or Guru?* New York, NY: Palgrave Macmillan.

Onuf, N. (1989). *World of our making: Rules and rule in social theory and international relations.* Columbia: University of South Carolina Press. Reissued 2013.

Onuf, N. (1998). Constructivism: A user's manual. In V. Kubalkova, N. G. Onuf, & P. Kowert (Eds.), *International relations in a constructed world* (pp. 58–78). London: M.E. Sharpe.

Onuf, N. (2002). Worlds of our own making: The strange career of constructivism. In D. Puchala (Ed.), *Visions of international relations* (pp. 119–141). Columbia: University of South Carolina Press.

Onuf, N. (2013). *Making sense, making worlds: Constructivism in social theory and international relations.* London: Routledge Taylor and Francis Group.

Onuf, N. (2014a). *Rule and rules in international relations.* Erik Castrén Institute of International Law and Human Rights, University of Helsinki. Retrieved April 24, from http://www.helsinki.fi/eci/Events/Nicholas%20Onuf_Rule%20and%20Rules%20%204-2-14.pdf

Onuf, N. (2014b). *Nicholas Onuf on the evolution of social constructivism, turns in IR, and a discipline of our making.* Retrieved from http://www.e-ir.info/2014/05/09/interview-nicholas-onuf/

Onuf, N. (2015). Theory Talk #70: Nicholas Onuf, Thursday. Retrieved July 2, from http://www.theory-talks.org/2015/07/theory-talk-70.html

Payne, R. (2001). Persuasion, frames and norm construction. *EJIR, 7*(1), 37–61.

Rathbun, B. (2012). Politics and paradigm preferences: The implicit ideology of international relations scholars. *International Studies Quarterly, 56,* 607–622.

Snow, D. A., & Benford, R. D. (1988). Ideology, frame resonance, and participant mobilization. In B. Klandermans, H. Kriesi, & S. Tarrow (Eds.), *International social movement research* (Vol. 1, pp. 197–217). Greenwich, CT: JAI Press.

Sunstein, C. R. (1996). Social norms and social roles. *Columbia Law Review, 96*(4), 903–968.

Teti, A. (2007). Bridging the Gap: International Relations, Middle East and Studies and the disciplinary politics of the Area Studies Controversy. *European Journal of International Relations, 13,* 117–145.

Teti, A. (n.d.). *Divide et impera: Notes on the interdisciplinary divide between IR and Middle East Studies.* Exeter: University of Exeter. Unpublished manuscript.

Tickner, A. B., & Weaver, O. (Eds.). (2009). *International relations scholarship around the world* (Worlding Beyond the West). London: Routledge.

Tversky, A., & Kahneman, D. (1986). The framing of decisions and the psychology of choice. In J. Elster (Ed.), *Rational choice* (pp. 123–141). Oxford: Basil Blackwell.

TRIP. Retrieved from https://trip.wm.edu/reports/2014/rp_2014/index.php

Walt, S. M. (1998). International relations: One world, many theories. *Foreign Policy, 110*(Spring), 29–46.

Weaver, O., & Tickner, A. B. (2009). Introduction: Geocultural epistemologies. In A. B. Tickner & O. Weaver (Eds.), *International relations scholarship around the world* (Worlding Beyond the West, pp. 1–12). London: Routledge.

Wyn Jones, R. (2001). Introduction. In R. Wyn Jones (Ed.), *Critical theory and world politics* (pp. 1–23). Boulder: Lynne Rienner.

Labour in Global Production: Reflections on Coxian Insights in a World of Global Value Chains

NICOLA PHILLIPS

University of Sheffield, UK

ABSTRACT   *This essay reflects on Robert W. Cox's work on global production, labour, and labour governance, and considers how his insights might illuminate the present conjuncture for labour in production. I work with an understanding of that conjuncture as involving the rise to pre-eminence of global production networks (GPNs) and global value chains (GVCs) as the contemporary expression of the ongoing globalization of production. The primary tasks of the essay are twofold: first, to explore the dynamics of labour and power in the GVC-based global economy, with a particular emphasis on labour exploitation; and second, to link these questions to those of the governance of the global economy, focusing on the shift towards transnational private governance as the dominant mode of contemporary governance, and on the evolving strategies of organized labour and the International Labour Organization in that context.*

When his work was most focused on the issue of labour in production in the 1970s, Robert Cox was observing the expansion of the multinational corporation (MNC) as the pivotal phenomenon in the international economy, and the associated consolidation of the hegemony and the economic dominance of the USA. Cox produced a series of reflections on the implications of this globalizing world economy for labour, the increasing global interconnectedness of labour relations, and the challenges for the union movement. He was also writing fascinating accounts of the politics of the pre-eminent international organization governing labour, the International

---

This is an Open Access article distributed under the terms of the Creative Commons Attribution-NonCommercial-NoDerivatives License (http://creativecommons.org/Licenses/by-nc-nd/4.0/), which permits non-commercial re-use, distribution, and reproduction in any medium, provided the original work is properly cited, and is not altered, transformed, or built upon in any way.

Labour Organization (ILO), seeking to locate its evolution within a story about the rise of corporatism in the USA and the 'deeper tendencies' of American hegemony and economic dominance. His insights into both the evolution of labour relations in the early globalization of production, and the political economy of the multilateral governance of labour relations, were unquestionably an inspiration for the future generation of scholarship on labour that has unfolded in the field of international political economy (IPE), although arguably still not come to command the attention that it deserves.

Forty years later, what can we say of the enduring relevance of Cox's work in understanding contemporary global production, labour, and labour governance? I approach my task here as a reflection on how global production has evolved since Cox was first writing about labour in the 1970s, and to bring to that reflection a consideration of the insights that Cox's work might provide in understanding the current conjuncture for labour in production. I advance an understanding of that conjuncture as involving the rise to pre-eminence of global production networks (GPNs) and global value chains (GVCs), as the contemporary expression of the ongoing globalization of production. The dominance of GVCs is such that, I suggest, all analyses of labour in production now need to accommodate an understanding of those structures. The 2013 *World Investment Report*, published by the United Nations Commission on Trade and Development (UNCTAD), estimates that around 80% of global trade now flows through GVCs led by transnational corporations (TNCs) (2013). The ILO estimates that one in five jobs world-wide is linked to GVCs (2015). These are arresting figures, and they add substance to a widely accepted proposition that GVCs have become the foundation of contemporary industrial organization: according to one recent contribution, they have become no less than 'the world economy's backbone and central nervous system' (Cattaneo, Gereffi, & Staritz, 2010, p. 7). In a process of striking convergence, all of the major international organizations now deploy the language and concept of GVCs as the foundation for their respective strategies (Gereffi, 2014), and many national governments have come to frame their development strategies as being about connecting to GVCs, securing integration with them, and achieving 'upgrading' within value chains.

As the structures around which global production and trade are increasingly and predominantly organized, it seems logical to suggest that an understanding of GPNs/GVCs needs to be central to a contemporary analysis and theorization of labour in global production. At the same time, it is undoubtedly the case that the GPN/GVC debates have been slow to incorporate labour in their analysis of global production, tending to treat it largely as a factor of production and to ascribe primary interest to the issue of labour costs determining the locational strategies of firms. Within the GPN/GVC field, calls to afford labour a more central place in the analysis have been heeded, but equally have tended to focus on the question through the prism of outcomes, exploring the consequences for labour standards of particular chain dynamics (Barrientos, Gereffi, & Rossi, 2011). This scholarship is fascinating and important, but, viewed from within the traditions of Cox's work, could fairly be said to fall short of contributing an integral account of labour in global production. In this sense, it becomes attractive to explore how Coxian and critical IPE-based insights in turn could usefully fertilize the GPN/GVC debate.

My task in this short essay is thus to consider how well Cox's work on labour travels in a very different world from the one in which he was writing in the 1970s and, subsequently, what his insights can contribute to our understanding of the contemporary GVC-based economy, and what is the extent of their enduring relevance. Given the richness of his contributions, such a task could open an expansive terrain of themes and questions, theoretical and empirical, linking to hegemony and counter-hegemony, states, multilateralism, international organizations, labour unions, firms, civil society, social marginalization, historical societal transformations, public policy, nationalism and transnationalism, and so on. Given present constraints on space, I will focus my energies in two areas, and organize this essay accordingly: first, exploring the dynamics of labour and power in the contemporary form of global production underpinned by GVCs, with a particular emphasis on labour exploitation; and second, linking these questions to those of the governance of the global economy, focusing on the dismantling of corporatism and the shift towards transnational private governance as the dominant mode of contemporary governance. A short descriptive outline of the contours of the GVC-based global economy is first warranted in order to frame the discussion.

Global Production and the 'GVC World'

The concept of GVC refers to a pattern of production coordinated by TNCs, which is geographically dispersed and in which the various stages and functions of production are fragmented (Gereffi, Humphrey, & Sturgeon, 2005; Milberg & Winkler, 2013). It rests predominantly on the trade of intermediate goods and services, wherein trade is no longer about the international exchange of final goods, but rather about 'trade in tasks' (Grossman & Rossi-Hansberg, 2008). The functional fragmentation of the production process is associated with its geographical fragmentation, as lead firms progressively outsource and/or offshore productive functions, resulting in patterns of specialization structured geographically by global asymmetries in production costs. As such, the trends identified by Frobel, Heinrichs, and Kreye (1980) in their early identification of a new international division of labour, and by Cox in his consideration of the expansion of MNCs and the shift of industrial manufacturing from what was often termed 'north' to 'south' (1976), have crystallized more recently in the consolidation of GVCs as the often staggeringly complex structures through which global production processes now flow. The focus of Cox and others on the power of MNCs—what in the GPN/GVC lexicon tend to be called lead firms—was apposite and relevant to the emerging understanding of economic globalization. Indeed, while the architects of the neoliberal globalization project envisaged a world of free market competition, what has instead emerged has been a 'highly leveraged form of managed trade' in which lead firms control production, not markets or states, and in which the value in the system is captured by the most powerful actors within it.[1] The GPN/GVC explanatory framework, in other words, re-conceptualizes global market engagement 'from a passive process involving the reaction of independent actors to market signals, as in international trade theories, to a set of industrial transformations constructed within system-wide dynamics of coordination and control by economic and non-economic actors' (Neilson, Pritchard, & Yeung, 2014, p. 1).

The concept of a 'value' chain is useful precisely because it goes beyond a description simply of how and where things are produced, to the question of how and where value is created, and where, how, and by whom or what it is captured. It is in this sense a key to understanding the continued evolution of power relations in the global economy, which is the core interest that has sustained Cox's work for half a century. The GVC-based pattern of production is driven, at root, by corporate strategies to create and harness global asymmetries of market power in the interests of generating and capturing profit. Creating these market asymmetries rests on securing a geographically differentiated structure in which firms at the top occupy oligopolistic positions, but competitive markets prevail among lower tier suppliers, as a foundational element of firms' cost-cutting strategies to help maintain cost mark-ups (Milberg & Winkler, 2013, pp. 123–124). Structures of this nature establish the mechanisms through which lead firms can transmit commercial pressures on conditions of price and supply along the length of value chains, maximize the process of value capture by varying these conditions at any point in time, and offload risk onto supplier firms, who in turn pass on the burdens to small producers and workers (Anner, Bair, & Blasi, 2013; Barrientos, 2013; Nathan & Kalpana, 2007). Through these pressures, 'entry barriers' are erected to safeguard the positions of the dominant firms, such that many suppliers, producers, and workers in the lower tiers are denied or squeezed out of advantageous participation in value chains (Gibbon & Ponte, 2005; Kaplinsky, 2005). The competitive struggle by firms within GVCs is waged to a significant extent on the terrain of factor costs, most notably labour input costs, but also rests on an array of institutional conditions (Milberg & Winkler, 2013, p. 103) ranging from market conditions, such as those relating to labour and technology, to the social conditions which in turn shape labour market conditions, and the political, policy, and regulatory environment that prevails in a given setting.

In the 1970s and the 1980s, Cox and others were observing the geographical shift of industrial manufacturing from 'north' to 'south', where the lead firms in the process were generally US and 'northern' corporations. In Cox's work, this was linked to a conceptualization of the global hegemony of the USA, in the process of being consolidated by the globalization of production, the rise of the MNC, and the pre-configuring of what later have become known as GVCs (1976). In the associated transformations of capitalism in the advanced economies to what he identified as a model of 'post-industrial' society and later 'evolved capitalism' (Cox, 1973–1974, 1999), the process was understood as one in which value chains came to connect production located in the low-cost economies of the 'south' to the consumer markets of the 'north'. Yet this empirical description—production in the south, end markets in the north—no longer holds. Trends in global industrial organization have been characterized by a shift in end markets and an increasing regionalization of value chains, such that dominant lead firms are no longer primarily (or not only) North American or European (Cattaneo et al., 2010; Gereffi, 2014; Kaplinsky & Farooki, 2010; Yeung, 2014). Likewise, the largest consumer markets are already—and increasingly will be—in China, India, possibly Africa, and elsewhere, fuelled by the explosive growth of the middle classes in those regions (Guarin & Knorringa, 2014).

This has significant implications for the governance of global production, including, as we will see shortly, the governance of labour and labour standards. It also has important consequences for the question that exercised Cox so much in his work on these issues, namely, the understanding of the transnational class structure that was and is still being ushered in by the forces of economic globalization and the consolidation of GVCs.

Labour and Labour Exploitation in Global Production

In a contribution in 1976, Cox identified this new social configuration as being threefold, dominated by a 'transnational managerial class' at its apex, running through a large class of 'established labour' in what at the time was beginning to be understood as the primary labour market, to the group of 'social marginals' who are either excluded from industrial production or integrated into the secondary labour market on the basis of markedly precarious forms of employment (Cox, 1976, pp. 351–352). In a later contribution in 1999, Cox modified his typology slightly, maintaining the core workforce of the highly skilled at the top, and envisaging them as flanked by a larger number of 'precarious workers', their condition resulting from fluctuating levels of demand for products, their lesser skill levels, and the premium placed on flexibility in the use of labour by firms. The third group is then identified as those excluded from international production (Cox, 1999, p. 9). While it might fairly be said that there was an implicit geographical categorization in the typology that Cox elaborated in the former article, by 1999 there was a much more explicit recognition of the transnational character of this social structure, where the excluded were to be found in both richer and poorer countries, capturing an important dimension of the social transformations brought about by the consolidation of GVCs.

Many of the forces pushing in these directions that Cox identified in the 1970s have continued and intensified as the globalization of production has advanced towards the consolidation of a GVC world. In many different types of GVCs, producers, suppliers, and employers seek to manage the aggressive competitive pressures transmitted by lead firms predominantly through the mechanisms of labour costs. What matters in shaping outcomes for working conditions is the manner in which multinational firms organize their production activities, and outsourcing emerges as the critical factor in that respect, representing the primary means by which lead firms in GVCs lower costs and increase the share of income taking the form of profit (Milberg & Winkler, 2013, pp. 14–16; Mosley, 2011; Phillips, 2013). For supplier firms too, outsourcing (particularly to smaller and household enterprises and to home workers) represents the key means of cutting costs and achieving flexibility in response to variable market conditions and the commercial pressures imposed by lead firms, as well as the primary mechanism by which they escape the pressures of social compliance and the reach of regulation and monitoring. A direct consequence is the continued expansion of precarious, insecure, and exploitative work as the hallmark of many contemporary GVCs, performed by a highly vulnerable and disenfranchised workforce, of which informal, migrant, and contract workers have come to be the primary constituents.

In this sense, Cox's insights into the 'far-reaching transformation' wrought by the expansion of the MNC (1976, p. 345) remain strikingly apposite, as do his insights into labour exploitation as, as Jeffrey Harrod later framed it, 'normal processes of power within production' (1987, p. 4; Davies & Ryner, 2006). Yet developments in three arenas offer a slightly different contemporary slant on how these processes are realized, and the conclusions that Cox draws for the challenges of labour governance. First, perhaps more in his earlier than his later work, Cox draws a distinction between workers employed directly by MNCs, and those who could be said to operate outside the MNC sector (1976, pp. 361, 363). The sense, implicit or explicit, was that the group of 'social marginals' fell into the latter category. At the time this may have been a fair characterization of the landscape, but this distinction has latterly been challenged by the evolution of GVC structures centred around the continued expansion of TNCs. The sheer scale and complexity of GVCs mean that now vastly more workers are integrated into what Cox was referring to as the MNC sector, even while very few of them can be said to be directly employed by the lead firm itself. Much of the inside/outside dichotomy suggests a parallel formal/informal dichotomy, wherein the MNC sector is deemed to represent the formal economy, and the rest the universe of informal workers and social marginals that are deemed to lie outside it. Instead, we now have a situation in which the MNC sector—which we could redefine as the structures of GVCs—incorporates vast swathes of the formal and informal economies to the extent that the distinction breaks down as a useful descriptor of the landscape of labour relations. The mechanisms of outsourcing mean that GVCs incorporate huge numbers of 'invisible' firms, entrepreneurs, and workers in the informal economy, even though the firms or enterprises in question may be subcontractors to registered firms. The implications for labour are that these firms and entrepreneurs generally lack any incentives to boost their profile of 'social legitimacy' in the context of cut-throat price competition (Knorringa, 2014), and the pressure on wages and working conditions is relentless.

In this sense, a proportion of the world's 'social marginals' identified by Cox may well exist in conditions of exclusion from employment in global production, but a far greater proportion is now integrated into it, not least as this type of employment has become the cornerstone of a development orthodoxy around poverty reduction (Milanovic, 2003). In relation to global production, the condition of most interest in the contemporary period could therefore be said to be not (or not only) exclusion, but rather the swelling ranks of workers integrated into GVCs on highly precarious and adverse terms. The concept of adverse incorporation has been developed to explain why, contrary to the orthodox view of employment as the key to poverty reduction, many integrated workers remain in conditions of chronic poverty (Hickey & du Toit, 2007; Phillips, 2011, 2013; Ponte, 2008; Wood, 2003). In 2012, the World Bank's poverty figures demonstrated the first aggregate decline in levels of extreme poverty in the developing world since it started monitoring in 1981, but also reported that the numbers living between the $1.25 per day extreme poverty line and the $2 per day poverty line had almost doubled between 1981 and 2008, to reach 1.18 billion people (2012). This is, essentially, the population of the global working poor—a category that orthodox economic and development policy thinking has long struggled to accommodate, and the arena of poverty that is shaped by the processes of adverse incorporation. The question of marginality in this sense has never been more pronounced or pressing, but marginality stems as much from the terms of inclusion as from a condition of exclusion.

The second issue is that, at the same time, a significantly decreasing number of workers are employed directly by TNCs or their upper-tier suppliers in the value chain. Outsourcing involves not only the functional disaggregation of the production process, but also the outsourcing of the functions and responsibilities associated with employment. Indeed, many workers in the lower tiers of GVCs have no knowledge of the fact that their labour is integrated into structures coordinated by TNCs, and have no knowledge of whether they are performing productive functions for a global branded retailer. More to the point, the outsourcing of employment functions facilitates a rupture in the traditional employment relationship. This implies both a significant dismantling of employers' obligations to workers and a considerable challenge for an organized labour movement, where the target of action is even less clear-cut than it was around the time that Cox was analysing the fragmented and partial responses of the union movement to the expansion of the MNC.

Add into this mix a further dimension of the outsourcing of employment, namely, the increasing outsourcing of labour recruitment to private labour contractors in GVCs, which represents 'a logical extension of the commercial dynamic through which global outsourcing is implemented by global buyers' (Barrientos, 2013, p. 1065). Labour contractors range from being legitimate and registered, to informal, unregulated, and essentially invisible, through to illicit and criminal with strong overlaps into trafficking networks. Workers are increasingly often employed directly by the labour contractor rather than the firm or enterprise which uses their labour, such that a further rupture is enabled in terms of labour rights and entitlements in GVCs. Even where lead firms take corporate social responsibility (CSR) seriously and impose social compliance requirements on suppliers, the outsourcing of contracting to third parties, and the consequent absence of a documented employment relationship, has enabled the latter frequently to evade responsibility for implementing these requirements and to disclaim the use of workers at any particular time. Workers recruited by contractors are usually bound to provide their labour to a particular employer, and, perhaps most significantly, the arrangement usually involves the payment of advance wages which are then owed as debts by the worker, enhancing already high levels of vulnerability and exploitation.

The third arena in which we can identify an acceleration of change from the time that Cox was most actively writing about these issues relates to the question of migration in constituting the global labour force. Cox was acutely conscious both of the dynamics of migration and the associated political challenges for national governments and unions in Western Europe. He noted how the importation of labour into Western European economies from Mediterranean countries was acting to '[transform] a geographical periphery into an internal social periphery' (Cox, 1976, p. 348)—a characterization of huge enduring relevance. What has perhaps changed, though, is that this is no longer, as Cox saw it, a phenomenon which distinguished Europe from the USA, where the preference was for offshoring productive functions rather than importing labour. In the USA, while different in nature from the European context, the dynamics of immigration have yielded the same reconfigurations of labour relations and the political landscape around labour issues. Moreover, the question of the migrant labour force has become properly global, no longer centred on Europe or on a 'south–north' movement from poorer to richer countries, but now in large proportion 'south–south' (United Nations Department of Economic and Social Affairs, 2013), strongly associated with the reorganization of global production and the consolidation of global and regional value chains. The key phenomenon in China and elsewhere is also that of massive internal movements of people, which have become as pivotal as cross-border movements in shaping the dynamics of labour in production. Global migration today takes the more traditional forms of movements into industrial manufacturing, such as flows of both internal and international migrants to the industrial zones of southern China, or less traditional forms associated with Cox's shift towards post-industrial society and the demand for service-providing labour fuelling post-industrial lifestyles. Again, this is not necessarily rooted in the 'evolved' capitalist economies of North America and Europe, but is also represented by, as an example, the significant flows of domestic workers within East and South-east Asia.

Globally, migration policy is frequently an integral element of neoliberal political strategies for the 're-commodification' of labour—a reassertion of the connection between the welfare of citizens and the price of their labour on an imagined free market, pursued through the rolling back of the strong welfare state, the deregulation of employment, and the transformation of citizenship and welfare arrangements (Schierup & Castles, 2011). The dynamics of precarious employment which Cox illuminated so forcefully are magnified through the exploitation of a global migrant labour force which lacks the power to engage in political action around wages and conditions, and whose condition of exclusion from rights and entitlements associated with citizenship or residency, as well as their condition of economic need, reinforce their vulnerability to the forms of 'adverse incorporation' and/or exclusion we explored earlier. This is not to claim that these positions are static or universal: there is an appreciable fluidity between the various levels of labour hierarchies, and migration remains a key to socio-economic advancement. But it also remains the case that processes of accumulation in the global economy and within GVCs both produce and reproduce the conditions in which the vulnerability and 'disposability' of the marginal workforce—and in specific ways for the migrant labour force—are for large parts of that workforce chronic and durable in nature. Global migration, in other words, is central to the forms of 'durable inequality' (Tilly, 1998) which remain a core feature of labour relations in contemporary global production.

Governance and Labour

Since the time that Cox was writing about the ILO and the organized labour movement, the political foundations of the global economy have quite dramatically been re-drawn. Driven by ideological imperatives on the part of states and the power of economic actors, the major shift has been the dismantling of corporatism, which Cox identified compellingly as the historical basis for the tripartite ideology of the ILO and the strategies of the organized union movement (1977). In its place, gradually, we have seen the emergence of a form of global economic governance that rests on the pre-eminence of private governance, wherein corporations are the primary agents of governance and the primary vehicle is that of voluntary corporate self-regulation. In part this mode of governance has been driven forwards by the rise of GVCs and the primacy of brand name loyalty in contemporary retailing, which have shifted the power to negotiate terms with companies decisively to consumers, away from governments and even further away from workers (Esbenshade, 2012). Yet there is a wider politics to this process, wherein, driven by neoliberal ideological imperatives and responsiveness to interests, powerful states have been the active agents of the shift to private governance, pursued through strategies of systematic deregulation and market facilitation, and an active role in shaping the evolution of the CSR agenda (Mayer & Phillips, 2015).

CSR represents a movement with a long history of multiple conceptual and political trajectories, reaching back to early notions of social responsibility in the late nineteenth and early twentieth centuries. Its contemporary connections with the ongoing process of neoliberalization stand at odds with some of its more socially progressive and anti-imperialist incarnations in previous eras. In the 1970s, these were represented by the early activism of such bodies as the World Council of Churches in the anti-Apartheid effort or non-governmental organizations (NGOs) involved in the boycott of the Swiss firm Nestlé, and the pivotal agenda of the United Nations in its creation of a Commission on Transnational Corporations and a Centre on Transnational Corporations (UNCTC). The reaction against this current in CSR thinking was driven by US corporations, the US government, and organizations such as the World Business Council for Sustainable Development, such that, at the 1992 UN Earth Summit in Rio de Janeiro, the final nail was driven into the coffin of UN proposals for a mandatory international code of conduct on transnational corporate activity (Sadler & Lloyd, 2009; Sagafi-Nejad, 2008).[2]

The drive towards greater regulation was thus replaced with a drive towards corporate self-regulation as the basis for a newly pre-eminent mode of private governance. The political argument against binding regulation had apparently been accepted fully—either from conviction or from pragmatism—by the time of the negotiation of the UN Guiding Principles on Business and Human Rights in the mid-2000s (see Ruggie, 2013). By moving in this context from a strategy of defensiveness to proactive leadership in relation to CSR, firms themselves were effective in both neutralizing opposition and capturing the power to shape the CSR agenda—a hegemonic strategy, in Gramscian terms, which has proved highly effective in insulating firms from oppositional activism, and ensuring that many issues relating to global injustice have remained essentially off-limits (Utting, 2008, p. 966). Together with an ongoing corporatization of civil society, a compelling argument presents itself that CSR has, in its dominant neoliberal incarnation, been emptied of much of its radical transformative potential (Shamir, 2004).

Unfortunately, space prevents a discussion of the limits of this dominant mode of transnational private governance in securing progressive outcomes for labour, the environment, or development. What is of most relevance for present purposes is its implications for two of the issues that have absorbed so much of Cox's interest, namely, the strategies of the organized labour movement and the strategies of the ILO. Let us take each in turn, necessarily briefly, as the conclusion to this essay.

Cox observed in 1976 that 'labor today has managed to generate only a confused, partial and lopsided response to the multinational corporation' (1976, p. 344). It would be fair to argue that much of that confusion and lopsidedness persists. Many of the limits to effective action also remain at least partially unresolved, including the difficulty the union movement has had in developing strategies that reach beyond the core of organized workers to the many millions working in the informal economy and in the darkest corners of the global economy, where the barriers to organization are in any case extreme. The arduous process through which many unions have passed in order to try to accommodate immigration and migration in their strategies remains tricky terrain, not least in view of the pronounced politics of anti-immigration which have come to prevail in many parts of the world. Equally, as Jill Esbenshade observes, the model of private regulation rarely empowers workers: workers have no formal role in this model of regulation, and considerable risk still attaches to their activism, both in terms of punitive retaliation from employers and managers, and in the consequences to the firm's business of exposure of labour rights violations (2012, p. 552). Yet, in general terms, we have seen some considerable movement in organized labour strategies in the context of a global economy dominated by TNCs, and interestingly it has not been in the direction that Cox perceived as the most likely in his horizon-scanning exercise in the 1970s.

Cox posed the challenge of a world dominated by MNCs for organized labour as a choice between a 'transnational' strategy of trying to negotiate directly with MNCs wherever they locate, on the one hand, and, on the other, a more 'national' strategy in which the unions would try to use their political leverage in their own nations to regulate and control the MNCs and protect jobs. Cox argued that it would only be in a minority of cases that the transnational strategy would be pursued, and that instead the focus would be on trying to influence national government policies to mitigate the impact on jobs of the globalization of production. Yet, from our vantage point in a world dominated by GVCs 40 years later, the transnational strategy has in fact become a more dominant mode of action than Cox expected, and the national strategy much less robust. A 'tentative transformation of the international union movement' (O'Brien, 2000) has been associated with attempts more robustly to pursue a transnational strategy of engaging directly with both international organizations and TNCs, developing transnational campaigning strategies and building 'transnational labour solidarity' (Bieler, 2014; Bieler, Lindberg, & Sauerborn, 2010; Seidman, 2008).

Robert O'Brien explains the roots of this shift as lying in the expulsion of unions from the corridors of power in key states, and in developing interactions with social movements and civil society organizations—facets of the 'reversal of corporatism' that Cox observed as resulting from the world crisis of capitalism of the 1970s (1999, p. 8). Neoliberal globalization is seen both to challenge the power of organized workers and to offer an opportunity for the transcending of national concerns and a dilution of 'working class nationalism' (O'Brien, 2000, p. 538), the latter being an important foundation of the national strategy that Cox identified as the most likely future focus for organized labour. Finally, O'Brien argues that we have seen a shift away from the support for US capitalism on which organized labour was premised around the time Cox was writing, and which he described as the underpinning of tripartism in the ILO (2000, p. 538). Instead, the union movement has become both more oppositional in character in relation to neoliberalism, but also more transnational in its strategic orientation. The traditional corporatist focus on the state, in other words, seems decisively to have been superseded.

One of the most interesting features of this engagement with TNCs, beyond the usual focus on collective bargaining, has been an attempt to work on the terrain of their private governance strategies. We might term this an attempt to leverage private governance mechanisms, particularly in relation to the incorporation of a focus on corporate codes of conduct into unions' and labour activists' strategies (O'Brien, 2000). It is unquestionably the case that private regulation and corporate codes of conduct have not been effective as mechanisms for dealing with labour exploitation in the global economy (Esbenshade, 2012; Locke, 2013; Taylor, 2011; Vogel, 2010;

Wells, 2007). Nevertheless, the interventions of organized labour, in conjunction with consumer groups, have added a layer of impetus and accountability to corporate self-regulatory initiatives which has contributed to ramping up pressure on TNCs to address egregious violations of labour rights. The interesting point is that this approximates something of the scenario Cox sketched when he described the possible transnational strategy for organized labour, not only in the emergence of such a strategy, but also in the marginal status within it of national states. Inasmuch as 'those who have cultivated this [transnational] vision have tended to regard the state as an obsolescent structure' (Cox, 1976, p. 354), many of the patterns of transnational engagement by unions have been targeted not at the state in their traditional corporatist mode of action, but at TNCs themselves, social movements of various descriptions, and international organizations.

It is nevertheless unquestionably the case that this shift towards a transnational mode of action remains complicated, patchy, and still limited. In this sense, Cox's assessment of the problems and obstacles to an effective strategy of this nature remains highly apposite (1976). He noted the myriad challenges relating to transnational organizing, in which he observed that MNCs held a significant advantage given their operational structures, and that unions were at a distinct disadvantage, particularly given the highly variable strength and capacities of union movements across the world. He noted that it would take a fragmentation of national labour organization in order to allow particular segments to pursue transnational integration. Equally, he saw the potential of the transnational strategy to be limited by the fact that it could only be realized by increasing the distance of the organizing bodies from the workers they purported to represent, wondering 'what guarantees [there would be] that a multinational union could hold all its members in different countries to a centrally negotiated agreement' (Cox, 1976, p. 354). Even while the path for a transnational strategy has been partially cleared since the time that Cox was writing, all of these challenges remain in place. As such, the corporatist conditions facilitating a national strategy have been eroded, and a national strategy is manifestly anachronistic in a world of GVCs and the challenges that such a world presents for labour. Yet, at the same time, a transnational strategy remains to be fully articulated, and transnational labour agency remains nascent rather than developed.

A transnational strategy for organized labour has thus become more dominant than Cox expected, but his assessment of some of the challenges to its articulation remains pertinent. At the same time, it should be observed that his scenarios for the national and transnational strategies reflected a preoccupation with labour unions as the key agents of labour activism. The combined consolidation of a GVC-based global economy and the rise of transnational civil society and social movements has instead put in place a labour politics that reaches more widely than its traditional trade union base. We noted earlier that, in the GVC context, the key relationship for firms has shifted to lie with consumers, not governments or workers—a shift that has run alongside the well-documented decline in union membership and the concerted maintenance or erection of barriers to unionization and collective bargaining across the global economy. In this context, the concept of transnational labour agency has expanded to go significantly beyond trade unions, and encompasses a wide variety of NGOs, activist organizations, alliances of informal workers, women's organizations, landless and peasant movements, and so on. There is an argument that this process acts to reinforce the distance that Cox observed, and thought to be problematic, between the organizations purporting to represent labour and the workers themselves. Alternatively, in some of its manifestations, and notwithstanding the potential for generating fragmentation and incoherence, it could be interpreted as a key means by which the transnational strategy now demanded of labour in a GVC economy has become more feasible than Cox might have envisaged in the 1970s.

Similarly, when we turn to the ILO in a consideration of the implications for governance of the GVC-dominated economy, we see a significant change from the time that Cox was writing about the connections between hegemony and multilateralism. This should not surprise us, given what we have already said about the dismantling of the corporatist state as the basis on which the tripartite ideology of the ILO was built. Inasmuch as the structure of power that Cox observed 'prevented the ILO from confronting effectively the real social issues of employment-creation, land reform, marginality, and poverty in general' (1977, p. 385), we might expect to see the reconfiguration of this power structure creating some change in the ILO's effectiveness as an international organization charged with addressing some of these issues.

To an important extent, this has been the case. The Decent Work platform is the ILO's flagship programme, which increasingly has been taken up by other international organizations in their attempt to say something about matters of work and employment in broader development agendas. Yet this is not a story of complete change: the 'hegemonic order' in the ILO can still be considered to be strongly influenced by the 'corporate/state-centric version of corporatism' which has always permeated its operations, and the Decent Work agenda to represent a 'skilful effort at mediating escalating tensions inside the ILO between global capital, backed by a majority of industrialized states, and an increasingly vocal group of member states, trade unions, women's organizations and other NGOs concerned with improving the lives of marginalized workers' (Vosko, 2002, p. 20).

The effort has not been entirely successful, and indeed many of the limits placed by US power on the functioning of the ILO remain intact. The tripartite structure remains a potential advantage for governance, but the agenda is continually defined by the politics of mediating those tripartite interests, and particularly the powerful corporate/state nexus. To this extent, the ILO struggles still to achieve critical force in much of its agenda, where the big questions of capitalism and globalization remain politically sensitive issues which are often skirted, and the question of the power relations in global production which produce systemic exploitation is left often untouched (Lerche, 2007; Phillips & Mieres, 2014; Rogaly, 2008; Selwyn, 2013). The ILO has come latterly to embrace the GVC concept along with other international organizations, in its case using the language of global supply chains. At the time of writing, the contours of its new agenda are not yet known. Given the nature of the ILO and its institutional architecture, one might expect a more progressive concern with the implications of GVCs for labour standards than that of many other international organizations which have adopted this framework of thinking, but still working within an assumption that improvements in labour conditions can be achieved by moving onto the terrain of a mode of governance informed by perceptions of the potential of TNCs to act as the primary agents of this improvement.

Conclusion

Together, these new dynamics of governance reveal starkly the tension that ran as a leitmotif through Cox's work: the challenges of governance in a transnational world, where the primary instruments of governance remain national. The ILO's provisions, as with the strategies of many other actors in the system, rest on national practice for their implementation and enforcement, and there still exists nothing akin to 'an international jurisdiction administered by an international authority to which MNCs could be made accountable' (Cox, 1976, p. 359). The influential development of the United Nations Global Compact and later its Guiding Principles on Business and Human Rights offer studies in one of the alternative forms of global governance that have emerged, based on the principle of voluntary self-regulation on the part of powerful firms. Yet they are two of many disparate initiatives and a huge number of similarly disparate organizations populating the increasingly crowded terrain of CSR and the governance of the GVC-based economy, stretching from left to right of the political spectrum and the approach to CSR, across the spectrum of modes of engagement with TNCs, and across the terrain of labour agency. At the same time, the level of engagement by TNCs with a CSR agenda remains extremely limited: in 2007, for example, the UNCTAD reported that the UN Global Compact, as the world's largest CSR initiative, had 3600 participating companies, while the universe of TNCs was calculated to stand at 78,000 TNCs and 780,000 affiliates (UNCTAD, 2007; Utting, 2010).

The world of CSR and labour governance is thus fragmented and incoherent, the articulation of transnational labour agency is similarly complicated, and meaningful challenges to the entrenchment of private regulation as the dominant model for delivering corporate accountability are few and far between. In such a context, we continue to lack clear alternative forms of transnational governance capable of mediating the power relations embedded in a GVC world and meeting the challenges of progressive governance. It becomes compelling to conclude that we remain, just as Cox worried, a long way from dealing with the potential for social conflict that is inherent in the increasingly consolidated transnational social structure of inequality.

Acknowledgements

I am grateful to two anonymous reviewers for the journal and the editors of this special issue, whose generous engagement with the paper and very constructive suggestions for improvement were most valuable. They will notice how I have drawn readily on their recommendations in the text. Needless to say, they bear no responsibility for the final product.

Disclosure Statement

No potential conflict of interest was reported by the authors.

Notes

1. I owe this formulation to a conversation with Frederick W. Mayer, and thank him for allowing me to use his phrase here.
2. I am indebted to one of the anonymous reviewers of my paper for her/his suggestions of some of the detail in this passage.

References

Anner, M., Bair, J., & Blasi, J. (2013). Towards joint liability in global supply chains: Addressing the root causes of labor violations in international subcontracting networks. *Comparative Labor Law and Policy Journal*, *35*(1), 1–43.

Barrientos, S. (2013). 'Labour chains': Analysing the role of labour contractors in global production networks. *Journal of Development Studies*, *49*(8), 1058–1071.

Barrientos, S., Gereffi, G., & Rossi, A. (2011). Economic and social upgrading in global production networks: A new paradigm for a changing world. *International Labour Review*, *150*(3–4), 319–340.

Bieler, A. (2014). Transnational labour solidarity in (the) crisis. *Global Labour Journal*, *5*(2), 114–133.

Bieler, A., Lindberg, I., & Sauerborn, W. (2010). After thirty years of deadlock: Labour's possible strategies in the new global order. *Globalizations*, *7*(1–2), 247–260.

Cattaneo, O., Gereffi, G., & Staritz, C. (2010). Global value chains in a post-crisis world: Resilience, consolidation and shifting end markets. In O. Cattaneo, G. Gereffi, & C. Staritz (Eds.), *Global value chains in a post-crisis world: A development perspective* (pp. 3–20). Washington, DC: World Bank.

Cox, R. W. (1973–1974). Labour relations and public policy: Perspectives on the future. *The Dalhousie Law Journal*, *1*(1), 82–104.

Cox, R. W. (1976). Labor and the multinationals. *Foreign Affairs*, *54*, 345–365.

Cox, R. W. (1977). Labor and hegemony. *International Organization*, *31*(3), 385–424.

Cox, R. W. (1999). Civil society at the turn of the millennium. *Review of International Studies*, *25*(1), 3–28.

Davies, M., & Ryner, M. (Eds.). (2006). *Poverty and the production of world politics: Unprotected workers in the global political economy*. Basingstoke: Palgrave.

Esbenshade, J. (2012). A review of private regulation: Codes and monitoring in the apparel industry. *Sociology Compass*, *6*(7), 541–556.

Frobel, F., Heinrichs, J., & Kreye, O. (1980). *The new international division of labor: Structural unemployment in industrialized countries and industrialization in developing countries*. Cambridge: Cambridge University Press.

Gereffi, G. (2014). Global value chains in a post-Washington consensus world. *Review of International Political Economy*, *21*(1), 9–37.

Gereffi, G., Humphrey, J., & Sturgeon, T. (2005). The governance of global value chains. *Review of International Political Economy*, *12*(1), 78–104.

Gibbon, P., & Ponte, S. (2005). *Trading down: Africa, value chains and the global economy*. Philadelphia, PA: Temple University Press.

Grossman, G., & Rossi-Hansberg, E. (2008). Trading tasks: A simple theory of offshoring. *American Economic Review*, *98*(5), 1978–1997.

Guarin, A., & Knorringa, P. (2014). 'New' middle class consumers in rising powers: Responsible consumption and private standards. *Oxford Development Studies*, *42*(2), 151–171.

Harrod, J. (1987). *Power, production and the unprotected worker*. New York: Columbia University Press.

Hickey, S., & du Toit, A. (2007). *Adverse incorporation, social exclusion and chronic poverty* (Chronic Poverty Research Centre Working Papers series, no. 81). University of Manchester.

International Labour Organization. (2015). *World employment social outlook: The changing nature of jobs*. Geneva: Author.

Kaplinsky, R. (2005). *Globalization, poverty and inequality*. Cambridge: Polity.

Kaplinsky, R., & Farooki, M. (2010). Global value chains, the crisis, and the shift of markets from North to South. In O. Cattaneo, G. Gereffi, & C. Staritz (Eds.), *Global value chains in a postcrisis world: A development perspective* (pp. 125–153). Washington, DC: World Bank.

Knorringa, P. (2014). Private governance and social legitimacy in production. In A. Payne, & N. Phillips (Eds.), *The handbook of the international political economy of governance* (pp. 261–278). Cheltenham: Edward Elgar.

Lerche, J. (2007). A global alliance against forced labour? Unfree labour, neo-liberal globalization and the international labour organization. *Journal of Agrarian Change*, *7*(4), 425–452.

Locke, R. (2013). *The promise and limits of private power: Promoting labor standards in a global economy*. Cambridge: Cambridge University Press.

Mayer, F. W., & Phillips, N. (2015, June 15–17). *Outsourcing governance: The politics of a 'global value chain world'*. Presented at the annual conference of the British International Studies Association, London, UK.

Milanovic, B. (2003). The two faces of globalization: Against globalization as we know it. *World Development*, *31*(4), 667–683.

Milberg, W., & Winkler, D. (2013). *Outsourcing economics: Global value chains in capitalist development*. Cambridge: Cambridge University Press.

Mosley, L. (2011). *Labor rights and multinational production*. New York, NY: Cambridge University Press.

Nathan, D., & Kalpana, V. (2007). *Issues in the analysis of global value chains and their impact on employment and incomes in India*. Geneva: International Institute for Labour Studies.

Neilson, J., Pritchard, B., & Yeung, H. W.-C. (2014). Global value chains and global production networks in the changing international political economy. *Review of International Political Economy*, *21*(1), 1–8.

O'Brien, R. (2000). Workers and world order: The tentative transformation of the international union movement. *Review of International Studies*, *26*(4), 533–555.

Phillips, N. (2011). Informality, global production networks and the dynamics of 'adverse incorporation'. *Global Networks*, *11*(3), 380–397.

Phillips, N. (2013). Unfree labour and adverse incorporation in the global economy: Comparative perspectives from Brazil and India. *Economy and Society*, *42*(2), 171–196.

Phillips, N., & Mieres, F. (2014). The governance of forced labour in the global economy. *Globalizations*. doi:10.1080/14747731.2014.932507: 1–17

Ponte, S. (2008). *Developing a 'vertical' dimension to chronic poverty research: Some lessons from global value chain analysis* (Chronic Poverty Research Centre Working Paper series, no. 111). University of Manchester.

Rogaly, B. (2008). Migrant workers in the ILO's global alliance against forced labour report: A critical appraisal. *Third World Quarterly*, *29*(7), 1431–1447.

Ruggie, J. G. (2013). *Just business: Multinational corporations and human rights*. New York, NY: W.W. Norton.

Sadler, D., & Lloyd, S. (2009). Neo-liberalising corporate social responsibility: A political economy of corporate citizenship. *Geoforum*, *40*, 613–622.

Sagafi-Nejad, T. (2008). *The UN and transnational corporations: From code of conduct to global compact*. Bloomington: Indiana University Press.

Schierup, C.-U., & Castles, S. (2011). Migration, minorities and welfare states. In N. Phillips (Ed.), *Migration in the global political economy* (pp. 15–40). Boulder, CO: Lynne Rienner.

Seidman, G. W. (2008). Transnational labour campaigns: Can the logic of the market be turned against itself? *Development and Change*, *39*(6), 991–1003.

Selwyn, B. (2013). Social upgrading and labour in global production networks: A critique and an alternative conception. *Competition and Change*, *17*(1), 75–90.

Shamir, R. (2004). The de-radicalization of corporate social responsibility. *Critical Sociology*, *30*(3), 669–689.

Taylor, M. (2011). Race you to the bottom ... and back again? The uneven development of corporate codes of conduct. *New Political Economy*, *16*(4), 445–462.

Tilly, C. (1998). *Durable inequality*. Berkeley: University of California Press.

United Nations Conference on Trade and Development. (2007). *Trade and development report 2007: Regional cooperation for development*. Geneva: Author.

United Nations Conference on Trade and Development. (2013). *World investment report 2013: Global value chains: Investment and trade for development*. Geneva: Author.

United Nations Department of Economic and Social Affairs. (2013). *International migration 2013: Migrants by origin and destination* (Population Facts no 2013/3). Retrieved from http://esa.un.org/unmigration/documents/PF_South-South_migration_2013.pdf

Utting, P. (2008). The struggle for corporate accountability. *Development and Change*, *39*(6), 959–975.

Utting, P. (2010). CSR and policy incoherence. In K. MacDonald, & S. Marshall (Eds.), *Fair trade, corporate accountability and beyond: Experiments in globalizing justice* (pp. 169–186). Farnham: Ashgate.

Vogel, D. (2010). The private regulation of global corporate conduct: Achievements and limitations. *Business and Society*, *49*(1), 68–87.

Vosko, L. F. (2002). 'Decent work': The shifting role of the ILO and the struggle for global social justice. *Global Social Policy*, *2*(1), 19–46.

Wells, D. (2007). Too weak for the job: Corporate codes of conduct, non-governmental organizations and the regulation of international labour standards. *Global Social Policy*, *7*(1), 51–74.

Wood, G. (2003). Staying secure, staying poor: The 'Faustian bargain'. *World Development*, *31*(3), 455–471.

World Bank. (2012, 29 February). *An update to the World Bank's estimates of consumption poverty in the developing world* (briefing note). Retrieved from http://siteresources.worldbank.org/INTPOVCALNET/Resources/Global_Poverty_Update_2012_02-29-12.pdf

Yeung, H. W.-C. (2014). Governing the market in a globalizing era: Developmental states, global production networks and inter-firm dynamics in East Asia. *Review of International Political Economy*, *21*(1), 70–101.

Global Governance and Universities: The Power of Ideas and Knowledge

JAMES H. MITTELMAN

American University, Washington, DC, USA

ABSTRACT   *So as to advance understanding of global governance, one can pick up on Robert Cox's critical formulations. Best known for his insights on the interplay of material conditions, institutions, and ideas, he later developed his framework by giving greater weight to the ideational dimensions of intersubjectivity. Yet it is usually deployed with regard to the former phase of his work while the latter phase goes unnoticed or is neglected. Cox's more recent conceptualization may serve as a springboard for thinking afresh about global knowledge production and dissemination. His approach can be stretched by exploring specific spheres of authority at particular sites. Focusing on universities as one of them, this article suggests a research itinerary that maps clusters of agents and guides empirical digging into how these structures operate. A complex of actors and processes, detailed in the findings, is redesigning global knowledge governance. The connective tissue in a cross-continental web of educational restructuring is gradually spreading. Cox's theorization may be fruitfully expanded to analyze this dynamic.*

Ever since the term global governance entered scholarly and popular discourses in the early 1990s, it has been promiscuously used. Often said to refer to formal and informal rules, regulations, and narratives, this loose language and field of study have become a catchall that warrants refinement. In this regard, Robert Cox's critical reflections are fruitful for characterizing the particular contents of global governance.

Picking up on the implications of his thinking, it is well to avoid locking into an overly confining definition or a fixed set of parameters for dynamic forces. That said, in the domain of knowledge production and diffusion across borders, global governance depicts the management, execution, and negotiation of different understandings of actions.

Scholars inspired by Cox's theoretical innovations rarely note that his academic work falls into three periods: initially, a historical and institutional focus (as in Cox & Jacobson, 1974); next, interactions among material conditions, institutions, and ideas (Cox, 1981, 1987); and, in the 2000s, deepening diagnosis of evolving consciousness (Cox, 2002, 2007, 2013).[1] This is not to suggest that Cox redesigned his approach, but rather to call attention to underappreciated ways in which he turned to multiple intersubjectivities.

Latterly, Cox emphasized that civilizations produce collective understandings, an entrenched 'common sense' in the Gramscian usage of fragmented values and beliefs that conform to a given social order. This awareness is based on the knowledge that is created and contested. The researcher's task is to enter into these mentalities so as to analyze a plurality of civilizations and their links to the global political economy.

Following from this point, I will peer into intersubjectivity, that is, shared meanings about the material world. The purpose of this article is to stretch Cox's conceptualization and offer a conceptual framework for further research. In what follows, I want to reach beyond Cox's earlier formulations for which he won critical laurels: namely, the distinction between problem-solving and critical theory, the coupling of social relations of production and forms of state, and propositions on the theory of hegemony (Cox, 1981, 1987). I will ground the analysis by examining a single sphere of global governance: knowledge production and dissemination, which is inextricably linked to universities.[2] The rationale is threefold: Cox's insights about intersubjectivity merit critical elaboration; knowledge as education is a crucial facet of the neoliberal world order; and International Relations (IR) scholars have seldom pursued in depth the study of universities as agents and structures in world order.[3]

Universities are important to world order because they transmit civilizational values from one generation to the next and sometimes undermine them. They serve as repositories of cumulative knowledge and incubators of new knowledge. The connection between universities and global governance is patent. Institutions of higher learning's mission is to foster inquiring minds, some entering the world of politics and as professional staff who can bring intellectual heft to governance units.

Although Cox began to explore the ways in which knowledge is constituted and how global governance agencies seek to universalize predominant ideas, he neither systemically scrutinized their production and the diffusion of civilizational values nor sought to account for IR's relative disinterest in this topic: relative because the cognate fields of international sociology, philosophy, and international education have carried out far more substantial research on this aspect of globalization (see Kennedy, 2015).

Inasmuch as higher education institutions are principal sites for knowledge generation, I hold that universities are intertwined with global governance. My core argument is that a loose meshwork of actors and processes is transforming this configuration. By meshwork, I mean a complex in which networks form and may reconfigure universities as knowledge structures.

A theme consistent with, rather than developed in, Cox's writing, a knowledge structure in Strange's manner (1988, pp. 117–119) is a system of power relations: who and what discovers, stores, and communicates knowledge. On this point, Cox and Strange's inquiries intersect. Intellectual mavericks with critical casts of mind, these two iconoclasts pioneered new directions in International Political Economy (IPE). For her part, Strange was particularly critical of US hegemony in our field of studies; and for his, Cox trained a critical eye on the hegemony of positivism in IR theory emanating largely from the US academy.

Just as Cox and Strange stressed ideological hegemony, it is important to underline that the story of the global university is linked to the American experience, which, in the eighteenth and nineteenth centuries, drew heavily on Cardinal Newman's Oxford in England and the Humboldtian tradition in Germany and then developed its own features. In the 2000s, the language of Wall Street concerning performance measures and impact factors, as well as the provenance of university rankings, evident in national commercial publications such as *U.S. News & World Report*, have gone global. The American model is inscribed in the narrative of a 'world-class university'. This discourse is used for the diffusion of the standards of US elite universities.

Distinctive national and regional trajectories should not however be discounted as mere attempts to replicate the USA. It would be a serious mistake to devalue diverse forms of intellectual production and transmission in varied contexts. These are not epiphenomenal even if some of them have come to parody the US system.

Still, with globalizing forces, knowledge structures are veering toward inter-elite consensus on global standards. And to explore consensus formation, let us first investigate segments of the whole. We can thereby unravel knowledge governance. Ten groups of agents seem most salient, though other catalysts could be identified as well. They propel change and fuel its processes. These actors are ensconced in the following institutions and milieus: (1) governments, (2) consultancies, (3) global governance agencies, (4) regional organizations, (5) accrediting bodies, (6) ranking boards, (7) higher education philanthropies, (8) think tanks, (9) technology communities, and (10) universities themselves. An objective in the following discussion is to offer what Clifford Geertz calls 'thick description', showing how these groups constitute important components of a globalizing knowledge structure.

Governments and Consultants

Education policies are anchored at the local and national levels. This is a fulcrum of restructuring universities. State funding or defunding spurs the repurposing of universities, even though the impetus is increasingly blended with extra-national factors. Finances are one among many mechanisms in this dynamic. State capacity, the reach of government departments and ministries, and the role of intermediary state agencies—buffers such as higher education commissions—are vital elements in regulatory reform.

States' basic principles in the area of university reform are reflected in their bilateral and multilateral education strategies. While governments bestow different names on their units, ministries of education and of international cooperation and development help formulate and execute strategies for university reform. To take one example, the U.S. Agency for International Development (USAID) *Education* Strategy 2011–2015 gives priority to supporting good governance, effective management, and learning outcomes (2011, p. 12). According to USAID, globalization demands a more highly skilled and competitive workforce; developing countries must therefore expand access to higher education, improve its quality and relevance, achieve greater equity, and construct a research agenda. USAID maintains that it can achieve its goals by partnering with the private sector and leveraging with other donors. In practice, this involves aligning more fully with the World Bank, because the Bank is a pacemaker in university restructuring and commands substantial resources. In tandem, these organizations coordinate awarding government contracts to private firms and building US-style universities in conflict-ridden areas such as Iraq and Afghanistan.

Partnerships between government agencies and the World Bank are highly influential. With its sizable contingent of researchers and means of dissemination through training programs and advisory services, the Bank transmits values and ideas. It identifies best practices, which are for specific purposes and which accord with the lenders' missions. Operationally, they favor problem-solving knowledge, not curiosity-driven, critical knowledge.

It may be argued that these agencies elicit local and national ownership of education projects. But many managers who run universities along with faculty throughout the world share the academic values of the transnational elites in governance agencies and are incentivized to embrace their missions. Typically, the intellectual formation of these elites in different countries bears commonality, albeit with secondary differences. Based on a knowledge structure, their training includes study abroad, exchange programs, grants, awards, and opportunities to publish with prestigious presses or in highly touted journals. The reward system embodies best practices defined in reference to market mechanisms.

Global Governance and Regionalism

Donors have sought to harmonize their higher education programs and the priorities of various stakeholders. The World Bank Group and the World Trade Organization (WTO) have been predominant trendsetters in restructuring higher education.

For the WTO, education is a service sector subject to trade liberalization.[4] The WTO administers the General Agreement on Trade in Services (GATS), which reduces trade barriers to cross-border flows of knowledge. GATS is a mechanism for facilitating greater mobility of professional educators and students. It may lead to long-term migration as well. Known as 'brain circulation', brain drain for some is brain gain for others. The regulatory framework for importing and exporting education services is of great importance in respect to licensing, accreditation, and quality assurance. It can augment national capacity but also undermine national efforts to strengthen higher education. For universities in some parts of the world, the substantial benefits offered by foreign suppliers are attractive. But others worry about the risks of Western hegemony and the dilution of local culture, particularly indigenous knowledge. The WTO approach can undercut the public good aspects of higher education. If the business of higher education institutions is to nurture democratic values, critical thinking, and unfettered academic freedom, the vagaries of the market inscribed in standards for international trade are not intrinsically linked to the university's basic purposes.

For its part, the World Bank rethought its higher education strategy in the late 1990s and early 2000s. When it designated itself as a 'Knowledge Bank', it came to regard higher education as a key factor in the global knowledge economy (World Bank, 1998). By this narrative, the Bank emphasized poverty alleviation and employed revised scripts: namely, local and national ownership, good governance, macroeconomic growth, and social sustainability

In higher education, the World Bank's impact largely comes from framing, developing, and brokering knowledge—soft governance traceable to technical assistance, policy advice (usually on a fee-for-service basis), training programs, and a website replete with vast datasets. In addition, the Bank's own publications on global knowledge and education appear as a spate of books, book chapters, working papers, and scholarly articles in peer-reviewed journals. According to the Bank, in one thematic area alone—the economics of education—its publications in journals are more numerous than those of 14 leading universities, with only Harvard approaching the same total (World Bank, 2011, p. 53).

In its 'Strategy 2020' agenda, the World Bank Group advocates education 'system reform'. This expansive concept takes in 'the full range of learning opportunities available in a country' in the public and private sectors for all stakeholders from teachers and administrators to students and their families, plus ways to address barriers outside the system as it has hitherto been delimited (World Bank, 2011, p. 5). To mobilize knowledge so broadly, the Bank asserts: 'It is not enough to simply get the technical details right; reforms must also navigate the challenges of a nation's political economy' (World Bank, 2011, p. 72). Concretely, this means learning from best practices, which are presented in handbooks on how to build 'world-class universities' atop their competitors (Altbach & Salmi, 2011; Materu, 2007, 2010; Salmi, 2009, 2010).[5] These practices are inventoried as checklists, negotiated, and stipulated in loan agreements.[6]

In the educational sphere, global governance is interwoven with regionalism. An exemplar is the European Commission's Bologna reforms, a regulatory framework that channels globalization to member countries and attempts to mitigate its unwanted features, including what some observers deem the undue influence of US norms at the expense of local values (Hartmann, 2008, pp. 207–220). The Bologna Process is a driving force for European standards, a regional strategy wherein universities internationalize and seek to harmonize their programs.

The impetus for the Bologna policies was the desire to make European higher education more competitive globally, promote citizens' mobility, and enhance students' employability (Bologna Declaration of 19 June 1999, 1999). Yet Bologna encountered student protests in countries such as Austria and Germany in reaction to a top-down structure said to be lacking democratic participation by stakeholders. At higher education institutions in Europe, there is concern that the Bologna Process is strengthening central management and spurring excessive market reforms, such the introduction of tuition fees and the reorganization of departments and universities, putting public education at risk (Bieber, 2011a, 2011b; Reichert, 2010, pp. 14, 16).

Common elements linking 'Bolognaization' and extraregional initiatives are the moves to identify best practices and harmonize quality assurance. Recognizing and periodically reviewing quality is the province of accrediting bodies and ranking systems. They set standards for programs and universities, and perform regulatory roles.

Accreditors and Rankers

Accreditation is meant to protect the rights of students and serve the public interest. This mechanism was developed to improve the caliber of higher education.

But accreditation is controversial because it normalizes certain practices and not others. Accreditors say that they act with integrity, provide value by ensuring that higher learning institutions furnish the public with accurate information about their programs and services, and foster accountability to an external organization. But their critics claim that they impose a hard-and-fast formula on institutions that require an accreditation committee's imprimatur. From their standpoint, accreditors are seen as powerful gatekeepers that safeguard their role as regulatory authorities so as to favor entrenched interests in fields like legal education, medicine, and engineering.

And do these regulatory authorities understand standards as the use of metrics and rubrics, which define performance, or as a democratic process? The integrity of this process is particularly worrisome in view of growing concerns about foreign degree mills (selling phony 'parchment' degrees), accreditation mills (selling fraudulent accreditations), and unscrupulous for-profit providers (lacking recognition by national agencies) (Knight, 2009, p. 118).

Similarly, unresolved issues pertain to global ranking systems. Like accrediting agencies, they are regulatory instruments that give universities marks. Yet the ratings are more directly a byproduct and driver of educational globalization.[7]

Prior to grappling with the broad import of global rankings, one should be mindful of their genesis. In the opening decades of the twenty-first century, the Shanghai Jiao Tong University Institute of Higher Education Academic Ranking of World Universities (ARWU) and the *Times Higher Education Supplement*'s/Quacquarelli Symonds (QS) World University Rankings (the THES) became staples of higher education in many parts of the world. In our conversation in Shanghai, Nian Cai Liu, director of the Center for World-Class Universities and dean of the Graduate School of Education at Shanghai Jiao Tong University, told me that in the late 1990s, China's political leaders prompted educators to prop up several 'world-class universities'. Liu and his colleagues then launched the ARWU rankings in order to better position their university relative to the standing of competing institutions (2013). According to him, the rankers are professors of education at Shanghai Jiao who have developed the ARWU system as a facet of their research and without external funding from government or private enterprise (Liu, 2013).

But the rankers cannot measure and compare performance in terms of the extent to which universities are cultivating character, intellectual curiosity, and love of learning. There is no way that such complexities of higher education institutions' performance on these mission-oriented issues can be accurately depicted by ratings numbers. It would seem, too, that it is a matter of self-interest for any university, including Shanghai Jiao Tong, to rank itself against its competitors. This brings us to the high stakes in the ratings race and who is sanctioned to serve as scorekeepers.

The potential rewards or losses from ranking systems are evident in both their tangible and intangible impact. University managers employ them in updating mission statements, fundraising, allocating resources, and offering incentives—bundles of carrots and sticks. Rankings also guide students and their families when they decide where to apply for admission. Eighty-five percent of international students indicate that global rankings and reputation are key factors in their choices, and one-third say that they are the most important consideration.[8]

In addition, ranking systems are linked to the social composition of a student body in countries such as Mongolia, Qatar, and Kazakhstan, where government sponsorship and scholarships for study abroad are restricted to students who gain entry to the top 100 global universities (Hazelkorn, 2011, p. 162).[9] Indonesia's Presidential Scholarships are tenable only at the world's 50 pre-eminently ranked universities. Rankings are pivotal for other linkages, too: Brazilian universities collaborate only with the foremost 500 universities in global rankings; Singapore, with the first 100; and the Netherlands and Denmark's immigration laws favor international students with degrees from the world's most prestigiously ranked universities (Guttenplan, 2013; Hazelkorn, 2011). Moreover, the governments of China, Germany, Indonesia, Japan, Malaysia, South Korea, Russia, and Taiwan have pledged to boost at least one of their universities into the upper 100 rank; and Nigeria has promised to catapult two to the front 200 (Fischer, 2013, p. A25; Hazelkorn, 2011, p. 162).

To realize these goals, higher education managers empanel committees or hire more administrators to design a strategy to climb the ladder to the super league of elite institutions. Their tasks are to prepare documents, issue reports, and strive to upgrade web presence. Additionally, some heads of universities receive bonuses if their institution moves up significantly in the rankings. Conversely, when a university drops in the rankings, its leader can suffer the consequences. Hence, in 2013, Sidney Ribeau, president of Howard University, abruptly announced his retirement after Howard fell sharply in a major national ranking (Anderson, 2013; Bidwell, 2013).

In brief, ranking exercises are important tools for managing and marketing universities. The global rankings contribute to the denationalization of standards. By identifying Harvard,

Cambridge, MIT, Caltech, or another elite university as the gold standard, these global systems are ordering and decontextualizing knowledge governance. The peril of emulating policies that conform to world rankings standards lies in a group mindset: a globalized prototype that shapes universities' purposes.

While the experts who produce the numerical systems are prepared to take criticism and improve their methodologies, they firmly believe that a university's value can be counted and do not doubt whether it is inherently uncountable. But can one really compare universities' results in different historical and cultural contexts, which, after all, present their own challenges? For example, why should the performance of South Africa's postapartheid universities, which face the formidable challenges of deracializing their faculty and student body, be rated relative to the accomplishments of Oxford or Yale? And do global rankings crowd out initiatives that do not fit the metrics of research output and reputation—say, clinical training by a law school for work in impoverished areas or for eroding gender hierarchies?

Issues of domination and subordination hardly show up on global ranking systems' measures, such as Internet surveys of universities' reputations, and in their descriptive statistics. Figuratively, rankings put higher education institutions on par with other commercial services—restaurants, cars, and hotels; they assign a number of stars to universities. Clearly, there are winners and losers in the global rankings race. The top finisher gets the gold medal, the high standard that other contestants strive to achieve. All competitors want to be in the premier league of 'world-class universities'.

There is limited mobility in the race for the upper echelon of the global scorecards. Most of the same elite universities appear in this tier year in and year out. Moreover, global league tables peg just the world's top research universities, not other higher education institutions. The main global rankings provide reliable data for about 700–1,000 universities of around 17,000 universities worldwide (Rauhvargers, 2011, p. 65). By rewarding or penalizing them on the basis of their categories and criteria, the ranking agencies are power brokers. They invite consent for and participation in repurposing universities. They extend the norms of competition. And ranking pressures induce conformism by bandwagoning best practices and punishing nonconformity. Ultimately, a numerical value cannot be placed on a society's priceless cultural institutions—libraries, museums, and universities.

Higher Education Philanthropy and Think Tanks

In their support for these institutions, international philanthropy expends large sums on higher education reform. As donors, private foundations dole out funds in line with their interests and priorities, including models of best practices of knowledge production and transmission. In the main, these contributions complement the foreign policies of the government in the home country where the philanthropists are chartered, as in the USA during the Cold War, and share the same basic values. At other times, they will diverge somewhat from official policy on specific issues such as human rights (Spero, 2010, p. 5).

Built on the vast fortunes of nineteenth and early twentieth century magnates such as Andrew Carnegie, John D. Rockefeller, and Henry Ford, US corporate philanthropy is sizable compared to that of other countries. The endowment assets of the largest 100 US family foundations by giving, though not total assets, exceed the total for the UK and the rest of Europe (Pharoah, 2008, p. 11).

In Europe and Japan, where state intervention in the economy has more scope than in the USA, private philanthropies like the Nokia and Toyota foundations, also rooted in corporate wealth, have made grants and scholarships available as well. In the global South, especially in emerging economies, newer foundations are building constituencies around education reform. As in the global North, they are relieving the state of some of its responsibilities and privatizing the public sphere (Wallis, 2013). A diverse group operating in different legal and policy environments, global institutional funders are attracted to market-based approaches to issues like mobility, benchmarks, measurable outcomes, completion of degrees, and productivity.

On the question of the undertakings of foundations and their worldview, Joan Spero, a former president of the Doris Duke Charitable Foundation, maintains that 'foundations are political actors pursuing foreign policies and playing an important role in the new global world' (2010, p. vii). She adds: 'Many old and new foundations are working together across national boundaries on global issues . . . .' (p. 37).

Criticism of corporate grant-makers influence centers on their nexus with the state. Some staff members have been moving back and forth between foundation and government jobs, with increased interplay of the two (Parry, Field, & Supiano, 2013, p. A22). Although one would not expect complete concurrence between them, increased collaboration of private philanthropies and the state is apparent. It is alleged that higher education projects sponsored by large philanthropists are skewed by the affinity of government and great wealth (Parry et al., 2013, p. A21).

Both the older and newer foundations target advocacy research. They provide prescriptive grants and, as said, try to shape public policy. The power of the purse lies in the ability to forge consensus. It is achieved by drawing together sundry organizations that do not necessarily concur with one another on higher education reform, and offering incentives for concerting their interests and rewards for carrying out the provisions of a common platform.

Like universities, several think tanks depend on corporate philanthropy and produce knowledge. Think tank pundits seek to influence policy on near-term problems and gain access to policy-makers. This is not to underestimate that think tanks are of different orientations on the right, center, and left of the spectrum. But in certain respects, they are alike. Their donors can color the research agenda. This is a matter of defining problems, posing the research questions that hired researchers are paid to answer. Corporate donations from companies like Bank of America, Citigroup, and Goldman Sachs, as well as backing by foreign governments, may lead to biased results by research groups, only some of which issue disclosures (Lipton, 2013). In addition, tanks of varied persuasions churn out enormous amounts of papers and postings. They produce rapid, functional knowledge.

Wherever think tanks are in play, their work is rarely subject to peer review. They largely produce in-house publications that do not clear blind reviews. Krugman (2005), a Nobel Prize-winning economist at the Graduate Center of the City University of New York and a *New York Times* columnist, put it less delicately, characterizing the world of think tanks as 'a sort of parallel intellectual universe, a world of "scholars" whose careers are based on toeing an ideological line, rather than on doing research that stands up to scrutiny by their peers'. Nonetheless, streams of advocacy reports and other opinion pieces issued by these organizations ripple through the world via media outlets and 'online exposure' with copious blogging. Modern technology thereby magnifies the power of knowledge.

Technology and University Communities

The influx of technology into universities can have cascading effects on research and teaching. Its uses may oblige universities to rethink their purposes.

In this vein, entrepreneurial professor-technologists, such as Cousera's founders Daphane Koller and Andrew Ng, hold that Massive Open Online Courses (MOOCs) can reconfigure learning, cut the work force, and contain costs. Irrespective of geographical constraints, students download lectures by distinguished professors at highly rated universities while their own instructors handle face-to-face communication. As indicated, it is also said that the global learning platforms are a means of democratizing higher education, furnishing opportunities for students who cannot pay for expensive institutions. They are seen as a way to overcome barriers to distributing global knowledge.

Technology critics, however, contend that MOOCs are a business model of higher education, impeding diverse viewpoints by teaching the same course at far-flung universities. Remembered as a great supporter of technological innovation on campuses, Charles Vest, a former MIT president who pioneered his university's OpenCourseWare project, commented on the promise of MOOCs in 2013. He remarked that while they reach a large audience, the *quality* of interactions among students and with their professors remains crucial. In our discussion shortly before his passing, Vest (2013) added: 'I had a nightmare that students across the world watch one big lecture.' Added to this, MOOCs skeptics hold that third-party online providers are contributing to dismantling departments and privatizing public universities. By offering courses and assessment of prior learning, alternative private providers are unbundling major aspects of higher education. The residential university, where students and faculty informally exchange views, often outside the classroom, and where cross-pollination among disciplines can flourish, is in jeopardy or already declining. Students who find that attendance and residency on a campus is too expensive or inconvenient can opt for courses that feature online chat sessions with instructors.

There are at least three reasons why intellectuals comply with this shift to increasingly entrepreneurial milieus. One explanation for consent is socialization: the training wherein personnel learn the disciplinary conventions of academic culture, including its regulations for rank order of many types (tenure, promotion, performance reviews). Professors used to grading are accustomed to marks, and most of them strive for high ones according to established criteria. Rankers spotlight the route and show them standards for excellence. Second, employees are reluctant to bite the hand that feeds them. And a growing proportion of instructors are working off the tenure track. Without job security, they are vulnerable to personnel actions. Third, playing by the rules offers the promise of research funding and forms of recognition. So, too, riding globalizing processes can provide additional tangible rewards like opportunities for travel, and administrators create incentives to compete for these privileges. When individuals are susceptible to competitive, globalizing market forces, coercion can take the form of penalties for nonconformity, including job loss or higher teaching loads at institutions that fare poorly in rating systems and contests for external revenue.

Modes of Conduct

In the absence of a single locus of educational reform, I have identified a plurality of actors and processes. These forces are diffuse. But they come together around meeting challenges of globalization and neoliberal reforms. The range of actors shares common reference points: broader scope for internationalization of the university, a more utilitarian approach to research, greater professionalization of degree programs, and an emphasis on science and technology. Time and again, specific instruments of reform include best practices, new forms of assessment, measurable learning outcomes, and quality assurance.

True, as Goodman (2011), president and CEO of the Institute of International Education, observed, '[i]nternational education is not lurching in any direction'. But even if the lurch is not down a single path, it would be remiss to fail to note that this early stage of educational globalization is marked by a growing intersubjectivity. Across borders, transnational elites are propagating discourses that reflect sameness. Amorphous catchphrases like 'training for global leadership' and 'pursuing excellence' are without substance unless this antiseptic wording is made specific. Some of the affinity among elites is an insipid consensus whose lure comes from constant and authoritative repetition of keywords to the point that educators hardly notice them and imbibe a way of thinking. Exercising influence in higher learning is thus not a matter of straightforwardly prescribing the content of courses. The latter would likely heighten contestation and infringe academic freedom.

While creating consensus on higher education reform is not superintended by any one knowledge group, a confluence of forces may be discerned at three junctions: working sessions of international nongovernmental associations, major convocations that advance higher education reform, and backstage conversations on how important participants in this process can strengthen linkages and build up American-style support services.

At points of articulation, large forums bring together knowledge communities from different countries. Emblematic of these gatherings are conferences of the European Universities Association, the All-Africa summit aimed at reaching a consensus for revitalizing higher education on the continent, and the annual World Innovation Summit for Education (WISE). The latter is supported by the Qatar Foundation and held annually in Doha. Akin to the World Economic Forum, which convenes leaders of the global economy to brainstorm in Davos, Switzerland, each year, WISE is designed to be the Davos of education—a conclave of ministers of education, heads of universities, foundation officers, professors, and student representatives. It gives prizes for best practices, promotes models for sustainable and scalable ventures, and finances projects.

At WISE and elsewhere, key players hold consultative meetings on higher education reform. The World Bank invites groups of US private foundations to Washington, DC, for closed-door sessions. The agenda is about process in higher education reform; the goal, to earmark common interests and possible avenues of collaboration.[10] The Bank provides funds and its imprimatur for facilitating some of the nongovernmental initiatives and caucuses mentioned above. This cross-fertilization establishes genial arenas where consensus can be forged. Just as US universities are expanding their programs and campuses across the world, so the American model of student services has spread. Many countries have introduced a US-kind of career services, mental health counseling, and leadership training. The International Association of Student Affairs and Services, launched in 2010, steps up this trend; it now includes around 600 members from over 50 countries (Lipka, 2012, pp. A1, A12, A14, A16, A17). Historical and cultural differences are of course central considerations. Nevertheless, a premise underlying student development philosophy is that the university should extend its reach in intellectual formation to the extracurriculum and be more directly involved in personal development.

The subtext in these moves is about realignments of regulation and self-regulation. They can span all the way to mentalities in the sense of basic outlook and orientation, as well as permeate the private lives of members of the academy. In activities such as career services and mental health counseling, education reform instills disciplinary power in daily existence.

So far, the bevy of actors and processes delimited above is weakly ordered. The institutions and organizations not only cooperate in certain instances but also compete with one another for resources and prestige. In terms of process, the monitoring of higher education reform is irregular, replete with tensions about scope, prerogative, and funding among national and international, public and private, authorities.

At this stage, the connective tissue in a web of cross-continental planning of educational reform is not yet substantially established but gradually spreading. To the extent that it is realized, syncing is unevenly prepared. Notwithstanding strategic planning at individual universities and organizations, transformations in higher education are occurring without a master plan. The strategic dimension pertains to accommodating globalizing pressures and local trends.

Conclusion

To round up my main points: Best known for his mid-career work on the interplay of material conditions, institutions, and ideas, Cox later developed his framework by giving greater weight to the ideational dimensions of intersubjectivity. Yet it is usually deployed in IPE with regard to the former phase of his thinking while the latter phase goes unnoticed or is neglected. The more recent conceptualization connects to other scholars, such as Strange and heterodox theorists concerned as they are with the role of ideas in history and politics. It can also serve as a springboard for thinking afresh about global governance and have transformative effects. It invites further reflections on the processes and mechanisms of global knowledge production and dissemination.

Cox's approach to global governance can be pushed by examining specific spheres of authority at particular sites. Focusing on universities as one of them, I have suggested a research itinerary that maps clusters of agents and guides empirical digging into how these structures operate. Hence, just as Cox decided to attach more importance to the power of ideas and knowledge, other scholars can profitably home in on intersubjectivity at a global level by explaining the ways that epistemic consensus is established and maintained by a lattice of actors and structures.

While Coxian historicism provides an open-ended theorization challenging the hegemony of mainstream IR theory in the academic establishment, much remains to be done in advancing this kind of critical scholarship and for identifying strategic moments. In the contemporary period, the countervailing pattern is still more potential than actual, though not ephemeral. To fortify it, the task of a community of thinkers—organic intellectuals—is to reformulate ideas and etch possibilities for a new common sense. In the sphere of knowledge governance, intellectuals and activists' roles are to articulate cogent critiques and express humane aspirations, an urgent undertaking for those who seek a global transformation.

Acknowledgements

Some of the material that follows is derived from James H. Mittelman, *Universities and international relations: The repurposing of higher education* (forthcoming). Nicholas Smith and Jan Westö provided stellar research assistance. And thanks to Shannon Brincat and *Globalizations*' anonymous reviewers for their helpful comments on an earlier draft of this paper.

Disclosure Statement

No potential conflict of interest was reported by the author.

Funding

I am grateful to American University and the Helsinki Collegium for Advanced Studies for supporting this work. It links to a collaborative project on 'Policy Instruments and Global Governance: Concepts and Numbers,' funded by the Academy of Finland.

Notes

1. I have engaged Cox's contributions from the early and mid-stages of his academic career in Mittelman (1997, 1998). Cox (2013) is memoir, offering a critical retrospective and prospective look at world order.
2. The discussion of sphere of global governance is informed by Rosenau's notion of 'sphere of authority' (2003, pp. 293–314).
3. Haas's work on epistemic communities (inter alia, 1992) provided a promising point of departure.
4. The passages below on the WTO draw on Knight (2003).
5. I have gleaned information from discussions with staff members at the Bank: especially Materu (2010), lead education specialist, World Bank, and Salmi (2010), tertiary education coordinator, World Bank.
6. For example, a 'Summary Checklist' appears in Salmi (2009, pp. 10–11).
7. Some passages below echo Mittelman (2013).
8. According to research cited in Fischer (2013, p. A25).
9. Salmi and Saroyan (2007), as cited in Hazelkorn (2011, p. 162).
10. Author telephone discussion with New York-based foundation program officer, 3 January 2011; author discussion with New York foundation officer, Kampala, Uganda, 21 May 2013.

References

Altbach, P. G., & Salmi, J. (Eds.) (2011). *The road to academic excellence: The making of world-class research universities*. Washington, DC: World Bank.

Anderson, N. (2013, October 1). Howard University president retires. *Washington Post*.

Bidwell, A. (2013, October 13). Campus life: Presidents in peril. *U.S. News & World Report*.

Bieber, T. (2011a, November 10). *Transatlantic convergence in higher education? Comparing the influence of the Bologna Process on Germany and the U.S.* Presentation at the American Institute for Contemporary German Studies, Washington, DC.

Bieber, T. (2011b, December 19). *Building a bridge over the Atlantic? The impact of the Bologna Process on German and U.S. Higher Education*. Retrieved from http://www.aicgs.org/publication/building-a-bridge-over-the-atlantic-the-impact-of-the-bologna-process-on-german-and-u-s-higher-education/

Bologna Declaration of 19 June 1999 (1999). *Joint declaration of the European ministers of higher education*. Retrieved from www.ehea.info/Uploads/Declarations/Bologna_Declaration1.pdf

Cox, R. W. (1981). Social forces, states and world order: Beyond international relations theory. *Millennium, 10*(2), 126–155.

Cox, R. W. (1987) *Production, power and world order: Social forces in the making of history*. New York, NY: Columbia University Press.

Cox, R. W. (2002) *The political economy of a plural world: Critical reflections on power, morals and civilization* (With Schechter, M.G.). London: Routledge.

Cox, R. W. (2007) 'The international' in evolution. *Millennium: Journal of International Studies, 35*(3), 513–527.

Cox, R. W. (2013) *Universal foreigner: The individual and the world*. Singapore: World Scientific Publishing.

Cox, R. W., & Jacobson, H. K. (1973). *The anatomy of influence: Decision making in international organization*. New Haven, CT: Yale University Press.

Fischer, K. (2013). American Universities yawn at global rankings. *Chronicle of Higher Education, 60*(5). Retrieved from http://chronicle.com/article/American-Universities-Yawn-at/141947/

Goodman, A. E. (2011, February 10). *Discussion with Mittelman*. Washington, DC.

Guttenplan, D. D. (2013, April 14). Vying for a spot on the world's A list, *New York Times*.

Haas, P. M. (1992). Epistemic communities and international policy coordination. *International Organization, 46*(1), 1–35.

Hartmann, E. (2008). Bologna goes global: A new imperialism in the making? *Globalization, Societies and Education, 6*(3), 207–220.

Hazelkorn, E. (2011). *Rankings and the reshaping of higher education: The battle for world-class excellence*. Houndmills: Palgrave Macmillan.

Kennedy, M.D. (2015). *Globalizing knowledge: Intellectuals, universities, and publics in transformation*. Stanford, CA: Stanford University Press.

Knight, J. (2003). Trade in higher education services: The implications of GATS. *Kagisano, 3*, 5–37.

Knight, J. (2009). New developments and unintended consequences: Whither thou goest, internationalization? In R. Bhandari & S. Laughlin (Eds.), *Higher education on the move: New developments in global mobility* (pp. 113–125). New York, NY: Institute of International Education.

Krugman, P. (2005, August 5). Design for confusion. *New York Times*.

Lipka, S. (2012). Campuses engage students, U.S.-style. *Chronicle of Higher Education, 58*(28). Retrieved from http://chronicle.com/article/Universities-Around-the-World/131128/?key=S2xycwQ8Y3YdbXtrZzgSZzdcaic5ZB4nN3ZKbHQtbltQEg%253D%253D

Lipton, E. (2013, December 14). Think tank lists donors, playing down their role. *New York Times*.

Liu, N. C. (2013, September 11). *Discussion with Mittelman*. Shanghai.

Materu, P. (2007). *Higher education quality assurance in Sub-Saharan Africa: Status, challenges, opportunities, and promising practices*. Washington, DC: World Bank.

Materu, P. N. (2010, December 21). *Discussion with Mittelman*. Washington, DC: World Bank.

Mittelman, J. H. (1997). Rethinking transformation in international studies: Global transformation at the turn of the millennium. In S. Gill & J. H. Mittelman (Eds.), *Innovation and transformation in international studies* (pp. 248–263). Cambridge: Cambridge University Press.

Mittelman, J. H. (1998). Coxian historicism as an alternative perspective in international studies. *Alternatives, 23*(1), 63–92.

Mittelman, J. H. (2013). Global university rankings as a marker of revaluing the university. In T. Erkkilä (Ed.), *Global university rankings: Challenges for European ranking systems* (pp. 223–235). Houndmills: Palgrave Macmillan.

Parry, M., Field, K., & Supiano, B. (2013). The gates effect. *Chronicle of Higher Education, 59*(42). Retrieved from http://chronicle.com/article/The-Gates-Effect/140323/

Pharoah, C. (2008). *Family foundation philanthropy: Report on the giving of the largest charitable family foundations in the US, the UK and the rest of Europe 2008*. Centre for Charity Effectiveness, Cass Business School, City University London. Retrieved from http://www.cass.city.ac.uk/__data/assets/pdf_file/0020/37280/famfoundationphil.pdf

Rauhvargers, A. (2011) *Global university rankings and their impact*. Brussels: European University Association. Retrieved from http://www.eua.be/pubs/Global_University_Rankings_and_Their_Impact.pdf

Reichert, S. (2010). The intended and unintended effects of the Bologna Reforms. *Higher Education Management and Policy, 22*(1), 1–20.

Rosenau, J. N. (2003). *Distant proximities: Dynamics beyond globalization*. Princeton, NJ: Princeton University Press.

Salmi, J. (2009). *The challenge of establishing world-class universities*. Washington, DC: World Bank.

Salmi, J. (2010, December 21). *Discussion with Mittelman*. Washington, DC: World Bank.

Salmi, J., & Saroyan, A. (2007). League tables as policy instruments: Uses and misuses. *Higher Education Management and Policy, 19*(2), 31–68.

Spero, J. E. (2010). *The global role of U.S. foundations*. New York, NY: Foundation Center.

Strange, S. (1988). *States and markets: An introduction to international political economy*. New York, NY: Basil Blackwell.

United States Agency for International Development. (2011). *USAID Education Strategy 2011–2015*. Washington, DC: Author.

Vest, C. (2013, March 11). *Discussion with Mittelman*. Washington, DC.

Wallis, W. (2013, February 8). Rash of African philanthropists aims to do more than fill the gap. *Financial Times*.

World Bank. (1998). *World Development Report 1998-99: Knowledge for development*. Washington, DC: Author.

World Bank. (2011). *Learning for all: Investing in people's knowledge and skills to promote development: Education strategy 2020*. Washington DC: Author.

'Behemoth Pulls the Peasant's Plough': Convergence and Resistance to Business Civilization in China

GEORGE KARAVAS* & SHANNON BRINCAT**

*University of Queensland, Brisbane, Australia
**Griffith University, Brisbane, Australia

ABSTRACT *It has been widely held that China's development was forged from a unique pathway to that of Western countries. As a result, it has been assumed that China's historical experience of modernization contains important lessons for other developing states. However, as we show, modernization in China can be seen as sharing many of the same assumptions of development as the West. Using insights from Cox's work on civilizations—particularly the notion of 'Business Civilization' (adapted from Susan Strange)—our paper examines how modernization theoretic assumptions underpin both Chinese and World Bank perspectives on agricultural development not only within China but also across their engagements, policies, and practices of development throughout Africa. We argue that development constitutes a political project historically inseparable from* La mission civilisatrice *of Business Civilization, extending a form of intersubjectivity and materiality, power and rationality, based on a specific civilizational worldview. This process retains a number of contradictions and points of conflict and we focus on the resistances of traditional forms of civilization in contestations around the imposition of commercialized agriculture.*

Civilization is something we carry in our heads which guides our understanding of the world... 'business civilisation'... defines the way of being and thinking of the agents of economic globalization... (Cox & Schechter, 2002, pp. 177, 142)

Introduction

China has become an increasingly large player in the context of global development. The recent opening of the Asian Infrastructure Investment Bank has fuelled suggestions that China is even attempting to rival the World Bank (Perlez, 2015), an institution with a long legacy of promoting development policy reflecting the interests of Western countries. China's provision of aid and other forms of assistance to African countries have attracted particular attention because unlike other major donors, China is not a member of the OECD Development Assistance Committee. Emphasizing the differences between Chinese and Western forms of engagement in Africa has often served as an analytical point of departure in efforts seeking to understand the impact of foreign actors and what it might indicate about future trends (Alden, 2007; Cheru & Obi, 2010). China's status as a 'developmental' and 'colonial' state are also grounds cementing this divergence from the West. In particular, China's development experience of agricultural modernization since the late 1970s—and its perceived role in reducing poverty and increasing standards of living following the turn to market-led approaches—is seen as having important lessons for other poor countries (Brautigam, 2015; Li et al., 2012; Ravallion, 2009). On this basis, some refer to 'the new politics of development cooperation' (Scoones, Amanor, Favareto, & Qi, 2016, p. 9) in relation to what they see as China's distinctive state-led interventionism in markets. In this narrative, differences between China and Western countries are at the heart of two contrasting development trajectories, with China potentially offering developing states greater knowledge, experience, and opportunities, than traditional donors along with more choice in future policymaking.

This narrative, however, constrains further analysis. That is, the extent to which China's unique experience as a developing country is assumed to distinguish it from the West serves to conceal the extent to which its approach to development shares many of the core modernization theoretic assumptions held by Western development and financial institutions. The fact that the World Bank champions China's unique experience of development and its potential for African agribusiness, as evidenced through initiatives such as the 'South-South Knowledge Exchange' (World Bank, 2012; see also World Bank, 2015) and its *World Development Report 2008* (WDR 2008) (World Bank, 2007) should give us pause to consider more closely areas of *convergence*. Analysis has yet to examine how such strategies of modernization, both Western and Chinese, are premised on shared assumptions regarding sequential and linear patterns of growth, a teleology of development towards industrialization, and an ideal endpoint of modernization defined by market imperatives of profit and competitiveness. Some have begun to detect this appearance of a *convergence* between China and Western development actors, practices, and principles (Kragelund, 2015). Power, Mohan, and Tan-Mullins (2012), for example, suggest that China's integration into the current world order may reflect forms of mimicry producing 'hybrid results that require us to think carefully about "non-Western" similarity/difference' (p. 14). In this article, we further this observation, arguing for a convergence toward what Cox, following Strange (1990, pp. 238–273), named 'Business Civilisation': 'the way of being and thinking of the agents of economic globalization ... [and] the mental frameworks through which they interpret global economic and political events' (Cox & Schechter, 2002, p. 142). We focus on agriculture as a key area in which this convergence between Chinese and Western approaches to development can be readily identified in a number of shared civilizational assumptions: an emphasis on modernization as development toward industrialization, the replacement of subsistence agriculture by commercial agriculture, and the integration of smallholder farmers into global markets. Business Civilization is not, however, purely material: it is promulgated through a nest of shared intersubjective meanings, symbols, and principals. These include the everyday, normalized practices—the 'being and thinking' (Cox & Schechter, 2002, p. 142) of Business Civilization—from the ideologies of consumption and individualism, to the curriculum of business schools, even common dress-codes. The convergence is also illustrated in the patterns of resistance by traditional civilizations forms against the imposition of Business Civilization.

Following Cox, we do not restrict the concept of civilization to geographical, cultural, or religious boundaries, however much this is the taken-for-granted view of civilizations. Such assumptions lead to parochial and anachronistic analysis, as if civilizations were bounded entities, closed, and non-developmental. As Cox posit in no uncertain language: to attempt to 'define the essence of a civilization reifies it in a non-historical way and reinforces exclusionary defensive tendencies' (Cox & Schechter, 2002, p. 179). Instead, we take Cox's view of civilization—developed from Innis (1986)—as the 'habits of thought' defining the reality of its participants. Under this conception, not only do multiple civilizations exist and overlap with each other, individuals may remain caught in the dilemma of 'dual civilizationship' of being in a traditional *and* modern civilization at the same time (Cox & Schechter, 2002, pp. 142, 167, 179–180). Taking up Cox's method for examining civilizations (esp. Cox & Schechter, 2002, p. 154) our article is divided into three sections that engage with the material conditions and mental (intersubjective) institutional structures that delineate Business Civilization, and, examine the marginal or subordinate social forces from which resistance may emanate from. We begin by outlining Cox and Strange's conception of Business Civilization, its materiality and intersubjective basis under which people view their reality. Secondly, we explore how this civilizational narrative of development emerged historically in China through various processes of integration into world order and how this has created a shared civilizational notion of agricultural development. Through examples of Chinese and World Bank policy, we examine how this narrative of agricultural development has been exported through particular development mechanisms in African agriculture—demonstrating the civilizational convergence around a core belief-system and vision of development. Finally, we engage with the forms of resistance as revealed in traditional civilizational struggles to the imposition of Business Civilization.

Business Civilization: Consolidation and Convergence

In his later work, Cox came to focus heavily on the concept of civilizations (esp. Cox & Schechter, 2002; Cox, 2013). For him, there are several factors constitutive of civilization: forms of social economy (how people are organized to satisfy material needs), the dynamics of dominance and subordination, spiritual consciousness (including the relation to cosmos and nature), and notions of time and space (Cox & Schechter, 2002, pp. 165–166). These inform and co-produce identity, culture, and material processes, in the context of a wider framework of meaning. In this way, Cox sees civilization as 'a fit or correspondence between material conditions of existence and inter-subjective meanings' (Cox & Schechter, 2002, p. 161). This should not be confused with civilizational identity that refers to the self-conscious affirmation of being in a civilization. Rather, civilization is the common-sense perceptions of a reality that are taken by a people, almost unconsciously, as 'universal and natural' (Cox & Schechter, 2002, p. 163); the way 'large aggregates of people interpret the world, respond to it, and shape projects for acting in it' (Cox & Schechter, 2002, p. 169). In language redolent of Innis, Cox defines civilizations as a development of mind—'the thought process' or 'habit of thought'—by which a people 'define their vision of reality' (Cox & Schechter, 2002, p. 148). Different intersubjective meanings may correspond to the same material conditions—what is required is that these 'make sense' for those people to 'conceive their future and to concert their activities towards certain ends' (Cox & Schechter, 2002, pp. 161–162).

Intersubjectivity, then, forms a critical element in Cox's conception of civilization extending it much further than the typical view of civilizations as merely 'a feeling of belonging'. Rather, the intersubjectivity of civilization refers to a 'people's shared idea of reality' including both normative guides of action (what is 'right and proper in ordinary behaviour') and perceptions of objectivity (what 'really is') (Cox & Schechter, 2002, p. 176). This includes the shared consciousness and symbols by which meaningful communication is made possible in the civilization (including religion, myth, and culture) but also particular forms of knowledge related to epistemology, theories of history, and conceptions of space/time (see esp. 2002, Ch. 10). What is common-sensical differs, of course, in time and space and is shaped by collective responses to material conditions (Cox & Schechter, 2002, p. 176). Each civilization, therefore, has their own form of intersubjectivity that provides access to forms of knowledge that view the world differently. It follows that as no civilization's vision or knowledge can be considered universal, they are engaged in interactions with each other in which there are no shared meanings, symbols of reality, or theory of historical change. The epistemological challenge of being able to 'enter' the intersubjective meanings of other civilizations is then a crucial precondition for peaceful coexistence (Cox & Schechter, 2002, pp. 155–156, 163). It also means that citizens of 'dual civilizations' may struggle to reconcile opposed duties between rival civilizations.

Cox's emphasis on intersubjectivity also leads to a broader definition of civilizations not bounded by territory, culture, or religion. Under accelerating processes of globalization, relationships between politics and place have altered along with ways in which space is re-imagined (Agnew & Corbridge, 1995, p. 6). In the same way, Cox insists civilizations are not 'fixed or bounded', they are not pre-given religious or cultural entities (like Islam or 'The West'), they have no 'fixed essence or spirit', and they do not 'remain static'. Instead, they are 'processes or tendencies' through which peoples run their lives: 'a product of collective human action, an amalgam of social forces and ideas that has achieved a certain coherence, but [are] continually changing and developing in response to changes both from within and from without' (Cox & Schechter, 2002, pp. 143, 162, 183). This conception has clear analytic advantages over reductive tendencies in mainstream approaches to civilizations that lead, at best, to fixed notions of civilizational identity frozen in time and place or, at worst, the inevitability of Huntington's 'clash of civilizations' between utterly closed cultural formations. Such conceptions cannot countenance the plurality of civilizations nor their 'mutual borrowings' from each other over-time (Braudel, 1994, p. 8; Cox & Schechter, 2002, p. 153).

The deliberate 'elasticity' in Cox's conception of civilization (Cox & Schechter, 2002, p. 158) has the benefit of emphasizing civilization as a 'community of thought', loosening them from geographic and statist boundaries. In this context, Cox affirms Susan Strange's account of a 'non-territorial "business civilisation"' as 'the way of being and thinking of the agents of economic globalization' (Cox & Schechter, 2002, pp. 142, 165). Cox sees Business Civilization as 'clearly pre-eminent' in world order, a 'vehicle for economic globalization', having its ideology expounded in business schools, media, and political rhetoric, and informally structured though a 'nébuleuse' of international bodies like the WTO, IMF, Bank for International Settlements, World Bank, OECD, and World Economic Forums. Though it originated as an offshoot of Euro-American civilization and has been rooted mainly in the geography of the US, it now 'cuts across' existing historical civilizations—arguably even colonizing American civilization in which New Deal or Golden Era liberalism are now almost unthinkable against 'the habit of thought' of market imperatives. Its key assumptions of individualism and competitiveness serve to epistemologically restrict conceptions of society, indeed, any bonds of solidity. Yet, for Cox, Business Civilization is still merely an ideal type, a 'projection into the future of some powerful tendencies in the present' (Cox & Schechter, 2002, p. 180). It does not constitute a form of global governance because it retains a 'weak centre' with an accepted number of 'common principles' in a fragmented world of 'different social practices and goals' (Cox & Schechter, 2002, pp. 180, 185).

The foundations of this idea came from Susan Strange who called it 'The International Business Civilisation' (1990, p. 260) and, like Cox, described it as being worldwide but not universal. She held a similarly elastic conception of civilization as Cox, in which they could combine territory, belief-systems, and formal structures, but also be non-territorial, *cives* (i.e. rights and duties), and exist informally. Whilst she traces the geographic core of Business Civilization in the nineteenth century to Britain, with a core in the 1990s located in New York, its authority was already then being diffused amongst non-state authorities, markets, bankers, scientists, corporate executives, transport, insurance, media, and entertainment. This process has only accelerated and expanded since the 1990s. For Strange, the central concerns of Business Civilization are to secure the authority of property rights, scientific objectivity, and finance markets. Its economic values are of efficiency and profit, with social values of competition and opportunity (1990, p. 265). Underpinning this civilizational expansion is the movement of power from the state to the market under which even the international institutions tasked with global management (such as the IMF and World Bank) are handicapped (1990, pp. 267–268, 271). A key part in this process is Mushakoji's idea of 'occultation', how dominated elites become displaced and absorbed in the new civilization (Cox & Schechter, 2002, p. 167). Cox and Strange describe how 'elites' of subordinated peoples may imitate the new civilization and how the 'people' may remain resistant throughout this process (Strange, 1990, pp. 261–265). This results in a hierarchy of agency at the core of Business Civilization in which its elites—the executives and managers—possess agential gravitas against which other marginal groups, whether class-based (such as the peasantry or industrial workers) or culture-based (such as traditionalists and non-commodified social forms), are rendered fixed, passive, almost *relics*. It is they to whom modernization is *applied* rather than in which they act as co-participants.

So what then constitutes the unconscious, shared idea of reality in Business Civilizations, both normatively and ontologically? The most powerful elements of Business civilization are how it promotes people to 'concert their activities towards certain ends': namely, competitiveness, profit, individualism, and consumption (Cox & Schechter, 2002, pp. 142, 162). Whilst it may seem, therefore, to overlap with Cox's conceptualization of globalization, it is neither synonomous or reducible to this. Globalization typically refers to the compression of space through communication, network society, and finance capital—that is, solely to material processes rather than the intersubjective dimensions mutually implicated in Cox's conception of civilization. Far more than just globalization, Business Civilization acts as a 'development of mind' through norms of behaviour (individualism and formal equality) but also objective assumptions of profit maximization and competitiveness: the universalization and naturalization of the *market*. It even holds a distinct notion of historical change that Cox calls 'the myth of the "end of history"' that helps Business Civilization to 'coast' its way against traditional forms of opposition and civilizations (Cox & Schechter, 2002, p. 154). Cox observes nationality and class being submerged, and traditional civilizations subordinated, though not eliminated, in this process. This conception has some overlap with McMichael's description of how the market has come to dominate notions of development through the 'progressive naturalization of its epistemological foundations' (Da Costa & McMichael, 2007, p. 590) to become 'not just a goal' but 'a method of rule' (McMichael, 2017, p. 50). Business Civilization operates through material cultures under which the very notion of development becomes 'anchored' in the 'being and thinking' of its subjects and understood as the material conditions and intersubjective naturalization of the market. This civilizing impulse has meant the expansion of Business Civilization across international development. A key example is how major International Financial Institutions require participants to the norms of economic liberalization—such as the conditions made on China's 2001 ascension to the World Trade Organization—thereby acting as institutions 'setting and enforcing international standards of civilization' (Bowden, 2006, p. 30). Under the assumed common-sense principles of market society, Business Civilization appears as 'homogenizing economic and cultural practices' despite corresponding forms of resistance to this imposition by marginalized and subordinate groups (Cox & Schechter, 2002, p. 157). The level of penetration of Business Civilization within a traditional civilization, however, can only be as deep as the consciousness of the 'universal and natural' order of market society itself—a determination that is therefore case-specific within each state or locale.

Convergence to Business Civilization: China and the World Bank on Agricultural Development

Developing the idea of 'pseudomorphology' from Spengler (1939, II: p. 189), Cox describes how the 'impetus' of a civilization can penetrate another, leading to partial transformation in which the persisting structures of the former civilization serve to constrain the latter (Cox & Schechter, 2002, p. 168). As such, there is no form of Business Civilization that is not enmeshed with other civilizational rivals—no 'uniform global capitalism' as Cox consistently reminds us—and he views the rise of China as a prime example of this type of 'morphing' of capitalism within a different civilizational tradition (Cox & Schechter, 2002, p. 146). So it is important to note that there is no claim to the erasure of Chinese civilization under the dominance of Business Civilization. Rather, the expansion of Business Civilization is in relation and contestation (*sic.* 'dialectical contradictions') with this traditional civilizational form, leading to a combination of development and modernity with 'Chinese Characteristics'. Here, taking a civilizational approach to help understand how modernization unfolded in China can help avoid the reductive tendency to conflate its assumed difference/separation from the West but also the tendency to over-emphasize specific periods of development in isolation from others. At the same time, it allows us to draw upon aspects of this civilizational convergence through a specific example: the principles and policies related to agricultural development shared by Chinese development practices and one of the leading institutions of Business Civilization, the World Bank.

China's development, the fraught process of struggle between competing visions on the role of tradition and the perceived need to embrace modernity, did not occur in isolation from the West. British civilizing missions in the East—the early core of Strange's Business Civilization, we must recall—were crucial in China's traumatic encounter with the expanding European international order (Suzuki, 2011, p. 275). Its experiences of unequal relations, typified in the treaty port system and its clear infraction of the formal principles of international society, not only saw China recognizing itself as a member of the international legal and political system that excluded it but that modernization was essential for strengthening the state and resisting foreign rule, that is, for China to secure its sovereignty (see Gong, 1984, pp. 140–147). The pursuit of modernization was predicated on this encounter between China and the West, hitching development to the creation of a strong national body in which the very 'thinking' of development was 'as a purpose-oriented, evolutionary and limited idea', a conception that persists to this day in Chinese developmental practices at home and what it promotes abroad (Barabantseva, 2012, p. 64). Underpinning this was a worldview of universal progress under a teleological, linear conception of development. Here, agricultural modernization was largely understood in relation to how it had underpinned industrialization in Europe: a transition from subsistence farming to industrialized agriculture through the greater use of technology, mechanization for the purposes of increasing production, whilst integrating peasants and smallholder farmers into markets.

Power et al. (2012, p. 13) have shown the convergence in the development narratives of China and the West that emerged through China's first encounters with European imperialism, and how they have remained a fundamental part of state-making/nation-building throughout the twentieth century. This historical experience serves not only as the context for the socialist vision of development in the first few decades of the People's Republic of China (PRC) (Wang, 1998, pp. 13–15) but also of the period during and after liberalization. For Mao, the 'uneven development' of China was considered the primary external and internal contradiction facing China, threatening it with imperialism (1975, pp. 162–163, 169, 263). Hence, Mao called not only for the removal of those classes hindering development but for the 'urgency' in experimental farms, agricultural research, and exhibitions, to 'stimulate the development of agriculture' (1975, pp. 13, 143). So even though modernization under Mao may have proceeded outside the capitalist world market, its premise was rooted in the same progressive teleology of development and the need to catch-up to Western industrialized countries. Indeed, the two great, rival ideologies shared this goal of industrial development under an over-arching civilizational framework. It would also make the revolution highly susceptible to the normative impetus of Business Civilization.

Whilst the specificities of pursuing socialist development in China contributed to the particular shape of central planning and the social contract between workers and the state, for Cox, the segmentation of labour under 'Real Socialism' kept the production process rooted in class-based politics similar to that of the capitalist market (Cox, 1991, p. 187). Upon visiting China in 1984, Cox witnessed a profound transition in the structure of society as socialist ethics was taken over by market rationality, a key intersubjective component of Business Civilization (Cox, 2013, p. 291). Similar observations were also made by Strange who saw how China 'opened' in the 1980s as a victory 'for the forces of the market'—a process in which China was 'join[ed] up with the business civilization' (Strange, 1990, p. 261). The concept of 'development' that emerged through China's historical experiences was thus central to this dramatic period of reform: it allowed the Chinese state to be able to jettison aspects of socialist doctrine whilst encouraging the market as an acceptable means through which to continue the pursuit of modernization and state-making. Viewed in this light, Deng Xiaoping's reforms could allow the market to reconfigure social relations domestically without challenging the legitimacy of the state or the civilizational framework. This logic is detectable today in the restructuring of agriculture that is made under the proviso that through such development rural populations will 'finally get their tickets to prosperity' (Zhang, Oya, & Ye, 2015, p. 303).

So for smallholders, whilst this process of rural restructuring has shifted from (socialist) cooperatives to (capitalist) markets, the motif has remained one of transformation from 'backward' into 'modern', from 'inefficient' to 'productive'. The promise of increasing productivity aided the emergence of a national discourse that framed all things rural as 'backward, unreformed and problematic' and in need of change (Zhang et al., 2015, pp. 301–303). A key shift in government policy has been towards de-peasantization through capital-intensive forms of agriculture and the active discouragement of small-scale farming (Yan & Chen, 2015, p. 367). Several initiatives in the *18th CPC National Congress Scientific Outlook of Development*

(SOD) revealed the intention to 'speed up the development of modern agriculture' (Hu Jintao quoted in Xinhua News, 2012). The SOD is particularly instructive for understanding the depth of penetration of Business Civilization. This report was to correct the developmental logic of 'develop for development's sake' in favour of a people-centred and sustainable vision as a transitional stage between capitalism and communism. Yet, it retained the notion of the necessity of development for 'exploration, accumulation, self-improvement and self-development' (Chen & Luo, 2009, pp. 60–65)—the very precepts of the intersubjectivity (normative and objective, or 'being and thinking') of Business Civilization. These ideas are central to the professed 'scientific view' of the annual *China Modernization Report* (Research Group for China Modernization Strategies, 2007), which provides a timeline of civilizational development on this basis: 'primitive' communities found upstream are those that engage in practices of agriculture thousands of years old, whilst those downstream are 'advanced', having embraced industrialization and modernization (Barabantseva, 2009, p. 72). The process of 'capital going to the countryside' has meant scaling-up production through the restructuring of 'specialised big households' and large agribusiness, 'dragon-head enterprises' (Yan & Chen, 2015, p. 371).

As described by Nyíri (2006), Chinese development actors carry with them a worldview framed in terms of progress and stability through a strong state—in other words, elements that combine Business Civilization with the unique historical experience of China and the perceived necessity of securing sovereignty through economic development. These norms and objectivities do not only operate internally but are now actively exported in China's development projects throughout Africa. *China's African Policy* (2006) (CAP) enshrines the principles of China's engagement with African countries along these civilizational terms, emphasizing development through the types of market reforms China has followed since the late 1970s (MOFA, 2006). This policy is pursued through a diplomatic apparatus, the *Forum on China–Africa Cooperation*, whose significant results already include unprecedented growth in trade, major contracts for infrastructure projects, and the substantial reduction in debts of many African governments. It presents development as a universal and progressive political project: 'promoting development', it claims, is a 'common desire of all peoples' and an 'irresistible historical trend' (MOFA, 2006, p. 1). The status of China and Africa as 'developing' are upheld as definitive categories by which their relations are secured on a shared basis for cooperation (MOFA, 2006, p. 1). Similarly, the *White Paper* (2013) *China–Africa Trade and Economic Cooperation 2013* (State Council PRC, 2013), frames China–Africa relations in terms of their shared status as 'developing' countries and as following a 'common path' to catch-up with developed states, in which agriculture is deemed 'crucial' for stable development and poverty reduction (p. 1). The CAP, for example, takes the view of what it terms 'long history' in which African struggles from colonial rule are said to have made possible the 'progress of civilization' by unleashing a 'huge potential for development' (MOFA, 2006, p. 2). What constitutes 'Africa' in the CAP is therefore quite narrowly conceived, its diversity and multiple histories folded into a homogenizing vision that equates the outcomes of all these struggles as a mere desire for development. In this sense, the document tends to equate all struggles as purposed toward the establishment of market civilization. The connection with the 'end of history' myth of Business Civilization is here self-evident.

Alongside these broad principles in convergence with Business Civilization, each document also contains a raft of policies related to agriculture. The CAP is particularly instructive with its focus on industrialization to increase productivity, and commercialization, to promote economic growth. Echoing the words of Mao almost 60 years earlier regarding the need for developing countries intent on catching up to the developed world, the policy focuses agricultural technology, training courses, and experimental/demonstrative agricultural projects (MOFA, 2006, p. 3). It also clearly recalls China's fear of the potential loss of sovereignty and threat of imperialism because of economic insecurity brought about by under-development (MOFA, 2006, p. 1). The two key development initiatives in the CAP center on the establishment of Special Economic Zone's and export of green revolution technologies (GRT). Both of these strategies had long histories in the development of China, the former as direct support of the Chinese state for market-driven strategies, the latter, the catalyst for rapid growth in food production from the 1960s. Some see them as a 'Grand Plan for Africa', a move to 'enclavization' based on China's experience of European imperialism through the treaty system (Davies, 2008, p. 136). Others suggest this reflects an attempt to export China's own development experience directly to Africa though with the potential to disrupt existing social arrangements which mostly impacts upon the traditional roles of women in relation to food production and accessibility to land tenure (Brautigam, 1992; Brautigam & Tang, 2009, p. 699).

The Forum on China–Africa Cooperation Johannesburg Action Plan 2016–2018 (FOCAC-JAP) demonstrates further the entrenchment of the core ideas of Business Civilization in strengthening agricultural cooperation by prioritizing food security and economic growth through 'agro-technology demonstration centers' (ATDCs) (MOFA, 2015a). The 23 ATDCs now located throughout African countries act to promote high yield agriculture (i.e. breeding, the production of seeds, and plant protection) and as training/vocational centres to provide Chinese agricultural technology and experience to African farmers (MOFA, 2015a, pp. 2–3). The importance placed on agro-technology runs across Chinese policies and practices featuring in the *White Paper* (2013) that documents a number of successful China–Africa ventures in agriculture (State Council PRC, 2013, p. 6) and the *China–Africa Science and Technology Partnership Plan* that announced the goal of improving capacities in African countries through the transfer of Chinese technology including joint laboratories/research centres and agriculture science demonstration parks (DICMST PRC, 2010, p. 3; MOFA, 2015a, pp. 6–8). Technology and industrial inputs are directed to increasing productivity in order to sell in markets, thereby strategically combining aid with commercial initiatives (Brautigam, 2009, p. 248). ATDCs offer a complementary platform for Chinese investment in areas where they are competitive (agricultural technology and seed cultivation) (Brautigam, 2009, p. 247), reflecting the FOCAC-JAP policy of creating 'an enabling environment for Chinese enterprises to invest and trade in agriculture in Africa' (MOFA, 2015a, p. 3). Of course, this has led many to question the extent to which these initiatives maintain a balance between their commercial and foreign aid objectives (Xu, Li, Qi, Tang, & Mukwereza, 2016, p. 7). Arguably, what is more significant is how Chinese companies have emerged as conduits of Business Civilization justifying their role in the promotion of business interests as coeval with development goals throughout a number of African states.

The *Programme for China–Africa Cooperation in Economic and Social Development* (PCACESD) furthers this concern to 'enhance' the 'capabilities' of China and African states to 'participate in globalization' and catch-up to industrialized countries (MOFA, 2009, p. 1). Whilst this document openly admits to concerns with the inequality of the existing world economy, these are made without deviating from how development is defined through the existing political and economic architecture of Business Civilization. In fact, the PCACESD explicitly serves to reinforce them:

> The Ministers stress the need to harmonize their trade policies and to participate actively in trade negotiation, including within the framework of the WTO, in order to ensure that the multilateral trading system contributes to enhanced competitiveness, economic growth and sustainable development of their countries. (MOFA, 2009, p. 2)

A more recent and detailed vision of the pursuit of development within the existing architecture of Business Civilization emerged in the *Declaration of the Johannesburg Summit of the Forum on China–Africa Cooperation* (2015) (MOFA, 2015b). This declaration included: opposing trade protectionism; applying WTO rules to help develop a 'open world economy'; reaching the Sustainable Development Goals (SDGs), and; honouring commitments to the G17 goals (MOFA, 2015b, p. 2). The policy defines development in the very terms of dominant international institutions, establishing 'an equivalence' between this specific China–Africa partnership and an open, multilateral commercial, and financial system that embodies Business Civilization (Amin, 2006, p. 4).

The development policies and principles underpinning Chinese policy on agricultural development are shared with the World Bank. Indeed, the claims that China is rivalling the World Bank in terms of market capture merely serves to reinforce this convergence. The World Bank maintains a commitment to overcoming subsistence and small-scale agriculture based on perceived inefficiencies in comparison to the productive capacity of large-scale commercial farming. *The World Development Report 2008* is the flagship policy document outlining its vision for agricultural development by integrating smallholders into markets, not merely as a poverty reduction strategy, but toward the goal of sustainable development and economic growth (World Bank, 2007, p. 8). It seeks to promote private investment in agriculture by encouraging agribusiness which is seen as a key area in which the World Bank can positively influence development in African countries. Importantly, the World Bank calls for pursuing more functional land tenure arrangements in Africa for the easier integration of agribusiness. As we have seen, China's policies on agricultural development in Africa share the same assumptions. Here, the integration of smallholders into global markets has followed the reform in China's rural economy since liberalization, introducing the market after de-collectivization, and changing land tenure property rights to create individual incentives (Ravallion, 2009, p. 307). Indeed, the World Bank claims that 'China's rapid growth in agriculture' was attributable 'to the household responsibility system, the liberalization of markets, and rapid technological change' (World Bank, 2007, p. 26).

In its reconstruction of the role of agriculture in development, the World Bank establishes three pathways out of poverty: through agricultural entrepreneurship, the rural labour market, and the rural nonfarm economy. It is unsurprising that agricultural development is conceived primarily as a market-led process (World Bank, 2007, p. 10). The report highlights the growth of input markets, such as those around seed and fertilizer markets, as ways to increase agricultural productivity (World Bank, 2007, p. 150). Yet, what is surprising is how smallholders are seen to play a vital role in the reconstruction of agriculture through commercialization when led by 'private entrepreneurs' in extensive value chains that link 'producers to consumers' (World Bank, 2007, p. 8). Their potential to increase agricultural productivity and make an important contribution to economic growth is because they are made to be the link between market, the state, and agribusiness (on this process see 2007, p. 8). This not only furthers the push to commercialized agriculture but does so in a way that transforms local forms of community and social reproduction towards market imperatives. The *Agriculture Action Plan 2013–2015* (AAP 2013–2015) (World Bank, 2013) remains largely consistent with the WDR 2008 promoting economic growth through agriculture and in which smallholders, once again, play the key 'linkage' role 'connecting farmers to local, urban, regional and global markets' (2013, p. 34). Investment plays a major role in driving this initiative in the AAP 2013–2015. In this plan, the World Bank promotes investment aimed at formalizing specific land tenure frameworks. Though justified as protective measures, they are aimed at ensuring that land be used more 'productively' so that smallholders are not restricted in their pursuit of the purpose of commercialization.

Other examples could be made not only in terms of agriculture but across economic fields and investment areas—though this would be beyond the bounds of this article. Regardless, the point is demonstrated: the way development actors in China and the World Bank conceive their future and concert their activities (Cox & Schechter, 2002, pp. 161–162) of agricultural development—from land tenure and smallholders, to technology or even food security—purposed towards the specific ends of increasing productivity, economic growth, and profitability in which universal progress and the efficiency of markets are naturalized through Business Civilization.

Resistance to Business Civilization

So far we have seen the convergence toward Business Civilization in the agricultural developmental practices advocated by China and the World Bank, and how the 'being and thinking' of this civilizational mind-set has been exported within a number of development policies and projects across Africa. This may give the impression of some uncontested march toward 'eternal' homogenization under 'one-civilization' (Cox & Schechter, 2002, p. 173). Yet, as Cox consistently affirms, in this dialectical process of civilizational interaction there is *always* resistance and conflict (Cox & Schechter, 2002, p. 157). Civilizations change through internal sources and inter-civilizational encounters: that is, the contradictions within them that pose choices for its future, *and*, external influences emanating from co-exiting that impact upon these choices (Cox & Schechter, 2002, pp. 177–179). Above all, however, for Cox, it is globalizing market forces that constitute the principle pressure on all traditional civilizations—the 'true generator of chaos' (Cox & Schechter, 2002, p. 142). This pressure is refracted through the structures of the existing civilization, shaping how economic forces are institutionalized and provoking conflict with internal social forces (Cox & Schechter, 2002, p. 146). As such, Business Civilization 'remains culturally specific' for different parts of the world have shaped its form through their historical experiences and for their social purposes (Cox & Schechter, 2002, pp. 166–167). This rootedness of Business Civilization in local traditions means that forms of resistance may result in desires for alternative visions of the future, or, people may turn to existing moral resources that can include a variety of deeply rooted cultural ideas/practices, including traditional civilizations. Here, traditional civilizations offer one source or alternative as they reflect forms of cultural diversity resistant to 'one-civilization' 'gradually absorbing and homogenizing what is left of cultural diversity' (Cox & Schechter, 2002, p. xxi).

Cox is matter-of-fact when describing this process: there are dominant and subordinate civilizations. The subordinate are not erased, however, but survive in hidden form (Cox & Schechter, 2002, pp. 142–143). Taking up Spengler's 'pseudomorphology' once again, Cox's primary analytic goal is to look to the 'kinds of crisis' that could lead to the rejection of the superimposed civilizational discourse by subordinate groups (Cox & Schechter, 2002, p. 168). Here, the key is to 'spot' the 'contradictions' within both the internal sources and inter-civilizational encounters (Cox & Schechter, 2002, p. 183). The question is whether society can 'generate both the bonds of solidarity' and 'the innovation in institutions' to create something new in the face of possessive individualism, consumerism, and the market (Cox & Schechter, 2002, pp. 141, 152, 183–184). For Cox, the 'rampant individualism' of Business Civilization has undermined social cohesion (Cox & Schechter, 2002, p. 180) and we could add now threatens the very environmental basis of its own reproduction. This leads to two versions of Business Civilization that Cox, unfortunately, does not systematically distinguish. The 'strong' Business Civilization thesis suggests that capitalist modernity has resulted in the consolidation of Business Civilization as a material and intersubjective web of meaning for many peoples based around norms and objectivity of market principles—and that these 'cut' across traditional civilizations, being endorsed and enforced by local elites. Alternatively, there is the 'weak' version that capitalist modernity is carried by local elites into existing, traditional civilizations in an attempt to co-opt them to the needs of profit/capital accumulation of the market under the 'thinking and being' of Business Civilization. Whilst both retain significant room for resistance, the latter has more salience because of the 'weak centre' in the governance of Business Civilization and the existence of a range of cultural practices in traditional civilization that serve to resist and 'morph' the actuality of Business Civilization.

Here, China presents a novel case. Cox upholds China as a force undermining the one-civilizational narrative of Business Civilization as its links to global capitalism are said to be constraining but also divergent (Cox & Schechter, 2002, p. 191). Moreover, whilst Chinese civilization is seen as in a subordinate role, its older traditions, such as Confucian norms of social responsibility and open attitudes to truth, survive (Cox & Schechter, 2002, p. 182). This struggle between the values of Business Civilization and traditional Chinese civilization has produced a number of 'profound historical contradictions' in modern Chinese economics and culture (1998, p. 15). Part of these contradictions involve the extent to which Business Civilization and its promotion of market-led development has rolled back the protections of the Chinese state and elements of the 'social contract' with workers. So (2013, p. 122) argues that it was the intensification of class struggle and extent to which the peasantry faced marginalization in China preceding the socialist revolution in 1949 that originally led to widespread support for land redistribution. For example, the state has had to manage the social effects of joining Business Civilization, addressing income polarization and inequalities particularly between the rural and urban areas. Rural issues have remained the key priority of the Central Committee for the 12th consecutive year revolving around the three problems of industrializing agriculture, urban-rural disparities, and reducing burdens on farmers (for a critical view see Wen, 2001). Widespread protests have become a regular feature of the political landscape (Perry & Selden, 2003), whilst the phenomena of 'ghost cities' reflects the extent of structural conditions challenging the government's ability to manage market forces (Shepard, 2015). Cox observes unequal distribution in wealth within other traditional civilizations as a condition that is ripe for manipulation by elites of Business Civilization (Cox & Schechter, 2002, p. 141). Strange refers to a similar problem regarding how elites are 'saved' from the volatility of the market by 'inflicting' it on other citizens—the peasants and marginal groups—who suffer in the 'periphery' of Business Civilization (1990, p. 268). In these outlying parts, the power of Business Civilization is 'diluted' with a number of dissidents and points of resistance (Strange, 1990, p. 264). This helps explain the number of social movements in China—the New Rural Reconstruction Movement is a prime example—that have emerged as a response to the changes in social relations through the privatization of property, land enclosures, and massive social upheavals that have attended the commercialization of agriculture in rural areas across China. Here, Cox's emphasis on resistance overlaps with two related studies of peasant resistance. Firstly, McMichael's idea of the 'alternative "peasantist" ontology' (McMichael, 2008) that contests the precepts of Business Civilization, rejects 'the universalisms of the project of modernity' (McMichael, 2005, p. 589), and challenges the 'epistemic privilege of the market calculus' (2010, p. 3). Secondly, the types of resistance located in the struggles of the Chinese peasantry reveals importance similarities to Scott's (1985) theories of peasant resistance in other parts of the world, indicating the existence of distinct subaltern movements against the same global, 'civilising' force.

There are also traditional, cultural aspects of Chinese civilization resistant to Business Civilization. In distinction to the progressive and linear beliefs of Business Civilization, Cox refers to the cyclical view of history and dyadic cosmology of Daoist 'yin and yang' in Chinese Civilization (Cox & Schechter, 2002, p. 165), whose emphasis on unity/harmony and activity/conflict could be made to serve a more harmonious economic alternative. The notion of harmony has been taken up even in Chinese foreign policy in the discourses of 'inclusionism' and neo-Tanxiaism. Similarly, Cox refers to Wang Gungwu's 'the long view' (Cox & Schechter, 2002, p. 123; cited in Cox, 2010, p. 15) as a way to conceptualize processes of global social change. Yet, the revival of Confucian thought by the Chinese state and various elites reflects a tension between traditional thought and the desire to achieve modernity. As with all cultural processes, such revivals are prone to absorption into the dominance of the new, imposed civilization. For some, Confucianism has appropriated the characteristics of modernization by becoming compatible with capitalism (Dirlik, 1995, p. 230). Here, a cultural form that was once seen as an 'obstacle' to development came to be regarded its 'facilitator' (Goody, 1996, p. 9). Cox acknowledges how the Chinese state's reassessment of Confucian values that emphasized order and stability helped legitimize the transition to a new political order (Cox, 2013, p. 291). We can detect a similar process of absorption in the national development discourse around *suzhi*, meaning 'essential' and 'nature' or the 'quality of human', encompassing wealth, health, education, and sophistication. The very notion of 'quality' was soon imprinted with the values of Business Civilization: to have low *suzhi* was to be considered backwards, to think and behave like a peasant. To raise one's *suzhi* was to work hard and obediently, becoming a conspicuous consumer and seeking self-improvement (Jacka, 2009)—that is, to act like one is part of the elite of Business Civilization within its hierarchy of agency.

Though research is yet under-developed on this phenomena, there are also irrefutable signs of forms of resistance against the imposition of Business Civilization regarding the commercialization and mechanization of agriculture across Africa. Green revolution technologies have a long history that has involved social and political contestations against agricultural modernization strategies that displace or challenges existing social and political arrangements, with local arrangements around land tenure and food production having a stronger hold at the local level than state control (Brautigam, 1992; Brautigam, 2009, p. 265). In Senegal, for example, Chinese development strategies in agriculture focused on commercialization have encountered local sources of resistance in its attempts to scale-up production and switch to high-cost inputs (Buckley, 2013). Research on the impact of some Chinese agricultural demonstration centres in Tanzania and Mozambique indicate that they face challenges of balancing priorities of commercial success and diplomatic goals and that local farmers are reticent about embracing some forms of agricultural technology such as high-yielding seed varieties that may incur high costs (Xu et al., 2016). This is not to argue that this is the inherent character of all Chinese investment and engagement in agriculture in African countries. Rather, the point is to situate the emerging research on responses to strategies aimed at agricultural modernization in the context of broader struggles against the same impulses from both Western and African actors pursing the same development strategies related to Business Civilization. Movements for agroecology against the GRT approaches (i.e. those pursued by the World Bank, NEPAD/ CAADP, and the Alliance for a Green Revolution in Africa) or peasant movements based around local concerns against the notion of food security (as pushed by the New Alliance for Food Security and Nutrition) are emergent forms of these types of struggle (such as African organizations that are members of the peasant movement La Vía Campesina). Indeed, in the near future we may expect an increase in such forms of resistance in the African context.

Conclusion

In this article, we have illustrated a remarkable convergence in China's agricultural development practices and those advocated by the World Bank. This process suggests the expansion and consolidation of Business Civilization first identified by Susan Strange and further developed in Cox's work on civilizations. Under this approach to civilizations, the 'being and thinking' of Business Civilization is seen to revolve around the values of individualism and consumerism, and the materialities of industrialization, commercialization, and profitability, in which 'development' is seen as a universal progression to the naturalization of the world market and its imperatives. The behemoth of Business Civilization has expanded beyond its cultural origins in the West, its geographical core in the US, and is now spread by elites across states in direct conflict with traditional civilizations and is provoking forms of resistance from subordinated social forces. Despite its expansion, Business Civilizations retains a number of 'dialectical contradictions'. Yet Cox offers a diagnostic not a prescription (Cox & Schechter, 2002, p. 154) and for him the question remains whether a 'coherent alternative to economic globalization' that could transcend these contradictions can be found (Cox & Schechter, 2002, p. 107).

It is no longer customary or vogue to think in civilizational terms in the social sciences, a category that seems so vast that any such engagement endangers generalization or essentializing. Our postmodern inclinations seem far more comfortable with the local and particular. Civilizational analysis seems to lack the subtlety—or the more popular term 'nuance' (see Healy, 2015)—that can only be conferred on micro studies that grapple with the empirics of the minutia and which are, therefore, deemed to be able to understand with sufficiency the complexity of thing or phenomena (or are the least likely to do violence to the 'Other'). Yet, just because we lack understanding of these processes, does not mean they are not present. Mittelman has bemoaned that recent studies of development in China have become 'atheoretical', either focusing on single problems like privatization or single projects like housing. This move entails prescribing piecemeal solutions—what Cox would deride as problem-solving approaches—to what are the structural challenges of development (Mittelman, 2006, pp. 377–380). Yet, Cox's approach to civilizations offers a way to understand China–Africa relations in historically grounded processes of dialectic transformation (Cox & Schechter, 2002, p. 182) in which encounters, relations, and contradictions between civilizations provoke responses to the pressures to modernize and integrate into the global economy. This level of analysis has fundamental things to tell us about the types of resistances we see on the ground. Indeed, we ignore these larger processes at the peril of inadvertently reifying the particular by not obtaining a clearer understanding of the whole in which they form a part. Our understanding of resistance would fail accordingly. By bringing in Coxian insights into civilizational processes we can draw out patterns of development that are lost when we look too closely at the coal-face.

Disclosure Statement

No potential conflict of interest was reported by the authors.

References

Agnew, J., & Corbridge, S. (1995). *Mastering space: Hegemony, territory and international political economy*. Routledge: London.
Alden, C. (2007). *China in Africa*. London: Zed Books.
Amin, S. (2006). The millennium development goals: A critique from the south. *Monthly Review, 57*(10), 1–15.
Barabantseva, E. (2009). Development as localization: Ethnic minorities in China's official discourse on the western development project. *Critical Asian Studies, 41*(2), 225–254.
Barabantseva, E. (2012). In pursuit of an alternative model? The modernisation trap in China's official development discourse. *East Asia, 29*(1), 63–79.

Bowden, B. (2006). Civilization, standards, and markets. In B. Bowden & L. Seabrooke (Eds.), *Global standards of market civilization* (pp. 19–33). London: Routledge.

Braudel, F. (1994). *A history of civilizations*. (R. Mayne Trans.). London: Penguin.

Brautigam, D. (1992). Land rights and agricultural development in West Africa: A case study of Two Chinese projects. *The Journal of Developing Areas*, *27*(1), 21–32.

Brautigam, D. (2009). *The dragon's gift: The real story of China in Africa*. Oxford: Oxford University Press.

Brautigam, D. (2015). *Will Africa feed China?* Oxford: Oxford University Press.

Brautigam, D., & Tang, X. (2009). China's engagement in African agriculture: "Down to the countryside". *The China Quarterly*, *199*(3), 686–706.

Buckley, S. (2013). Chinese land-based interventions in Senegal. *Development and Change*, *44*(2), 429–450.

Chen, X., & Luo, Q. (2009). The scientific outlook on development and changes in the mode of human existence. *Social Sciences in China*, *30*(1), 54–67.

Cheru, F., & Obi, C. (2010). Introduction – Africa in the twenty-first century: Strategic and development challenges. In F. Cheru & C. Obi (Eds.), *The rise of China and India in Africa: Opportunities and critical interventions* (pp. 1–9). London: Zed Books.

Cox, R. W. (1991). "Real socialism" in historical perspective. *Socialist Register*, *27*, 169–193.

Cox, R. W. (2010). Historicity and international relations: A tribute to Wang Gungwu. In Y. Zheng (Ed.), *China and international relations: The Chinese view and the contribution of Wang Gungwu* (pp. 3–17). Routledge: London.

Cox, R. W. (2013). *Universal foreigner: The individual and the world*. Hackensack, NJ: World Scientific.

Cox, R. W., & Schechter, M. G. (2002). *The political economy of a plural world: Critical reflections on power, morals and civilization*. London: Routledge.

Da Costa, D., & McMichael, P. (2007). The poverty of the global order. *Globalizations*, *4*(4), 588–602.

Davies, M. (2008). China's development model comes to Africa. *Review of African Political Economy*, *35*(115), 134–137.

DICMST (Department of international cooperation ministry of science and technology of the People's Republic of China). (2010). China-Africa science and technology partnership program (CASTEP).

Dirlik, A. (1995). Confucius in the borderlands: Global capitalism and the reinvention of Confucianism. *Boundary 2*, *22*(3), 229–273.

Gong, G. (1984). China's entry into international society. In H. Bull & A. Watson (Eds.), *The expansion of international society*. Oxford: Clarendon Press.

Goody, J. (1996). *The east in the west*. Cambridge: Cambridge University Press.

Healy, K. (2015). *Fuck nuance*. Paper presented at the Theory Section Session on "The Promise and Pitfalls of Nuance in Sociological Theory", American Sociological Association Meetings, Chicago, IL.

Innis, H. (1986). *Empire and communication*. (D. Godfrey Ed.). Toronto: Press Porcépic.

Jacka, T. (2009). Cultivating citizens *suzhi* (quality) discourse in the PRC. *Positions: East Asia Cultures Critique*, *17*(3), 523–535.

Kragelund, P. (2015). Towards convergence and cooperation in the global development finance regime: Closing Africa's policy space? *Cambridge Review of International Affairs*, *28*(2), 246–262.

Li, X., Qi, G., Tang, L., Zhao, L., Jin, L., Guo, Z., & Wu, J. (2012). *Agricultural development in China and Africa: A comparative analysis*. London: Routledge.

McMichael, P. (2005). Globalization. In T. Janoski, R. Alford, A Hicks, & M. Schwartz (Eds.), *The handbook of political sociology: states, civil societies, and globalization* (pp. 587–606). Cambridge: Cambridge University Press.

McMichael, P. (2008). Peasants make their Own history, but not just as they please … *Journal of Agrarian Change*, *8*(2 and 3), 205–228.

McMichael, P. (2010). Changing the subject of development. In P. McMichael (Ed.), *Contesting development: critical struggles for social change* (pp. 1–14). New York, NY: Routledge.

McMichael, P. (2017). *Development and social change: A global perspective*. Thousand Oaks, CA: Sage.

Mittelman, J. (2006). Globalization and development: Learning from debates in China. *Globalizations*, *3*(3), 377–391.

MOFA (Ministry of Foreign Affairs of the People's Republic of China). (2006, January 12). *China's African policy*. Forum on China-Africa Cooperation. Beijing: Author.

MOFA (Ministry of Foreign Affairs of the People's Republic of China). (2009, September 25). *Programme for China-Africa Cooperation in Economic and Social Development*. Forum on China-Africa Cooperation. Beijing: Author.

MOFA (Ministry of Foreign Affairs of the People's Republic of China). (2015a). *The Forum on China-Africa Cooperation Johannesburg Action Plan (2016–2018)*. Beijing: Author.

MOFA (Ministry of Foreign Affairs of the People's Republic of China). (2015b, December 10). *Declaration of the Johannesburg Summit of the Forum on China-Africa Cooperation*. Beijing: Author.

Nyíri, P. (2006). The yellow man's burden: Chinese migrants on a civilizing mission. *The China Journal, 56*(2), 83–106.

Perlez, J. (2015, December 4). China creates a world bank of its own, and the U.S. Balks. *New York Times*.

Perry, E., & Selden, M. (2003). Introduction: Reform and resistance in contemporary China. In E. Perry & M. Selden (Eds.), *Chinese society: Change, conflict and resistance* (2nd ed., pp. 1–30). London: Routledge.

Power, M., Mohan, G., & Tan-Mullins, M. (2012). *China's resource diplomacy in Africa: Powering development?* Houndmills: Palgrave Macmillan.

Ravallion, M. (2009). Are there lessons for Africa from China's success against poverty? *World Development, 37*(2), 303–313.

Research Group for China Modernization Strategies. (2007). *China modernization report outlook (2001–2007)*. Beijing: Peking University Press.

Scoones, I., Amanor, K., Favareto, A., & Qi, G. (2016). A New politics of development cooperation? Chinese and Brazilian engagement in African agriculture. *World Development, 81*(1), 1–12.

Scott, J. C. (1985). *Weapons of the weak: Everyday forms of peasant resistance*. New Haven, CT: Yale University Press.

Shepard, W. (2015). *Ghost cities of China: The story of cities without people in the world's most populated country*. London: Zed Books.

So, A. (2013). *Class and class conflict in post-socialist China*. Hackensack, NJ: World Scientific.

Spengler, O. (1939). *The decline of the west*. (One Vol. ed.). (C.F. Atkinson Trans.), New York, NY: Knopf.

State Council PRC (The State Council of the People's Republic of China). (2013). China-Africa economic and trade cooperation (2013). Information office of the state council, The People's Republic of China.

Strange, S. (1990). The name of the game. In N. X. Rizopoulos (Ed.), *Sea-Changes: American foreign policy in a world transformed* (pp. 238–273). New York, NY: Council on Foreign Relations.

Suzuki, S. (2011). Why does China participate in intrusive peacekeeping? Understanding paternalistic Chinese discourses on development and intervention. *International Peacekeeping, 18*(3), 271–285.

Tse-Tung, M. (1975). *Selected works of Mao Tse-tung* (Vol. I). Oxford: Pergamon Press.

Wang, H. (1998). Contemporary Chinese thought and the question of modernity. *Social Text, 55*, 9–44.

Wen, T. (2001). Centenary reflections on the 'three dimensional problem' of rural China. *Inter-Asia Cultural Studies, 2*(2), 287–295.

World Bank. (2007). *World Development Report 2008*. Washington, DC: Author.

World Bank. (2012, May 21). *China and Africa share experience in development*. The World Bank Group. Accessed January 12, 2016. http://www.worldbank.org/en/news/feature/2012/05/21/china-africa-share-experience-in-development.

World Bank. (2015, January 13). *Lessons for Africa from China's growth*. The World Bank Group. Accessed January 12, 2016. http://www.worldbank.org/en/news/speech/2015/01/13/lessons-for-africa-from-chinas-growth.

Xinhua News. (2012, November 8). Scientific outlook on development becomes CPC's theoretical guidance. Xinhuanet.

Xu, X., Li, X., Qi, G., Tang, L., & Mukwereza, L. (2016). Science, technology, and the politics of knowledge: The case of China's agricultural technology demonstration centers in Africa. *World Development, 81*(1), 1–10.

Yan, H., & Chen, Y. (2015). Agrarian capitalization without capitalism? Capitalist dynamics from above and below in China. *Journal of Agrarian Change, 15*(3), 366–391.

Zhang, Q., Oya, C., & Ye, J. (2015). Bringing agriculture back in: The central place of agrarian change in rural China studies. *Journal of Agrarian Change, 15*(3), 299–313.

Rethinking about Civilizations: The Politics of Migration in a New Climate

SAMID SULIMAN

School of Humanities, Languages and Social Science, Griffith University, Nathan, QLD, Australia

ABSTRACT *In this paper, I will lay out some useful conceptual/theoretical markets that will help us to understand, and resolve, significant political challenges to 'action' on climate change migration. Thus, while this paper is concerned with climate change and migration responses, it is also concerned with understanding* how we understand *migration in the context of climate change, and how climate change forces a radical shift in such understandings. To do so, I pick up on the work of Robert W. Cox and push it in a different direction. In particular, I am interested in his work on civilizations, and how this civilizational account of world politics opens up space for thinking about climate change broadly, and climate change migration specifically. I argue that Cox's account of 'inter-civilizational' politics helps us to solve a pressing analytical problem: how to rethink the coordinates of contemporary cosmopolitics in the 'Anthropocene', and reconsider the frames of analysis that we adopt to understand and respond to climate change migration. I demonstrate this by considering two distinctly different 'civilizational' accounts of migration and mobility in the Asia-Pacific/Oceania region (one territorial and the other maritime), and consider how these might reveal an important source of future change. By sketching out this approach, my intention is to mobilize the resources offered by Cox in order to further his project of envisaging alternative world orders, and post-hegemonic political relations therein.*

Introduction

Robert Cox sits in the pantheon of critical political studies. His cross-disciplinary work, spanning the fields of international relations, international political economy, and political and social theory, remains as impactful as it was decades ago. Cox's continuing influence over the study of global politics is testament to the originality and even iconoclastic nature of his inquiry. Not satisfied with the strictures of the grand disciplinary debates in International Relations, Cox posed difficult and probing questions about both the nature of the world *and* our understanding of our place/s therein. By drawing our eye to the importance of intersubjectivity within material worlds, Cox helped to make attention to meaning as important as attention to process and outcome in global politics. But it was also his attention to the productive role of knowledge and research, and his recognition of the need for a reflexive and critical understanding of the domain of scholarship, that have significantly altered the traditionally dour epistemological landscape of International Relations (see Mittelman, 1998). While critics abound (see Schechter, 2004, *passim*), it is difficult to overstate either the force of Cox's work, or its impact on the fields of International Relations (IR) and International Political Economy (IPE). But this is not hagiography. In this paper, I am interested in engaging with Cox's *oeuvre* as a way of thinking critically, and differently, about a seemingly intractable global problem: climate change migration.

The starting point for this essay is that the world is not as it used to be. Anthropogenic climate change—attributed to global warming as a result of industrial carbon emissions (IPCC, 2014)—is radically transforming the physical world as much as it is collapsing seeming stable coordinates of global politics, processes that have an important epistemological dimension (Jasanoff, 2010). As I show in the first part of the paper, climate change is also rendering a new political climate, one in which epistemological quandaries abound, complicating obvious material concerns about the projected impacts of climate change (e.g. Castree et al., 2014; Hulme, 2015).

In the case of migration, climate change makes critical thinking about political boundaries, identities, and institutions, as well as the relationship between past, present, and future, even more urgent. For this reason, I propose that Cox provides some important methodological tools needed to analyze this period of acute uncertainty. I am interested in his thinking on post-hegemonic politics (Cox, 1992), his work on civilizations (Cox, 2000), and the ways that his civilizational account of world politics—distinct from the 'civilizational analyses' canvased by Bhambra (2014)—opens up space for thinking about how to deal with migration in the context of a rapidly changing climate, and, in turn, considering alternative prospects for future world order in uncertain times.

However, the utility of Cox's work only holds if we read him with reverence and infidelity in equal measure. Rather than using Cox's contributions as a methodological blueprint, I seek to use his work as the basis for an engagement with novel questions that have arisen in the present conjuncture. Thus, I seek to push Cox's work in a different direction from the one he himself contemplated. In doing so, I will lay out some useful conceptual/theoretical markers that will help us to both understand and, in future, resolve significant political barriers to 'action' on climate change migration. But there is a dual purpose here: while this paper is concerned with climate change and migration, it is also engaged with the epistemological landscape in which climate change migration is occurring. In order to countenance possible futures for migration in a changing climate, we also need to understand *how we understand* migration, and how climate change forces a radical shift in such understandings.

Thus, I argue that Cox helps us to solve a pressing analytical problem: how to rethink the referents of contemporary cosmopolitics, and reconsider the frames of analysis that we adopt to understand present political challenges and future political change. I demonstrate this by considering two distinctly different 'civilizational' accounts of migration and mobility in the Asia-Pacific/Oceania region (one territorial and the other maritime), and consider how the relationship between these might reveal an important source of future change. By sketching out this approach, my intention is to mobilize the resources offered by Cox in order to further his project of envisaging alternative future world orders and post-hegemonic political relations therein.

Migration in a New Political Climate

> Future weather will not be like past weather; future climates will not be like past climates. (Hulme, 2010, p. 1)

Climate change not only poses a challenge to present and future visions of world order and development. Climate change is—or, rather, ought to be—considered a critical irruption of the extant social order. We have entered into a *new political climate*, in which climate change compounds long standing crises and catalyzes new ones. Both the material and ideational bases for the geopolitical expansion of the 'development project' to encompass the entire globe (i.e. the 'globalization project') have made this climate crisis tragically inclusive (see McMichael, 2010, 2012). The single-minded focus upon enclosing the commons has constrained our collective political imagination, to the extent that the extreme political project of commodification has made all forms of life on the planet susceptible to the vagaries of the 'market', itself a symbolic construct that both expresses and conceals the wide variety of human actions that are concerned with the basic activities of accumulation and exchange. This has been the driving force of the development project, the goal of which has been 'to sustain energy, capital and commodity flows for purposes of military and political security' (McMichael, 2009, p. 248), even as the ecological consequences of global industrialization accumulate, themselves most apparent in anthropogenic climate change and associated environmental impacts.

Climate change, to echo Naomi Klein (2014), changes everything. Not only does climate change pose problems for the material bases of both global and local economies (not to mention the interactions between global and local economic systems), but it also presents an immense challenge to both the politico-legal basis of global capitalism (i.e. commodification and enclosure) and the ideological justification of this (i.e. the virtue of the 'free market'). But the challenge cuts deeper still. Climate change makes the social scientific models and frameworks heretofore central to the endeavor to explain and understand social and political transformation untenable (if they ever were tenable in the first place). However, the politics of climate change remains inherently bound up in hegemonic institutions and knowledge structures, and this begs questions about whether extant ideas and institutions can produce the kind of change that is necessary to answer cries for action and redress claims of injustice (Barnett, 2007).

Hegemonic knowledge frameworks and dominant institutions have been problematized by a novel form of historical agency that has been rendered visible by the manifest effects of carbon emissions. Famously, the term 'Anthropocene' emerged in the context of geological research, which set out to understand the impacts of human activity upon the global ecology (Crutzen & Stoermer, 2000). From the perspective of the earth sciences,

> The Anthropocene represents a new phase in the history of the Earth, when natural forces and human forces become intertwined, so that the fate of one determines the fate of the other. Geologically, this is a remarkable episode in the history of the planet. (Zalasiewicz, Williams, Steffan, & Crutzen, 2010, p. 2231)

It is, one could easily argue, also remarkable for important anthropological reasons. As Mike Hulme suggests,

> [...] physical manifestations and cultural representations of climate change are interacting in ways that have no historical analogues from which we can learn. And they are doing so in ways that continue to surprise us. The past, through historic emissions of greenhouse gases, is constraining the future in new ways that are still only crudely understood, whereas the future, through scientific predictions and artistic depictions of climates to come, is making new incursions into the present. The idea of climate change is a consequence of this interpenetration of past, present, and future is acting as a powerful and novel motor for cultural change. (Hulme, 2010, p. 1)

The very real (but, as yet, unknown) risks posed by a warming climate are already impinging on social, cultural, and political relations, in profound ways, on a world scale. And this makes climate change an acutely political problem. The big issues of our time —migration, development, trade, terrorism, international stability, and security—all become complicated by the temporal conundrum of the Anthropocene.

However, the political implications of climate change will not be easily registered if we continue to rely upon explanatory (and predictive) social science models. This is because both political challenges and political meanings are being radically transformed *in relation to a changing climate*. Not only is the climate changing, but so too are the parameters and purpose of knowledge production (Rose et al., 2012). In so far as we humans have become an active agent in the transformation of the physical world—as is argued in writings on the shift from the Holocene to the Anthropocene—humankind has come to insert itself into deep historical processes. This, it is argued, has also irrevocably changed the relationship between the social sciences and humanities and the objects of their inquiry (i.e. the social and the human):

> This is why the need arises to view the human simultaneously on contradictory registers: as a geophysical force and as a political agent, as a bearer of rights and as author of actions; subject to both the stochastic forces of nature (being itself one such force collectively) and open to the contingency of individual human experience; belonging at once to differently-scaled histories of the planet, of life and species, and of human societies. One could say, mimicking Fanon, that in an age when the forces of globalization intersect with those of global warming, the idea of the human needs to be stretched beyond where postcolonial thought advanced it. (Chakrabarty, 2012, pp. 14–15)

If taken seriously, Chakrabarty's claims have serious ramifications for the ways in which we (as analysts of political order and political change) come to understand our own work. It also has profound consequences for the ways in which social and political change will come about, as societies will struggle to reconcile the competing and contradictory demands of extant political allegiances, cultural affiliations, and (self-)identifications, on the one hand, and the slow moving disaster of climate change, on the other hand. But, as Chakrabarty (2009, p. 212) notes elsewhere, the realization of climate change both as an outcome of human agency and as a recalibration of human experience due to its (our?) new role as a geological force should not lead to perceiving the politics of the Anthropocene *only* through a critique of capitalism. Thus, climate change cannot be reduced to an economic, or even a technical, issue: it also draws into question the seemingly settled political coordinates, raising questions about the limits of established ways of thinking about political order and political change.

These challenges are acutely apparent when it comes to contemporary migrations in the context of climate change. Ultimately, we have entered into a period of profound uncertainty, in which the prospect of mass migration looms large. However, equitable and just solutions to climate change-induced displacement have (so far) failed to materialize. While 'the dynamics of the interaction of mobility with climate change are multifaceted and difficult to establish' (Adger et al., 2014, p. 767), the fact is that migration will become an increasingly prominent issue, and an increasingly likely prospect for those peoples whose lives and livelihoods are most threatened by climate change and associated environmental transformations (Reuveny, 2007, pp. 513–514; Tacoli, 2009). As we know, the national and international mechanisms that are used to govern migration are failing spectacularly in terms of protection and security for many migrants—be they recognized refuges, rejected 'asylum seekers', or mere 'economic migrants'—and it is exceedingly unlikely that there will be a place for 'climate migrants' in the future (Betts, 2013, 2011). Compounding this, within the current global order, migration has been constituted as a vector for global inequalities (see Green, 2011; Marchand, 2008; Suliman, 2014, 2016). In the Asia-Pacific/Oceania region, particularly in island communities, climate change all but guarantees a future of migration and/or displacement. Prospects for *in situ* survival are increasingly grim, and options to move remain poor. Where options do exist—such as the purchase of land, asylum claims, or participation in established labor migration channels—they neither afford collective rights for affected peoples, nor guarantee equality with citizens.

Climate change has been an incredibly divisive issue, in terms of formal politics and public discourse (Beeson & McDonald 2013, p. 331). But given the stakes raised so far, extant arrangements must not be taken as the parameters for future debate and action. In this new political climate, the very coordinates by which we can speak and act meaningfully about climate change migration have also changed. The problem that requires new, critical thinking to resolve is a very simple one: if existing ideas, political institutions, and economic structures cannot accommodate the future migrations that will, in all likelihood, emerge in a changing climate, can we rethink and refashion the conditions of world order to accommodate those who are displaced in a changing climate?

The key lesson from the foregoing discussion is that climate change has disrupted the coordinates of political life irrevocably. The radical displacement of human–ecological relations in Anthropocene has, therefore, destabilized available frameworks for understanding (and effecting) political change. The advent of a new global condition also draws into question the ways in which we understand, interpret, and act upon contemporary issues such as climate change migration. At the very least, contemporary conditions necessitate that we revisit our analytical frameworks to see if they are indeed fit for purpose.

Rethinking Change in the New Political Climate

> Hegemony frames thought and thereby circumscribes action. (Cox, 1992, p. 179)

I will now outline several key markers laid by Robert Cox in his work on civilizations, and how this civilizational lens can be focused on the problems outlined in the previous section. The disjuncture between the historical conditions of belonging and the present conditions of being requires innovative thinking about the possibilities for, and likelihood of, future change. I argue that Robert Cox's account of 'inter-civilizational' politics helps us to solve a pressing analytical problem: how to rethink the coordinates of contemporary cosmopolitics in the Anthropocene, and reconsider the frames of analysis that we adopt to understand and respond to climate change migration.

The instability of the current world order, and the fragility of ideological and normative commitments to 'development' by which it is bolstered, has not been lost on Robert Cox. Writing at 'the turn of the new millennium', Cox highlighted a contradiction between 'the real economy and the biosphere' (Cox, 1999, p. 17). To resolve such a contradiction, for Cox, would require a series of profound transformations, no less than 'revolution in social practices and in the structure of social power' (Cox, 1999, p. 17).

Thinking about the future, and the sources of such future change, requires a mode of theorizing that does not take the status quo for granted. 'Theory is always *for* someone and *for* some purpose'. Thus wrote Cox in his seminal article 'Social Forces, States and World Orders: Beyond International Relations Theory' (1981, p. 128). Theory, for Cox, has always served actors and their interests. A primary goal of Cox's scholarship, as we all should know, was to eschew problem-solving approaches in favor of critical theory, which, he argues,

> [...] allows for normative choice in favour of a social and political order different from the prevailing order, but it limits the range of choice to alternative orders which are feasible transformations of the existing world. A principal objective of critical theory, therefore, is to clarify the range of possible alternatives. (Cox, 1981, p. 130)

Cox's historical materialism impresses the importance of understanding change, far beyond a simple plotting of linear time. The dialectical understanding of development and change presented by Cox is one that foregrounds complex relationships between the material and the ideational, the synchronic and the diachronic, and the past and the present. For Cox, the source of such change emerges not from the contradictions in the material conditions of life alone, but from the transformations in 'historical structures', a concept he deploys as heuristic for capturing the changing relationships between ideas, institutions, and material capabilities (Cox, 1981, p. 137). The methodological device of the 'historical structure' allows for an analysis that encompasses the full scope of social and political change, rather than presuming that change is rendered exclusively from the top down, or the bottom up, or that it is unidirectional.

Within this scheme, ideas play an important role, and it in this domain that I want to dwell for a moment. For Cox,

> Ideas are broadly of two kinds. One kind consists of intersubjective meanings, or those shared notions of the nature of social relations which tend to perpetuate habits or expectations of behavior [...] These notions, though durable over long periods of time, are historically conditioned [...] It is possible to trace the origins of such ideas and also to detect a weakening of signs of them [...] The other kind of ideas relevant to an historical structure are collective images of social order held by different groups. These are differing views as to both the nature and the legitimacy of prevailing power relations, the meanings of justice and public good, and so forth. Whereas intersubjective meanings are broadly common throughout a particular historical structure and constitute the common ground of social discourse (including conflict), collective images may be several and opposed. The clash of rival collective images provides evidence of the potential for alternative paths of development and raises questions as to the possible material and institutional basis for the emergence of an alternative structure. (Cox, 1981, p. 136)

A major pillar of Cox's project was the development of an expansive account of hegemony, by incorporating the role and nature of ideas into the political analysis of social change. According to Adam David Morton, '[b]y including the intersubjective within a theory of hegemony, it is also possible to begin appreciating alternative conceptions and different understandings of the world' (Morton, 2003, p. 157; see also Cox 1996, 2000, 2001). Contrary to established theoretical paradigms within International Relations, Cox's approach enables a greater appreciation of differences within specific historical conjunctures, and a deeper understanding of different ideational complexes, and the relations between them, as being potent sources of historical change. Conversely, Cox's concern with understanding the importance of intersubjectivity within hegemonic structures also enables a deeper understanding of why and how social forces that agitate for change are not successful in their aims (see Cox, 1983).

FROM INTERNATIONAL RELATIONS TO WORLD CIVILIZATIONS

The heuristic model of the 'historical structure' has proven to be quite adaptable in Cox's work, in so far as he engaged this way of thinking about the hegemony of the international system in order to consider the complexities of global order and global change, complexities that both envelope and exceed the domain of the 'international'. In repudiation of the kinds of 'civilizational' accounts of global conflict offered by Huntington (1993) and others, Cox (1995, 1997, 2000, 2001) proposed an engagement with inter-civilizational relations as a way of understanding possibilities for conflict, cooperation, and change on a world scale. Importantly, Cox averred that '[t]he universalistic notion of civilization has [...] remained a characteristic of Western consciousness, and an intellectual obstacle to recognition of the ontological equality of other civilizations' (see also Bowden & Seabrooke, 2006). Thus, Cox reframes the question of civilization as one that is open ended, non-teleological, and analytically open to diversity and difference: *'So a working definition of civilization can be a fit or correspondence between material conditions of experience and intersubjective meanings'* (Cox, 2001, p. 110, italics original). In other words,

> Civilizations are ways of being, ways of understanding the world, ways of acting upon that understanding. They shape people's perceptions and thus how they react to events. They exist in the realm of intersubjectivity—those shared ideas that constitute the sense of reality for large groups of people, what they think of as the natural order of things. (Cox, 1995, p. 11)

There are two important elements of Cox's account of civilizations that are worth highlighting. The first is that civilizations are not fixed, immutable, all-encompassing, and mutually exclusive entities:

> The important thing is that it [i.e. civilization] conveys a sense of reality to the people concerned. Of course, there is nothing fixed or immutable in this fit. Material conditions change. So do the meanings that people share intersubjectively. Civilizations are thus in slow but continuing development. *Change is of their essence.* (Cox, 2000, p. 220, emphasis added)

The second, following the first, is that 'civilizations' in Cox's scheme allow for a much more open and change-oriented account of politics than those described (or imagined) by state-centric approaches. For as Cox notes, 'states and civilizations are not equivalent entities' (Cox, 1995, p. 11), and civilizations may coexist *within* a territory, *within* an individual, and *within* relations of domination and subordination, but always in relation to each other. Civilizations, in other words, are not premised on exclusivist or exclusionary understandings of subjectivity or identity, but instead exist and unfold relationally. To this end, thinking in terms of civilizations as the primary intersubjective concern (as opposed to national identities) would be central to any political project concerned with countering the kinds of civilizing missions underpinning hegemonic globalization (see Bowden & Seabrook, 2006; Gill 1995, 2002) and dealing with the displacement of the current (international) world order in the Anthropocene:

> In a global perspective, a balance is to be struck between the distinctiveness of different traditions of civilization and values that can become the common basis for coexistence and mutual enrichment of these traditions. (Cox, 1997, p. 111)

The concept deployed by Cox is a 'big' one, in so far as 'civilization' (despite sitting in the background of consciousness much of the time) manifests routinely in thought and deed. It is also 'big' because it transcends and undercuts methodological premises that hinge on the nation-state and associated developmentalisms; the concept of civilizations offered by Cox complicates the fantasy of neat boundaries and immutable blocs. For Cox, therefore, the present conditions of 'globalization'—exemplified in the turbulent forms of migration that press at the seams of the formally bordered world (see Papastergiadis, 2000)—demand a more nuanced account of civilizational encounters and change. Constant transformation through contact and transmission is the source of historical change, and—contrary to more vulgar materialist accounts—Cox proposes that civilizational matrices are in a state of flux (despite appearances to the contrary) because they are always in contact. Importantly, given that almost all forms of social relations are less determined by geography than they used to be, the terrain of civilizational politics is no longer to be found in space, but rather in mind. Thus, 'we need to know more about the modes of thought characteristic of different civilizations, how these modes of thought came about, and how they may be changing' (Cox, 2000, p. 220).

This account of inter-civilizational encounter posits a very different understanding of contact, conflict, and cooperation from that posited by Eurocentric epistemologies. The great conceit of the auto-narration of 'Western civilization' is that it purports to have resolved the historical problem of political change. However, this has come at the cost of petrifying a specific account of politics, whereby

> [t]he demarcation and policing of the boundary between the 'inside' and 'outside' of the political community defines the problem of difference as *between and among* states; difference is marked and contained as *international* difference. This construction of difference allows us to 'solve' the problem by negotiating a modus vivendi among political communities. (Inayatullah & Blaney, 2004, p. 39)

While this absolves the hegemonic order from dealing with the cracks in this myth, it does so at an enormous cost to those different political/cultural orders that neither assent nor assimilate. Cox proposes a different set of encounters, less to do with resolving differences in the abstract, and more to do with understanding how civilizations change *in relation to each other*.

> Development and change in civilizations today has to be approached from two aspects: first, the contradictions within civilizations that pose choices among visions of the future; and second, the external influences coming from coexisting civilizations that have an impact on these choices. (Cox, 2000, p. 224)

For Cox, the emphasis should be on the 'processes of change', rather than attempts to draw boundaries around civilizations, or to account for change as though civilizations were bounded. This concern for civilizational change and inter-civilizational relations repudiates the state-centrism that continues to limit the scope of political possibilities in a more mobile world, and that IR has not yet relinquished when posing 'solutions' to contemporary problems. Moreover, the focus on intersubjective relations within and between civilizations (already recognized as *not* being spatially determined or defined) allows a greater understanding of potentials for future change than we can glean from the resources assembled by understandings of politics that assume a linear and bounded temporality of development: 'Up to now, international studies have been concerned primarily with states, the inter-state system, and markets. [In contrast,] [c]ivilizations explain the potential of societies to espouse new directions for development' (Cox, 2000, p. 228). This approach to political analysis is useful for identifying contradictions within specific world orders, in different times and places, and 'to assess the possible directions for change' (Cox, 2000, p. 229). The pressing task, from this perspective, is to think about how we can undo hegemony, which Cox understands being 'expressed in universal norms, institutions and mechanisms which lay down general rules of behavior for states and for those forces of civil society that act across national boundaries—rules which support the dominant mode of production' (Cox, 1983, pp. 171–172).

At present, the hegemony of 'Western' civilization is apparent, and has had deleterious consequences for other civilizations (especially those subject to colonial, and later, neo-liberal rule). However, while hegemonic orders can and do change, the active pursuit of a common future must also use contradictions as the starting point for different kinds of inquiry, so as to avoid the repetition of banal—but deeply problematic—universalist maxims. As Cox notes,

> Previous hegemonic orders have derived their universals from the dominant society, itself the product of a dominant civilization. A post-hegemonic order would have to derive its normative content in a search for common ground among constituent traditions of civilization. What might be this common ground? (Cox, 1992, p. 180)

In the final section, I pick up this search for the common ground in inter-civilizational relations. I suggest that while climate change migration is a seemingly intractable problem, its intractability arises from the persistent hegemonic territorial account of community, which emerged in the Euro-American tradition, and is now embedded in all state-forms, often sitting uneasily with different civilizational accounts of polity, community, and mobility. The formation of political space has been contingent upon domesticating—in a very specific way—movement and migration. Yet, this is not the only form of mobility practice, and the relationship between exclusive space and the sovereign right to include (or exclude) coheres with only one specific political project: the system of territorial nation-states. This is contingent, not natural, and is routinely circumscribed and circumvented by other spatio-kinetic political arrangements. In this brief exploration, I suggest that we can apprehend the political significance of migration in the terms set out by Cox: rather than an outcome of changes rendered by climate change, migration is a site, or vector, for a different politics in a changing climate. This is because migration is a social domain in which inter-civilizational encounters unfold virtually all the time. Interestingly, the common ground sought by Cox might not be ground at all.

The Sea as Common Ground

> [...] *indeed,* the movement creates *the relation of an archipelago.* (Stratford et al., 2011, p. 125, emphasis original)

When it comes to migration (particularly maritime migration) in the Asia-Pacific/Oceania region, we have seen a turn toward fortification, detention, and forced return, with the overriding goal to scupper unauthorized arrivals before they cross the shoreline. One of the most powerful regional states—Australia—has been particularly hostile to claims of migrancy by regional others, and others who travel through the region. Recognition of legitimate movement is delimited, and migration between islands and the hegemonic mainland has, for quite some time, been disciplined by imperial and capitalist concerns, adding to the mythology of superiority that envisages the 'white' settler nations in the region as providing the moral leadership for development and peace among its island neighborhood. This is to say nothing of the ways that mobility has been highly circumscribed for Aboriginal peoples of Australia, who have been either detained or displaced according to the whims and wants of racist (post)colonial institutions (see Long & Memmott, 2007; Taylor & Bell, 2004; Young & Doohan, 1989).

When talking about intensifying political challenges in the Asia-Pacific/Oceania region that are emergent in the Anthropocene, such as climate change migration, we can no longer start with the premise of 'Australia' (for example) as though it were a bounded entity. In fact, it was a mistake to even do so in the first place. 'Contrary to conventional belief', writes the poet John Mateer (2006, p. 89), 'Australia is not an island—it's an archipelago, culturally porous and edgeless'. Instead of trying to force climate change migration back into the box of international law and national sovereignty, perhaps we can look to a range of civilizational orders, and the relations between them, to rethink the *common grounds* for shared inter-civilizational institutions, at a time when the social and political coordinates in the Anthropocene are completely up for grabs.

Another vision of this region, and the mobility politics therein, is posed by Epeli Hau'ofa (1994), who writes instead of a 'sea of islands', where the ocean does not separate, but rather connects peoples through departure, journey, and arrival. The seas have, for Hau'ofa, a very different ontological significance, which he makes evident in his preference for a different nomenclature of the region and its peoples:

> 'Oceania' connotes a sea of islands with their inhabitants. The world of our ancestors was a large sea full of places to explore, to make their homes in, to breed generations of seafarers like themselves. People raised in this environment were at home with the sea. They played in it as soon as they could walk steadily, they worked in it, they fought on it. They developed great skills for navigating their waters, and the spirit to traverse even the few large gaps that separated their island groups [...] Theirs was a large world in which peoples and cultures moved and mingled unhindered by boundaries of the kind erected much later by imperial powers. From one island to another they sailed to trade and to marry, thereby expanding social networks for greater flow of wealth. They travelled to visit relatives in a wide variety of natural and cultural surroundings, to quench their thirst for adventure, and even to fight and dominate. (Hau'ofa, 1994, pp. 153–154)

The territorial sea has long impinged upon this sea of islands. The colonial encounter consigned islands to the margins: 'inferior islands in opposition to superior continents and mainlands' (Farbotko, 2010, p. 52). Existing migration arrangements do little to change this fact. Importantly, however, and contrary to the mainland-ism and territorialism of state practice and foreign policy in the region, the seas and oceans that surround the Australian mainland are inhabited in ways that consistently defy the ordering logic by which they are governed. It is in the interstices between the 'ordered sea' and the 'lived sea' that irruptive political transformations are occurring, and where we can train our eye to locate future possibilities in a changing climate.

And the importance of this onto-political shift is even more important when we contemplate the actualities of climate change migration in the Asia-Pacific/Oceania region today. While climate change negotiations press on for another year, and another decade, the real-world effects of climate change are becoming more and more acute for many communities around the world. For many coastal and island people, the effects of climate change are becoming ever too real. And this both poses problems for reorganizing the economy and society of islands, and represents a substantial threat to the ongoing viability of life in these places. These problems are particularly acute for island nations in the Asia-Pacific/Oceania region.

A key problem is that when the island community is comprised as a sovereign nation-state, the possibilities for relocation or mass migration are limited. Island states have struggled to make themselves heard in the domain of climate politics for quite some time, and in proposing/pursuing more radical solutions of individual and collective migrations, they face even less surmountable obstacles (see McAdam, 2012; Vaha, 2015). Indeed, the proposition of the migration of entire states to new territories seems almost implausible as the notion that entire communities will be willingly resettled in just and humane ways (cf. McAdam, 2014). International refugee law is silent on protections of people (and peoples) forced to move because of environmental change, and national laws of signatory states have proven inflexible to the new migration claims within the new political climate that we now find ourselves in.

There is no clear fit between the international mechanisms that exist to govern 'exceptional' forms of migration (such as 'survival migration'), and the empirical reality of climate change migration that is unfolding under conditions induced by hegemonic forms of political organization (such as the globalization of the world economy). What is clear, however, is that recourse to the discourses and mechanisms for protection that have emerged from the civilizational ordering of world politics through the universalization of the nation-state system and the insistence upon 'development' are inadequate, if not harmful (see McNamara & Gibson, 2009). But despite the resistance to a future dictated by the excesses of industrial (or market) civilization, migration will be unavoidable for the adaptation and survival of island peoples. Thus, exchanges of social resources to manage mobility, beyond the exclusionist approach that predominates, will likely be in order (see Farbotko & Lazrus, 2012, p. 388).

Indeed, many island peoples have very different traditions and inhabit cultures of mobility that look very different from the hegemonic conception of migration as the 'severance of ties, uprootedness, and rupture' (Lilomaiava-Doktor, 2009, p. 1). For example,

> The Samoan concept *Malaga*, usually translated as 'travel' or 'movement', implies going back and forth [...] The Samoan idea of *vā*, or social space, engages the power within and between spaces and places arrayed in opposition to each other. (Lilomaiava-Doktor, 2009, p. 1)

This might represent a kind of archipelagic thought—distinctive from the territorial, Westphalian imagination—that has emerged in a variety of disciplinary contexts as a way of thinking about the social relations *between* spaces and places that are represented as discrete and bounded. Whereas hegemonic institutions and knowledge structures privilege containment and enclosure, archipelagic thought subverts these ordering principles to reveal a dynamic history of movement and relation (see Carter, 2011; Glissant, 1999; Minter, 2013). I would suggest that this archipelagic thought reflects the 'common sense' of many peoples in the Asia-Pacific region, and as such makes possible a different kind of political order from that which we see at present. I would also suggest that we can see this as the basis of different kinds of mobilization that draw on a historical 'civilization of mobility', and the insertion of these civilizational resources into regional climate change politics.

At the state level, island leaders are appropriating the current enthusiasm of the 'migration for development' discourse (i.e. an embrace of labor migration as a key economic development strategy; see Suliman, 2016; Sutherland, 2013) to prepare their peoples for a future of geographical dispersal and eventual relocation as sea levels rise. Kiribati President Anote Tong is well aware that '[i]f nothing is done, Kiribati will go down in to the ocean' (cited in Goldberg, 2013). In addition to strident climate change activism in international fora, he has attempted to 'transnationalize' the Kiribati archipelago by encouraging his people to link in to skilled migration channels (see McAdam, 2012, p. 205), thus closing the spatial distance denoted by the vast ocean through strategic engagements with regional neighbors (such as purchasing land in Fiji and rallying with other Pacific Island leaders to advocate for an alternative to industrial multilateralism), and foreign labor markets. Importantly, this gives the sense that Tong sees the I-Kiribati future in old and new connections across the sea. In a different register, the transnational collective *The Pacific Climate Warriors* (n.d.) are mobilizing culture to render acutely visible the connections between the Australian government's rapacious energy and industrial policies and threats to the cultural survival of Pacific Island peoples. Their motto is 'We're not drowning, we are fighting' (http://world.350.org/pacificwarriors/).

Perhaps this represents a political future in the region where political power does not conspire against public interest, but rather political authority is situated within a polyvalent and open set of publics that are open to exchange. But we might also look to everyday practices of migration and movement in the region, while keeping in mind the necessity to work against those assumptions that we derive from the 'common-sense' of the social sciences, which are nested within—and claimed by—the developmentalism of the West.

In our inter-civilizational archipelago, migration and mobility are polysemic, meaning different things to different peoples, depending upon where they reside within any given civilizational imaginary. For those invested in the Westphalian world, maritime mobility—interpreted primarily as a kind of unsanctioned migration—is all about transgressing national borders (for good or for ill). For many island cultures, mobility is about connection. Oftentimes, these different meanings abrade each other as the physical movement of traveling from here to there, or back again, unfolds. While one conception may predominate the other in the current historical conjuncture, migration and mobility can never be reduced to the static, statist imaginary by which international mobility is largely governed today.

Rather than seeing these points of contact and contestation as a political problem *per se*, Cox's approach permits a substantive engagement with the ideas that underpin material processes. This may allow us to level out inequalities between the epistemological resources that different civilizations may have to offer in grappling with the collective and inescapable problem of climate change, and negotiate the problems that will eventually arise when people are compelled to migrate in our new political climate, in which the boundaries of politics are completely up for grabs. It may also enable a post-hegemonic and open-ended understanding of 'us'.

Cox asked, 'What might be this common ground?' We might answer, 'the sea'.

Conclusion

The future is at an impasse. As the foregoing discussion has intimated, the spatial and temporal framework of 'development' is becoming undone, through climate change and all the contradictory processes that both cause and amplify these planetary transformations. The temporality of the supposedly universal industrial/market civilization, while always historically contingent, has been rendered acutely unstable. Meanwhile, 'climate change refugees' sit at the fraying edge of this auto-ethnography of a fortified civilization. There is a need to unwind the intellectual fixing of space that was integral to the ascendency of state sovereignty as the guiding principle of world affairs, itself a contingent practice that has become a cornerstone of the civilizational imaginary of 'international society' (see Walker, 1990, pp. 172–173).

The focus on inter-civilizational encounters, and the attendant possibilities of (inter-)civilizational change, offers a productive avenue for understanding contemporary ructions surrounding climate change migration, and possibilities for institutions to govern these emergent challenges. In this paper, I have considered how the work of Robert Cox might be drawn upon to reframe political analysis in the contemporary period. A deep understanding of how civilizations are changing, and how they change through interactions, is essential to reimagine the possibilities for cooperative and even collective action to ensure that all peoples have a future in the changing climate, and not just the historically privileged few. The possibilities for a post-hegemonic politics lie in the capacity for civilizations to change, and for these changes to be manifest in the political institutions and ideals through which societies are governed. Civilizational exchanges may prove to be the lifeboat we need for figuring out how we are all going to get along in a warmer world. Cox (2004, p. xxi) wrote that 'in the contemporary world we have to think of civilizations as existing in the mind rather than on a plot of land'. To do so, we also need to break down the hegemony of the territorial imagination in order to be open to change. In this new political climate, we have much to learn from lives lived in the archipelago.

Disclosure Statement

No potential conflict of interest was reported by the author.

References

Adger, W. N., Pulhin, J. M., Barnett, J., Dabelko, G. D., Hovelsrud, G. K., Levy, M., ... Vogel, C. H. (2014). Human security. In C. B. Field, V. R. Barros, D. J. Dokken, K. J. Mach, M. D. Mastrandrea, T. E. Bilir, ... L. L. White (Eds.), *Climate change 2014: Impacts, adaptation, and vulnerability, part A: Global and sectoral aspects, contribution of working group II to the fifth assessment report of the intergovernmental panel on climate change* (pp. 755–791). Cambridge: Cambridge University Press.
Barnett, J. (2007). The geopolitics of climate change. *Geography Compass*, *1*(6), 1361–1375.
Beeson, M., & McDonald, M. (2013). The politics of climate change in Australia. *Australian Journal of Politics & History*, *59*(3), 331–348.
Betts, A. (Ed.). (2011). *Global migration governance*. Oxford: Oxford University Press.
Betts, A. (2013). *Survival migration: Failed governance and the crisis of displacement*. Ithaca, NY: Cornell University Press.
Bhambra, G. K. (2014). *Connected sociologies*. London: Bloomsbury.
Bowden, B., & Seabrooke, L. (Eds.). (2006). *Global standards of market civilisation*. Abingdon: Routledge.
Carter, P. (2011). Archipelago: The shape of the future. *Antithesis*, *21*, 11–25.
Castree, N., Adams, W. M., Barry, J., Brockington, D., Büscher, B., Corbera, E., ... Newell, P. (2014). Changing the intellectual climate. *Nature Climate Change*, *4*(9), 763–768.
Chakrabarty, D. (2009). The climate of history: Four theses. *Critical Inquiry*, *35*(2), 197–222.
Chakrabarty, D. (2012). Postcolonial studies and the challenge of climate change. *New Literary History*, *43*(1), 1–18.
Cox, R. W. (1981). Social forces, states and world orders: Beyond international relations theory. *Millennium – Journal of International Studies*, *10*(2), 126–155.
Cox, R. W. (1983). Gramsci, hegemony and international relations: An essay in method. *Millennium – Journal of International Studies*, *12*(2), 162–175.
Cox, R. W. (1992). Multilateralism and world order. *Review of International Studies*, *18*(2), 161–180.
Cox, R. W. (1995). Civilizations: Encounters and transformations. *Studies in Political Economy*, 47 (*Summer*), 7–31.
Cox, R. W. (1996). Civilisations in the world economy. *New Political Economy*, *1*(2), 141–156.
Cox, R. W. (1997). An alternative approach to multilateralism for the twenty-first century. *Global Governance*, *3*(1), 103–116.
Cox, R. W. (1999). Civil society at the turn of the millennium: Prospects for an alternative world order. *Review of International Studies*, *25*(1), 3–28.
Cox, R. W. (2000). Thinking about civilizations. *Review of International Studies*, *26*(5), 217–234.
Cox, R. W. (2001). Civilizations and the twenty-first century: Some theoretical considerations. *International Relations of the Asia-Pacific*, *1*(1), 105–130.
Cox, R. W., & Schecter, M. G. (2004). *The political economy of a plural world*. London: Routledge.
Crutzen, P. J., & Stoermer, E. F. (2000). The anthropocene. *IGBP Newsletter*, 41.
Farbotko, C. (2010). Wishful sinking: Disappearing islands, climate refugees and cosmopolitan experimentation. *Asia Pacific Viewpoint*, *51*(1), 47–60.
Farbotko, C., & Lazrus, H. (2012). The first climate refugees? Contesting global narratives of climate change in Tuvalu. *Global Environmental Change*, *22*(2), 382–390.
Gill, S. (1995). Globalisation, market civilisation, and disciplinary neoliberalism. *Millennium – Journal of International Studies*, *24*(3), 399–423.

Gill, S. (2002). Constitutionalizing inequality and the clash of globalizations. *International Studies Review, 4*(2), 47–65.
Glissant, É. (1999). From introduction to a poetics of the diverse. *Boundary* 2, *26*(1), 119–121.
Goldberg, J. (2013). *Drowning Kiribati, Bloomberg Business*. Retrieved from http://www.bloomberg.com/bw/articles/2013-11-21/kiribati-climate-change-destroys-pacific-island-nation
Green, L. (2011). The nobodies: Neoliberalism, violence, and migration. *Medical Anthropology, 30*(4), 366–385.
Hau'ofa, E. (1994). Our sea of islands. *The Contemporary Pacific, 6*(1), 147–161.
Hulme, M. (2010). Mapping climate change knowledge: An editorial essay. *Wiley Interdisciplinary Reviews: Climate Change, 1*(1), 1–8.
Hulme, M. (2015). Changing what exactly, and from where? A response to Castree. *Dialogues in Human Geography, 5*(3), 322–326.
Huntington, S. P. (1993). The clash of civilizations? *Foreign Affairs, 72*(3), 22–49.
Inayatullah, N., & Blaney, D. L. (2004). *International relations and the problem of difference*. London: Routledge.
Intergovernmental Panel on Climate Change (IPCC). (2014). *Climate change 2014: Synthesis report, contribution of Working Groups I, II and III to the fifth assessment report of the intergovernmental panel on climate change* [Core Writing Team, R.K. Pachauri & L.A. Meyer (Eds.)]. Geneva: IPCC.
Jasanoff, S. (2010). A new climate for society, theory. *Culture & Society, 27*(2–3), 233–253.
Klein, N. (2014). *This changes everything: Capitalism vs. the climate*. New York, NY: Simon and Schuster.
Lilomaiava-Doktor, S. I. (2009) Beyond 'migration': Samoan population movement (Malaga) and the geography of social space (Vā). *The Contemporary Pacific, 21*(1), 1–32.
Long, S., & Memmott, P. (2007). *Aboriginal mobility and the sustainability of communities: Case studies from north-west Queensland and eastern Northern Territory*. Alice Springs: Desert Knowledge CRC.
Marchand, M. (2008). The violence of development and the migration/insecurities nexus: Labour migration in a North American context. *Third World Quarterly, 29*(7), 1375–1388.
Mateer, J. (2006). Australia is not an island. *Meanjin, 65*(1), 89–93.
McAdam, J. (2012). *Climate change, forced migration, and international law*. Oxford: Oxford University Press.
McAdam, J. (2014). Historical cross-border relocations in the pacific: Lessons for planned relocations in the context of climate change. *The Journal of Pacific History, 49*(3), 301–327.
McMichael, P. (2009). Contemporary contradictions of the global development project: Geopolitics, global ecology and the 'development climate. *Third World Quarterly, 30*(1), 247–262.
McMichael, P. (Ed.). (2010). *Contesting development: Critical struggles for social change*. London: Routledge.
McMichael, P. (2012). *Development and social change* (5th ed.). Thousand Oaks, CA: Sage.
McNamara, K. E., & Gibson, C. (2009). 'We do not want to leave our land': Pacific ambassadors at the United Nations resist the category of 'climate refugees'. *Geoforum, 40*(3), 475–483.
Minter, P. (2013) Archipelagos of sense: Thinking about a decolonised Australian poetics. *Southerly, 73*(1), 155–169.
Mittelman, J. H. (1998). Coxian historicism as an alternative perspective in international studies. *Alternatives: Global, Local, Political, 23*(1), 63–92.
Morton, A. D. (2003) Social forces in the struggle over hegemony: Neo-Gramscian perspectives in international political economy. *Rethinking Marxism, 15*(2), 153–179.
The Pacific Climate Warriors. (n.d.). *The Pacific Warrior Journey*, August 14. Retrieved from http://world.350.org/pacificwarriors/
Papastergiadis, N. (2000). *The turbulence of migration*. Cambridge: Polity.
Reuveny, R. (2007). Climate change-induced migration and violent conflict. *Political Geography, 26*(6), 656–673.
Rose, D. B., van Dooren, T., Chrulew, M., Cook, S., Kearnes, M., & O'Gorman, E. (2012). Thinking through the environment, unsettling the humanities. *Environmental Humanities, 1*(1), 1–5.
Schechter, M.G. (2004). Critiques of Coxian theory: Background to a conversation. In R. W. Cox & M. G. Schecter (Eds.), *The political economy of a plural world* (pp. 1–25). London: Routledge.
Stratford, E., Baldacchino, G., McMahon, E., Farbotko, C., & Harwood, A. (2011). Envisaging the archipelago. *Island Studies Journal, 6*(2), 113–130.
Suliman, S. (2014). The politics of migration and the North American free trade agreement. In H. Weber (Ed.), *The politics of development: A survey* (pp. 193–220). London: Routledge.
Suliman, S. (2016). Mobility and the kinetic politics of migration and development. *Review of International Studies*. doi:10.1017/S0260210516000048
Sutherland, P. D. (2013). Migration is development: How migration matters to the post-2015 debate. *Migration and Development, 2*(2), 151–156.
Tacoli, C. (2009) Crisis or adaptation? Migration and climate change in a context of high mobility. *Environment and Urbanization, 21*(2), 513–525.

Taylor, J., & Bell, M. (2004). Continuity and change in indigenous Australian population mobility. In J. Taylor & M. Bell (Eds.), *Population mobility and indigenous peoples in Australasia and North America* (pp. 13–44). London: Routledge.

Vaha, M. E. (2015) Drowning under: Small island states and the right to exist. *Journal of International Political Theory*, *11*(2), 206–223.

Walker, R. B. J. (1990). Sovereignty, identity, community: Reflections on the horizons of contemporary political practice. In R. B. J. Walker & S. H. Mendlovitz (Eds.), *Contending sovereignties: Redefining political community* (pp. 159–185). Boulder: Lynne Rienner.

Young, E., & Doohan, K. (1989). *Mobility for survival: A process analysis of aboriginal population movement in Central Australia*. Darwin: North Australia Research Unit.

Zalasiewicz, J., Williams, M., Steffan, W., & Crutzen, P. (2010) The new world of the anthropocene. *Environmental Science & Technology*, *44*(7), 2228–2231.

Index

Note: Page numbers in **bold** type refer to figures
Page numbers in *italic* type refer to tables
Page numbers followed by 'n' refer to notes

absolute historicism 33, 42
Academic Ranking of World Universities (ARWU) 114
Accolti, B. 25
accreditation 113
accreditors 113–15
activism 102–3
actors 8, 16, 27, 36, 109–11; alienated 5; central 36; Chinese development 129; civil society 6; development 132; economic 6, 101; foreign 123; individual 36; non-state 91; political 6, 27, 82; social 43
Afghanistan 55, 111
Africa 50, 56, 98, 123, 129–34
African American (USA) 56
African Policy, China's (CAP) 129
Agency for International Development (USAID) 111; Education Strategy (2011–15) 111
agriculture: commercialized 122; development 127–32; modernization 123
Agriculture Action Plan 2013–15 (AAP) 131
agroecology 134
agrotechnology 130
agrotechnology demonstration centres (ATDCs) 130
Aguelli, E. 49
Alamuti, M.M. 74
alienated actors 5
All-Africa summit 118
American hegemony 34, 43, 96
American Hegemony and the Trilateral Commission (Gill) 53
anachronism 27–9; systematic 21, 29
Anatomy of Influence, The (Bloom) 7, 35
Anglo-American IR split 87–9
Angola 56
Anthropocene 138–52
anti-immigration 103

apartheid 16
Approaches to World Order (Cox) 44n3, 45n14
Arab Revolution 57
ascending hierarchy 24
Ashley, R. 23
Asia 101
Asia-Pacific/Oceania region 138, 142, 146–7
Asian Infrastructure Investment Bank (AIIB) 123
asylum seekers 142
Augelli, E. 50; and Murphy, C. 50, 53, 60n2
Australia 52, 87–9, 92n2
Austria 113
autonomy 24

Bakunon, M. 38
Bank of America 116
Banks, M. 88
Barkawi, T., and Laffey, M. 51, 55, 58
Beckert, S. 53
Beier, M. 51
benevolent hegemony 53
Benford, R.D., and Snow, D.A. 81
Bentham, J. 89
Bhambra, G.K. 139
Bieler, A., and Morton, A.D. 15
Blair, A. (Tony) 57
Bologna reforms (European Commission) 113
Bolognaization 113
Booth, K. 23, 68, 77n4
Boulding, K. 81
Braudel, F. 8, 33–4, 38–43, 45n9, 45n11, 45n13, 59, 69, 74
Bretton Woods 4, 41
Brincat, S.K. 7–10, 64–78; and Karavas, G. 8, 122–37; Lima, L. and Nunes, J. 51, 84
British Empire 56
Bruni, L. 25

INDEX

Business Civilization 9
Butler, J. 51

Canada 52, 87–9, 92n2
capitalism 3, 24, 56–9, 70–2, 98, 127–9, 141; global 58; neoliberal 3–4; US 103; war 53
carbon emissions 139
Carnegie, A. 115
Carr, E.H. 8, 14, 33–4, 38–43, 44n8, 45n9–10, 69, 83
Cartesian philosophy 27–8
Cartesian structuralism 49
casualties, Western and Third World (1886–2006) 54–5, 54
central actors 36
Chakrabarty, D. 141
Chatterjee, P. 50
China 8–9, 18, 98, 101; Shanghai Jiao Tong University 114
Chomsky, N. 5
Citigroup 116
citizenship 101
civil persona 25–8
civil society 3, 27, 44n3, 45n12, 75, 102, 145; actors 6; organizations 103
civilization 39; business 9
class: transnational managerial 98; working 59, 71
classical Marxism 86
classical realism 3–4
climate change 3, 4, 9
Clinton, W. (Bill), Administration (USA) 57
cognitive psychology 81
Cohen, B. 91
Cold War (1945–92) 3–4, 40, 56, 115
collective activity 38
collective subjectivity 39
Collingwood, R.G. 8, 33–43, 44n5–6, 69, 73–4
colonization 49
Columba Peoples 51
commercial humanism 28
commercialization 9, 129–35
commercialized agriculture 122
common sense 110, 149
communism 129
communities, university 116–17
conceptualization 109
conquest, violent 57
consensual hegemony 55
consensus–coercion nexus 51
constructivism 19, 79–83, 87; soft 81–3, 88
consumerism 135
conventional ontology 12
convergence 122–37
Copernican Revolution 73
corporate social responsibility (CSR) 100
corporations, transnational (TNCs) 96–9, 103–6

corporatism 101
counterhegemony 17, 59, 96
covert operations/support 57
Cox, R.W. 1, 2–6, 7–10, 35–47, 109–11, 119, 120n1
Critical International Theory (CIT) 65
critical theory 2, 5, 11–13, 16–19, 22–5, 30, 30n4, 49
critical thinking 12, 17–19, 21
cross-disciplinarity 90
cross-fertilization 118
Crow, J. 56
Cruickshank, N.G., and Kubálková, V. 92n1

Decent Work Platform (ILO) 105
defensive neorealism 60n3
Dehio, L. 25
democracy, liberal 41
denationalization 114
Denmark 114
Depelchin, J. 59
Descartes, R. 70
descending hierarchy 24
destabilization, violent 55
Deutsch, K. 4
developing countries 123, 129
Devetak, R.R. 69; and Walter, R. 8, 21–32
dialectical production of history 23–4
dichotomy 85, 99
diplomacy 57, 87, 91
Discourse on Method (Descartes) 70
dominant states 4
domination, racial 56
Donation of Constantine 29
Dostoyevsky, F. 38
Doty, R. 51
dual civilizationship 124–5

East 127
ecology, global 140
economic actors 6, 101
economic globalization 97–8, 122–5, 135
economic growth 132
economy: global 8, 95–7, 101–3, 135; international 95; political 21, 24, 70, 110; social 124; world 3, 24
Education Strategy (USAID, 2011–15) 111
Egypt 57
eighteenth century 89, 111
Eisenstadt, S. 92
emancipation 84
empirical materialism 43
empowerment 3
Engels, F. 58, 86
enlightened hegemony 53
epistemology 125

INDEX

Esbenshade, J. 103
ethnic violence 56
Euro-America 48, 51, 58–9
Eurocentrism 59, 73, 77n6
Europe 4, 56–8, 101, 113–15, 128
European Commission 113; Bologna reforms 113
exploitation, labour 8, 98–101
extremism 5

Falk, R. 2–6, 8
fifteenth century 29
Fiji 148
folklore 37
forces redux 17–18, **18**
Ford, H. 115
foreign actors 123
Forum on China–Africa Cooperation Johannesburg Action Plan 2016–18 (FOCAC–JAP) 130
Foucault, M. 80, 89–91
Frame Analysis (Goffman) 81
framework for action 67
France 56
Frankfurt School (FS) 65, 76n1, 77n2, 83–6, 91, 92n1
Freud, S. 86
Frobel, F., Heinrichs, J. and Kreeye, O. 97
Fukuyama, F. 4, 40

Gadaffi, M. 57
Gaza, Israeli invasion of (2008–9) 51
Geertz, C. 111
General Agreement on Trade in Services (GATS) 112
genetic historicism 49
genocide 57
Germain, R. 8, 33–47
German Idealism 65, 69
Germany 56, 72, 89, 111–13
Gilbert, F. 26
Gill, S.R. 49, 53, 60n1; and Law, D. 50
global capitalism 58
global ecology 140
global economy 8, 95–7, 101–3, 135
global hegemony 53–5
global industrialization 140
global migration 101
global neoliberalism 56
global North 116
global order 34
Global Political Economy, The (Gill and Law) 50
global production networks (GPNs) 95
global South 116
global warming 3
globalization 57–8, 73, 77n5, 95–9, 103–5, 125–6, 141; economic 97–8, 122–5, 135; hegemonic 144; neoliberal 3, 97, 103
Globalization Syndrome, The (Mittelman) 50

Goa 56
Goffman, E. 81
Goldman Sachs 116
Goodman, A.E. 117
Google Scholar 34, 44n1
Gramsci, A. 17, 33–5, 41–3, 44n5, 45n9, 45n16, 50, 56, 69, 77n5
Great Britain 24, 126
green revolution technologies (GRT) 130
Grovougi, S.N., and Leonard, L. 53
Grundrisse (Marx) 85

Haas, P.M. 120n3
Habermas, J. 23, 65, 86
Haddock, B.A. 27
Hamati-Ataya, I. 69
Harrod, J. 99
Hegel, G.W.F. 23, 65, 69, 72
hegemonic globalization 144
hegemonic knowledge 140
hegemonic order 145–6
hegemonization 59
hegemony 14, 41–2, 48–50, 52–3, 60n3, 96, 119, 143–4; American 34, 43, 96; benevolent 53; consensual 55; counter 17, 59, 96; enlightened 53; global 53–5; intellectual 87; neo-Gramscian theory 8; political 24; primitive 51–9; US 87–8, 110; Western 112
Heinrichs, J., Kreye, O. and Frobel, F. 97
Held, D. 58
hierarchy, descending 24
historical idealism 8, 33–4, 40–3
historical materialism 33–4, 40, 143
historical mode of thought 34–42
historical ontology 22
historical structure 39, 45n10, 49–51, 67
historicism 8, 25, 33–5, 42, 66–8, 73; absolute 33, 42; genetic 49; praxis 33
historiography 8
History and Class Consciousness (Luckas) 49
Hitler, A. 86
Hobsbawm, E. 35
Hobson, J. 59
Hoffman, M. 85
Honneth, A. 65, 75
Horkheimer, M. 8, 84–5
Hulme, M. 140
human association, as civilization coexistence 73–5
human reproduction 19
human rights 16, 57, 115
humanism 25–7, 30; commercial 28; Renaissance 25–6
humanity 39–40, 65, 73, 91
Hunter, I. 30
Huntington, S.P. 40, 144
hyperliberalism 69

INDEX

Ibn Khaldun 2, 41, 45n14, 73–4
idealism 37; German 65, 69; historical 8, 33–4, 40–3; philosophical 43
ideology 3, 19, 52, 69, 85, 125; tripartite 102
Image, The (Boulding) 81
immigration 103; anti- 103
imperialism 66, 128–30
Imperialism: Pioneer of Capitalism (Warren) 58
India 56, 98
individual actors 36
individualism 124–6, 135
Indonesia 114
industrial carbon emissions 139
industrialization 123, 128–9; global 140
Innis, H. 41, 124
innovative ontology 16
Institute of Higher Education, Academic Ranking of World Universities (ARWU) 114
institutionalism, neoliberal 52
intellectual hegemony 87
inter-civilization politics 9
internal violence 56
international economy 95
International Historical Sociology 7
International Labour Organization (ILO) 7, 35–6, 95–6, 101, 105; Decent Work Platform 105
International Organization 36
International Political Economy (IPE) 7, 11–12, 17–19, 33, 96, 139
international society 127
international theory 49, 59
internationalism, liberal 4
internationalization 73, 117
intersubjectivity 15–17, 82, 109–10, 118–19, 125, 139, 143–4
intra-Euro-American relations 48–9, 52
Iraq 111
Israeli invasion of Gaza (2008–9) 51
Italy 29

Jackson, P.T. 90–2
Jahn, B. 68
Japan 115
Jay, M. 86
Jones, S.W. 51

Kahneman, D. 81
Kaldor, M. 58
Kant, I. 85
Kantian philosophy 68
Karavas, G., and Brincat, S.K. 8, 122–37
Keohane, R. 35
Klein, N. 140
knowledge 64, 79–80, 90, 100; hegemonic 140; self- 37, 71, 74; social 82
Knowledge Bank 112

Koller, D. 117
Korean War (1950–3) 55
Kreye, O., Frobel, F. and Heinrichs, J. 97
Krugman, P. 116
Kubálková, V. 8, 76, 79–94; and Cruickshank, N.G. 92n1
Kuhn, T.S. 88

labour 8
Lacan, J. 89
Laffey, M., and Barkawi, T. 51, 55, 58
Lancet, The 55
Law, D., and Gill, S.R. 50
legitimacy 128, 143; social 99
Leonard, L., and Grovougi, S.N. 53
Leysens, A. 83–4, 92n1
liberal democracy 41
liberal internationalism 4
liberal order 23–4
liberalism 43, 49, 52, 68; hyper- 69
liberalization 128, 131
Liberty Before Liberalism (Skinner) 29
Lima, L., Nunes, J. and Brincat, S.K. 51, 84
Linklater, A. 23
Livy (Titus Livius) 26
Luckas, G. 49

Machiavelli, N. 2, 25–7
McMichael, P. 126, 133
Mamdani, M. 56
managerial class 98
Marcuse, H. 65
marginality 100
marginalization 133; social 96
marginals, social 98–9
Marx, K. 38–40, 43, 58, 65, 70–3, 85–6
Marxism 13, 35, 49, 58, 85–6; classical 86; Western 86
Massive Open Online Courses (MOOCs) 117
Mateer, J. 146
material capabilities 14–15, 18
materialism: empirical 43; historical 33–4, 40, 143
Mayer, F.W. 106n1
Mearsheimer, J. 52, 60n3
Meinecke, F. 25
Merleau-Ponty, M. 86
Method of Historical Structures (Cox) 8
Middle East 56–7, 60n5
migration 9, 100–3; global 101
Millennium 7, 11, 15–16, 35, 49, 79
Mitrany, D. 4
Mittelman, J.H. 8, 49–50, 109–21, 135
mobility 112–13
mobilization 5, 148
modern world system 48

INDEX

modernity 70–2, 87, 127, 132–4
modernization 8, 122, 127–9, 134; agricultural 123
Mohan, G., Tan-Mullins, M. and Power, M. 123, 128
Moore, B. 58
Morgenthau, H. 60n3
Morton, A.D. 60n2, 143; and Bieler, A. 15
Mozambique 56, 134
Mubarak, H. 57
multilateralism 44n3, 69, 96, 105
multinational corporations (MNC) 95–9, 103
Murphy, C. 49–50, 83–4, 92; and Augelli, E. 50, 53, 60n2

nation-states 146–8
National Images and International Systems (Boulding) 81
national sovereignty 147
nationalism 73, 97
naturalization 126, 135
neo-Gramscian theory of hegemony 8
neo-realist theory 35
neocolonialism 59
neofunctionalism, technocratic 4
neoliberal capitalism 3–4
neoliberal globalization 3, 97, 103
neoliberal institutionalism 52
neoliberalism 34, 43, 68, 82, 103; global 56
neoliberalization 102
neorealism 3–4, 13, 33–4, 49, 52, 66, 82; defensive 60n3; offensive 52, 60n3
Netherlands 114
Neufled, M. 68
New Science (Vico) 27
New York Times 116
New York (USA) 120n10, 126
New Zealand 52
Newman, Cardinal 111
Ng, A. 117
nineteenth century 24, 38, 53, 89, 102, 115, 126
Nokia 115
non-agential structuralism 49
non-governmental organizations (NGOs) 102–5
non-state actors 91
nonconformity 115
norm-entrepreneur 80–2
normative choice 67
normativity 69
norms, social 80
North, global 116
Nunes, J., Brincat, S.K. and Lima, L. 51, 84
Nye, J. 52
Nyíri, P. 129

O'Brien, R. 103
OECD (Organization for Economic Cooperation and Development) 123–5

offensive neorealism 52, 60n3
On the Study Methods of Our Time (Vico) 28
ontology 13–17, 76; conventional 12; historical 22; innovative 16
Onuf, N. 82
optimism 4, 43, 65
organizations: civil society 103; non-governmental (NGOs) 102–5
organized labour 8
orthodoxy 19, 100
Other 51, 74–5
Out from Underdevelopment Revisited (Mittelman and Pasha) 50

Paris Agreement on Climate Change (2014) 3
participatory silence 55
Pasha, M.K. 49–52
Pasrsons, T.H. 53
Pax Americana 53
Pax Britannica 53
Peace of Westphalia (1648) 24
Persaud, R.B. 8, 48–63, 76
pessimism 4–5, 43
philanthropy 115–16
Phillips, N. 8, 95–108
philology 27–8
philosophical idealism 43
philosophy 26, 33–47, 68, 86–8, 110; Cartesian 27–8; Kantian 68
Philosophy of History (Hegel) 72
Pocock, J.G.A. 28–30
political actors 6, 27, 82
political economy 21, 24, 70, 110
Political Economy of a Plural World, The 40–1
political hegemony 24
political relations, post-hegemonic 138–40
politics, inter-civilization 9
Popper, K. 88
Portugal 56
positivism 65, 82–4, 87–8, 110
post-colonial era 3
post-hegemonic political relations 138–40
post-industrial society 98, 101
post-Westphalian world order 3
postcolonialism 48
poverty 100, 112, 131
power, state 52
Power, M., Mohan, G. and Tan-Mullins, M. 123, 128
power relations 21, 97, 105
pragmatism 19–20, 102
praxis historicism 33
Presentation of Self in Everyday Life, The (Goffman) 81
primitive hegemony 51–9
Prison Notebooks, The (Gramsci) 45n16
private sector 112

INDEX

privatization 135
problem-solving theory 11–16, 19, 21–2, 34, 49, 64–78
production 17
Production Power and World Order (Cox) 7, 23–4, 34–5, 38–40, 45n9, 45n11
productivity 116, 129, 132
professionalization 117
Programme for China–Africa Cooperation in Economic and Social Development, The (PCACESD) 130
Promoting Polyarchy (Robinson) 50
pseudomorphology 127, 132
psychology 81; cognitive 81
public sector 112
public sphere 116

Qatar Foundation 118

racial domination 56
racism 8
Radice, H. 50, 59
rankers 113–15
Rathbun, B. 80
rational choice theory 81
rational society 71–2, 75
realism 3, 25, 49, 80, 88; classical 3–4; neo 3–4, 13, 33–4, 49, 52, 66, 82
regionalism 112–13
Renaissance humanism 25–6
reproduction 15–17; human 19
Rhodesia 56
Ribeau, S. 114
rights, human 16, 57, 115
Robinson, W.I. 49–50, 58, 60n2
Rockefeller, J.D. 115
Rolland, R. 45n17
Ruggie, J. 73
Rupert, M. 49
Rwanda 57

Said, E. 5
Sallust (Gaius Sallustius Crispus) 26
Salmi, J. 120n5
Salutati, C. 25
Saudi Arabia 57
Scala, B. 25
Schechter, M. 16, 20
Scholasticism 25
Scientific Outlook of Development (SOD) 128–9
Scott, J.C. 133
Searle, J.R. 14, 18–19
self-knowledge 37, 71, 74
Senegal 134
Shanghai Jiao Tong University (China) 114
Sinclair, T.J. 8, 11–20

sixteenth century 81
Skinner, Q. 29–30
Slater, D. 52
slavery 56, 65
Smith, S. 87
Snow, D.A., and Benford, R.D. 81
social actors 43
social change 21, 23
social dynamics 16, 19
social economy 124
social facts 15–16, 81
social forces 7, 48, 51, 66, 76, 80, 135
social knowledge 82
social legitimacy 99
social marginalization 96
social marginals 98–9
social norms 80
social order 67, 110, 140–3
social relations 37–8, 110, 128, 143, 148
social responsibility 133; corporate 100
social science 12–15, 35–6, 64–5, 79–82, 141, 149
social structure 8, 21, 98
social transformation 67
social world 82
socialization 52, 117
sociology 81–2, 88, 110
soft constructivism 81–3, 88
soft power 52
Somalia 50
Sorel, G. 44n2, 69, 73
South, global 116
South Africa 56, 115
sovereignty: national 147; state 149
Soviet Union 12, 23, 55, 86
Spengler, O. 40–1, 73, 127, 132
Spero, J. 116
spheres of activity, three levels 14–15, **14**
spheres redux 17–19, **18**
Spivak, G.C. 50
state power 52
state sovereignty 149
state-centrism 3
Strange, S. 9, 33, 76, 91, 110–11, 123–8, 135
structuralism: Cartesian 49; non-agential 49
subjectivity 37; collective 39
Suliman, S. 9, 138–52
supremacy 50
Sustainable Development Goals (SDGs) 131
systematic anachronism 21, 29

Tan-Mullins, M., Power, M. and Mohan, G. 123, 128
Tanzania 134
technocratic neofunctionalism 4
technology 116–17; green revolution (GRT) 130
Teti, A. 89–90

INDEX

Thatcherism 18
Theory of International Politics (Waltz) 12
Think Tanks 115–16
Third World 8
Thomas, C. 58
Thompson, E.P. 35, 45n15
Times Higher Education Supplement's/Quacquarelli Symonds (QS) World University Rankings 114
Tong, A. 148
Toynbee, A. 40–1
Toyota 115
Traditional Theory (TT) 65–8
transformation, social 67
transnational corporations (TNCs) 96–9, 103–6
transnational managerial class 98
transnationalism 97
tripartism 103
tripartite ideology 102
Tversky, A.N. 81
twentieth century 2, 83, 102, 115, 128
Twenty Years Crisis, The (Carr) 38, 83
twenty-first century 3, 19, 53, 83, 91, 114
typology 98

unionization 104
United Kingdom (UK) 86–91, 92n2, 115
United Nations Commission on Trade and Development (UNCTAD) 96, 106
United Nations Commission on Transnational Corporations and a Centre on Transnational Corporations (UNCTC) 102
United Nations (UN) 4, 7, 56; Global Compact 105–6; Guiding Principles on Business and Human Rights 105
United States of America (USA) 12, 56–7, 80–1, 86–91, 92n2–3, 95–8, 111–15, 135; African American 56; Agency for International Development (USAID) 111; capitalism 103; Clinton Administration 57; hegemony 87–8, 110; New York 120n10, 126; Wall Street 111
Universal Foreigner (Cox) 35
universalization 126
USSR (Union of Soviet Socialist Republics) 12, 23, 55, 86
utopianism 5

Valla, L. 29
verum-factum principle 37, 40
Vest, C. 117
Vico, J.T.G. 8, 33–43, 45n9–10, 69

Wall Street (USA) 111
Walt, S.M. 80
Walter, R., and Devetak, R.R. 8, 21–32
Waltz, K. 12, 21, 60n3
war capitalism 53
Warren, B. 58
Wealth of Nations (Smith) 28
Weber, M. 44n2
well-being 3
Wendt, A. 73
West 4, 51–6, 72, 86, 93n4, 122–3, 135, 149
Western civilization 145–6
Western countries 48
Western hegemony 112
Western Marxism 86
Western social theory 22
Western and Third World casualties (1886–2006) 54–5, *54*
Wight, M. 92–3n4
Winch, D. 28
working class 59, 71
World Bank 9, 100, 111, 118, 120n5, 122–32
World Development Report (2008) 123, 131
world economy 3, 24
World Innovation Summit for Education (WISE) 118
World Investment Report (2013) 96
world order 2–5, 8–9, 23, 48–51, 80, 138–42, 145; post-Westphalian 3
World Trade Organization (WTO) 112, 120n4, 125–7, 130–1; General Agreement on Trade in Services (GATS) 112
World War I (1914–18) 56
World War II (1939–45) 12, 51–2, 56
world-systems theory 4

Xiaoping, D. 128

Yashar, D. 58
Yemen 57